Welfare Justice

Neil Gilbert

Welfare Justice: Restoring Social Equity

Yale University Press
New Haven and London

Published with assistance from the Kingsley Trust
Association Publication Fund established by the Scroll
and Key Society of Yale College.

Designed by Deborah Dutton.
Set in Janson text type by Marathon Typography
Service, Inc., Durham, North Carolina.
Printed in the United States of America by Vail-Ballou
Press, Binghamton, New York.

Library of Congress Cataloging-in-Publication Data
Gilbert, Neil, 1940–
    Welfare justice : restoring social equity / Neil Gilbert.
        p.   cm.
    Includes bibliographical references and index.
    ISBN 0-300-06202-8 (alk. paper)
    1. Public welfare administration.   2. Social policy.
3. Welfare state.   I. Title.
HV51.G55   1995   94-38146
361.6'1—dc20   CIP

A catalogue record for this book is available from the
British Library.

The paper in this book meets the guidelines for
permanence and durability of the Committee on
Production Guidelines for Book Longevity of the
Council on Library Resources.

10   9   8   7   6   5   4   3   2   1

Contents

Acknowledgments

This book was written over several years, in the course of which I benefited from the generous assistance of many friends and colleagues. A major portion of the work was completed during a sabbatical in 1992, when I had the good fortune to serve as a visiting scholar at the International Social Security Association (ISSA) in Geneva. I am indebted to Dalmer Hoskins for making this remarkable opportunity available. The ISSA research unit is an incomparable source of information on social security programs around the world. It also provided a stimulating and congenial atmosphere in which to work, thanks to the good offices of Roland Sigg, Xenia Scheil-Adlung, Mike Gautrey, Judy Raymond, and Donatella Fabbri-Lovatti. During this period, my sense that significant changes were reshaping the American welfare state was reinforced by what I learned from European colleagues, who told of similar experiences in their countries. In this regard I particularly thank Christoph Badelt, Betty Duskins, Pieter Hermans, Berl Kutchinsky, Fiona Mejan, Rainer Munz, and Reink Prins for sharing their views and insights.

My wife, Barbara, read the entire manuscript, exercising her critical faculties with much vigor on my behalf and suggesting a number of thoughtful ideas that I freely incorporated as my own. I am also grateful to Harry Specht for his perceptive comments on drafts of the chapters. Rick Barth, Jill Duerr Berrick, Marcia Meyers, and our students at the Family Welfare Research Group (FWRG) in the School of Social Welfare at the University of California, Berkeley, created a lively forum for intellectual exchange, while Susan Katzenellenbogen managed the FWRG office with unfailing good humor. Although my work on this book gained from their encouragement and wise counsel, none of these people bears any responsibility for errors that remain or conclusions that are drawn about where the welfare state is headed and where it should be going.

Earlier drafts and sections of chapters in this book appeared in various journals. I am grateful to the publishers of the following articles for their permission to reprint revised versions or selected portions of these works: "Caring for Children: The Unfinished Business of Welfare Reform," *Society* (March–April 1987); "Teaching Children to Prevent Sexual Abuse," *The Public Interest* (Fall 1988); "Social Responsibility and Social Accounting: Time for a New Ledger," *The Responsive Community* (Winter 1992–93); "From Entitlements to Incentives: The Shifting Philosophy of Social Protection," *International Social Security Review* 45, no. 3 (1992); "Gender Equality and Social Security," *Society* (May–June 1994); "Touch and Stop," *Reason* (March 1994); "Why the New Workfare Won't Work," *Commentary* (May 1994); "Miscounting Social Ills," *Society* (March–April 1994); "Social Security and Family Relations: Choices for Change," *International Social Security Review* 47, nos. 3–4 (1994), which I also presented in a plenary address to the National Social Policy Conference in Sydney, Australia, on July 1993; "Violence Against Women: Social Research and Sexual Politics," *American Enterprise* (September–October 1994).

Special gratitude is owed to the family members who established the Milton and Gertrude Chernin Chair in Social Services and Social Welfare at the University of California, Berkeley; occupying the chair gave me time to ruminate about social welfare policy and made available the resources to follow lines of research that were not always high on the agendas for institutional support. Finally, I wish to thank my sons, Evan and Jesse, for remaining a constant source of warmth and wonderment.

Introduction

There are, of course, always plenty of frustrated querulants, and they play a not altogether insignificant role in every Western country. But the general mood of the ordinary citizen in the advanced Welfare State can be observed to be one of quiet satisfaction—although combined with a ubiquitous urge, but also a reasonable hope to get more and more of the good things of life. —*Gunnar Myrdal*, Beyond the Welfare State *(1960)*

Welfare-state expenditures were poised for a historic takeoff in almost every Western democracy in 1960. The public contentment sensed by Gunnar Myrdal at that time might well have derived from the increasing entitlements to social benefits, shortly to come due in advanced welfare states. The mood changed, however, as the growth in spending leveled off after 1975. Over the next decade, the guarded optimism of quiet satisfaction with modern welfare states was replaced by the language of crisis and retreat. Part of the difficulty was that as programs matured, expenditures could not keep up with the rising needs of aging populations and the lingering expectations that government would provide for more and more of the good things of life. By the mid-1990s quiet satisfaction had turned to manifest discontent with conventional welfare arrangements. In Europe the Organization for Economic Cooperation and Development advocated a shift from "passive" welfare policies that undermined initiative to "active" policies that would reinforce the work ethic. In the United States, President Clinton promised to enact policies that would "end welfare as we know it."

Not only have costs mounted and grown burdensome, but troubling questions have emerged about the fundamental consequences of the welfare state, particularly in the United States. The questions center on concerns for social equity. Over the past several decades welfare payments and policies have become increasingly unfair. Married women who work and pay social security taxes often qualify for old-age pensions that are no larger and sometimes even smaller than those awarded as dependents' benefits to wives who have never worked. Demands for social rights by groups self-identified as victims (on the basis of ethnicity, gender, addictions, disabilities, age, or sexual orientation) have proliferated without reference to personal responsibilities. New victims of social ills are constantly being detected by advocates who often employ extremely tentative evidence to verify that they have uncovered problems of immense magnitude requiring huge investments of public resources for immediate relief. Many low-income workers earn less than the combined value of cash grants and in-kind benefits received by those on welfare. While government has come under pressure to reduce welfare spending for the poor, a hidden welfare state has evolved. It delivers enormous subsidies (for health, housing, day care, and pensions) to the middle and upper classes through tax expenditures that are excluded from the conventional audit of welfare spending.

According to the conventional audit, the American welfare state administers a vast array of programs that currently distribute about $1 trillion directly in social benefits. Billions more are allocated indirectly through welfare-related tax expenditures that go largely uncounted. The massive governmental apparatus is built on legislative foundations and philosophical views formulated half a century ago during the New Deal. In the 1930s Harry Hopkins, Frances Perkins, Rexford Tugwell, and other New Deal architects devised blueprints for social protection against poverty, unemployment, and insecurity in old age; in many ways these blueprints continue to guide contemporary policies.

To understand the New Deal's legacy to the welfare state, we must appreciate the social norms, political ideology, and scientific knowledge that framed welfare planning back then. Norms of family life prescribed that wives stay at home to care for children and elderly relatives, so planners augmented social security benefits with a dependent's allowance. Social rights to welfare were customarily limited; public assistance thus was designed initially for the dependent children of widows and was expected to wither away as these widows became eligible for survivors' insurance under the newly organized social security system. With the applied policy-related social sciences still in their formative years, data on social needs and problems were meager. It was also a time when, as Joseph Schumpeter ([1942] 1950:63) observed, hostility to capitalism was so widespread that "whatever his political preference, every writer or speaker hastens to conform to this code and to emphasize his critical attitude, his freedom from 'complacency,' his belief in the inadequacies of capitalist achievement, his aversion to capitalist and his sympathy to anti-capitalist interests."

All that was in the 1940s. Since then, norms governing the division of labor in family life have changed; increasing gender equality has eroded the need for dependents' benefits under social security and created new needs for child-care services. Social rights to welfare have proliferated, raising concerns about the appropriate balance between the rights and the responsibilities of citizenship. Social scientists have assumed a more active role as advocates for victim groups, often submitting questionable estimates of social ills, which muddle policy deliberations. With the fall of communism, public approval of capitalism has resurged, lending impetus to the privatization of social services and the use of fiscal instruments that dispense indirect cash transfers. These changes have created new sets of problems that draw into question the fairness of traditional welfare-state programs and policies.

This book is about social trends and public policies that have fostered inequities in the American welfare state and how these inequities might be redressed. In the first five chapters I examine issues of fairness emanating from increasing gender equality and the changing character of family life (Chapter 1), the expansion of social rights (Chapter 2), the emerging emphasis on social obligations (Chapter 3), the rise of advocacy research (Chapter 4), and the privatization of welfare activities (Chapter 5). I suggest that to restore a sense of equity, policymakers need to recognize the social and economic contributions of women working both at home and in the marketplace, to develop programs that create a better balance between social rights and responsibilities, to require stronger evidence of social ills before allocating funds to remedy "epidemics" that may not exist, and to formulate a new ledger for social accounting that affords a full reckoning of who benefits from government transfers.

Although the response to these needs for reform has been slow, in recent years the methods and philosophy of social protection have begun to change, transforming the essential character of the welfare state. In the final chapter I analyze the welfare state in transition as it moves from expansion of social entitlements toward promotion of private responsibility. In this new approach to social protection, which is increasingly characterized as the "enabling state," citizens are treated not as passive recipients of public benefits and care but as individuals capable of looking after themselves with occasional assistance from the government. Policies that emphasize public support for private responsibility favor what Thatcherites have called the vigorous virtues —initiative, fair play, diligence, commitment, and enthusiasm—over the gentle virtues of charity, patience, tolerance, kindness, and sympathy (Letwin, 1992). Here the course of change is guided more by regard for encouraging fairness and independence than by concern for promoting a gentler society.

The dictates of gentleness and fair play do not necessarily afford the same guidelines for social policy; still, there is no inherent contradiction between these objectives. The danger lies elsewhere. Whereas policies emphasizing private efforts may increase fairness and independence for those most capable of assessing alternatives and exercising initiative, they may also foster a meaner and uncaring society for those least capable. Owing to personal incompetence as well as to social forces beyond their control, some people are temporarily or permanently unable to fulfill the ordinary responsibilities of citizenship. Can public officials restore social equity without cracking down too harshly on dependency? Moving beyond the welfare state in directions that Myrdal did not anticipate, we face an immediate challenge: to create a system of social protection that enables private responsibility while maintaining a reliable framework of public care for those unable to help themselves.

Welfare Justice

Chapter 1

Strengthening Family: Social Security and Gender Equality

When the American social welfare system took shape during the New Deal, married life embodied both the traditional division of labor—husband at work, wife at home caring for children—and hierarchical gender relationships. Much about families has changed since then. Although the changes are often characterized as liberating for women, freeing them from the despotic patriarchy of the mid-twentieth century, traditional Victorian family life was considerably more oppressive than the oft cited (and rather amiable) relations between Ozzie and Harriet. Trollope's novels testify to the suffocating state of wedlock frequently experienced by women in Victorian times, even among the upper classes. One's wife, as Mr. Kennedy declares in *Phineas Finn*, "was subject to her husband by the laws of both God and man." Unable to endure the crushing boredom of Mr. Kennedy's presence, his wife, Lady Laura, fled the country—a solution to marital discord available only to the privileged few in those days.

Since the Victorian era, events have reshaped the conventions of marital life for both men and women, most significantly over the past forty years. The character of family life was transformed after World War II by rising divorce rates, declining birthrates, and the expanding participation of women in the labor force. In 1950 there were more than four marriages for each divorce; by 1990 there were two marriages for each divorce, at which rate almost half of all couples being joined in wedlock could expect their unions to dissolve. The trends toward fewer children and more liberal access to divorce have eased some of the customary restraints of family life (Goode, 1993). At the same time, wives have gained a degree of liberation from the traditional division of labor through increasing levels of employment outside the home. Steadily on the rise, the labor-force participation rate of married women with children under age eighteen climbed from 24 percent in 1950 to 41 percent in 1970 to 67 percent in 1990 (Cherlin, 1988; U.S. Bureau of the Census, 1992). These were not all women with older children. In 1990 more than half of all wives with children aged three or younger were in the labor force. Sociologists have called these developments in family life a shift from traditional familism to individualism (Whitehead, 1992) or from child-centeredness to adult-centeredness (Popenoe, 1988).

The move away from hierarchical gender relationships in which wives are financially dependent on their husbands, socially acquiescent, and legally constrained in family matters manifests the increasing value accorded to equality in family life. There are, however, different ideas about the calibration of equality in human affairs. Social policy in race relations, for example, is sharply divided between measures favoring equality of opportunity and those favoring equality of results (Glazer, 1975). The Aristotelian distinction between numerical and proportional equality poses the choice of distributive principles: treating everyone the same or granting similar treatment to people of similar merit (Vlastos, 1962). In the matter of gender equality, feminists are not all of the same mind. Some believe that the goal should be simply to erase formal and informal discrimination; others would aim instead at "a thoroughly genderless world in which roughly as many fathers as mothers are in primary charge of children, and roughly as many women as men hold top military positions" (Dworkin, 1993:27). As the traditional guidelines for domestic arrangements dissolve, two schools of feminist thought offer alternative perspectives on the meaning of gender equality in family life. They address not only the way husbands and wives should divide their labor to fulfill joint responsibilities but also the appropriate design of social policies in support of the new conventions.

Changing Gender Roles: Radical and Conservative Outlooks

To liberate family life from the traditional hierarchy of male dominance, radical egalitarians recommend a model of gender relations marked by complete functional equality. The model represents a system of belief organized around four tenets: negation of gender roles, devaluation of traditional activities, celebration of paid employment, and recognition of the individual as the primary unit of concern for policy.

The elimination of all gender distinctions is a prerequisite for functional equality. Radical egalitarians are explicit on this point. As Cynthia Fuchs Epstein (1988:160) observes, they call for "destruction of the traditional family in order to restructure society and abolish all gender roles." Susan Okin (1992:171), for example, argues that in a just future "one's sex would have no more relevance than one's eye color or the length of one's toes. No assumptions would be made about 'male' or 'female' roles." Because innate or natural differences between men and women are viewed as trivial, the fact that women tend to be more involved than men in caregiving and domestic activities is credited almost entirely to socialization.

Advocates of functional equality view caregiving and domestic work as servile, tedious, mind-numbing, and of limited value (Kaminer, 1990).[1] The liabilities attributed to domestic work contrast sharply with the presumed benefits of wage labor. From this perspective, paid employment imparts autonomy and self-respect as it liberates women from the repressive confinement of childcare and housekeeping. The assumption is that women can achieve self-determination in the labor market but not in the family (Tilly and Scott, 1989). Thus, equality between husbands and wives is possible only if women participate in the paid labor force to the same extent as men. Toward this end, several policy initiatives are typically advanced to facilitate the shift of women's labor from the household to the market

---

1. The low regard in which this work is held by radical feminists creates a curious dilemma. "If work in family wraps one in a haze of domesticity and enrolls one in a cult of domesticity that blunts all talents," Suzanne Gordon (1992:127) inquires, "why would any man volunteer for this social lobotomy?"

economy. First, an infrastructure of public family services is required to provide social care and deal with other traditionally female tasks. At the same time that women are freed to compete in the labor market, men must be encouraged to increase their involvement in domestic activities—for example, through parental leave policies, as in Norway, where several weeks of paid leave are reserved solely for fathers (Leira, 1994).

More generally, efforts to liberate women from domesticity are guided by the principle that the individual rather than the family should be taken as the focal unit for policy design. This principle has been advocated for some time. Almost twenty years ago Constantina Safilios-Rothschild (1974), for one, suggested that the United States adopt the Swedish model and abolish all social policy distinctions based on family status so that the law would always treat women and men as independent individuals. The principle has been recently endorsed by the Organization for Economic Cooperation and Development (OECD).[2] As the OECD Group of Experts on Women and Structural Change in the 1990s reports: "In most OECD countries the tax system is now based on the individual as the unit of assessment. Applying the same rule to social security enhances consistency and promotes the principles of personal autonomy and economic independence" (OECD, 1991:28).

Beyond stimulating autonomy and independence, OECD social policies focused on individuals are seen as a way to discourage role differentiation in family life "with regard to the division of time between paid employment, domestic duties, and leisure" (OECD, 1985). To achieve this state of affairs, OECD officials acknowledge the need to engage in the "social construction of gender," a process through which individual-oriented policies are reinforced by media messages that encourage men and women to adopt a functionally equal division of labor in family life (OECD, 1991).

2. The OECD's (1991b:7) blueprint for the "active society," discussed below in Chapter 3, not only proposes the replacement of "passive" social-welfare supports with schemes designed to stimulate employment but also "demands a new perspective on the role of women as economic actors."

The ideal model of functional equality is characterized by a family in which both spouses work, maintain separate accounts, pay separate taxes, and contribute more or less equivalent sums to the family's financial support. Household and caregiving tasks performed outside the hours of paid employment are divided equally between husbands and wives, with each contributing the same amount of time to the full range of domestic responsibilities (so that they do not fall back into the traditional division of labor, in which men take out the garbage and protect the household while women mop floors and change diapers). The domestic and caregiving tasks to which the spouses cannot attend are performed through arrangements with state-subsidized public providers or private service providers, for which any remaining charges are born equally by the spouses. Extending into the realm of more intimate behavior, Safilios-Roth-schild (1974:118) describes a model marriage contract in which even the practice of contraception is equally divided—"half the time she uses a diaphragm, the other half he uses a condom."

As an alternative to both functional equality in marital life and the traditionally conservative hierarchy of male dominance, neoconservative feminists embrace a model of family relations based on domestic partnership. Unlike the radical feminists, for whom the family represents a voluntary union in which members' rights are derived from their status as individuals, neoconservatives regard the family as a corporate entity that confers certain rights and duties upon its members (Fox-Genovese, 1992). They view marriage as a partnership built on economic interdependence, mutual adjustment, and self-realization through a combination of domestic activity and paid employment. Couples decide how to divide their labor most effectively to satisfy personal needs and family responsibilities (Kersten, 1991). This flexible approach contrasts with the functional equality model of family relations, which prescribes a division of labor that encourages economic independence, personal autonomy, and self-realization through a career of paid employment, with domestic responsibilities split evenly down the middle. The egalitarian assumption is that the particulars of a satisfying life are entirely the same for men and women (Levin, 1986).

Supporters of both the traditional hierarchy of marital relations and the tenets of functional equality subscribe to a more restrictive view of gender roles than do advocates of the partnership model, who assume that a productive and fulfilling division of labor in family life can take many forms. In some families a wife or husband may want to stay at home to manage childcare and domestic affairs for an extended time; in some families it may be convenient for a partner to divide his or her labor between the household and part-time paid employment or for both partners to work part-time in paid employment and part-time at home; and in other families both members may work full-time and make alternative arrangements to fill caring and domestic functions. The domestic partnership model acknowledges that however spouses decide to allocate their labor, both are contributing to the management of a joint enterprise and deserve to share equally in the benefits that accrue over time; this has distinct implications for social policy.

Indeed, each of these models of family relations—traditional hierarchy, functional equality, and domestic partnership—advances and is reinforced by different policy choices. Table 1.1 illustrates a range of policies concerned with pension benefits, retirement age, childcare, and the social rights of cohabitation, summarizing the various measures aligned with alternative perspectives on gender roles in family life.

Separate Accounts or Split Entitlements?
The case of social security is instructive. In the United States and many other industrial nations, pension policies were introduced at a time when wives were not expected to have paid careers. Among married couples, a woman's right to old-age pension benefits is typically derived from her dependent status as a wife under social policies that support the traditional hierarchy in family relations. The dependent's benefit remains a major feature of most public pension schemes in modern welfare states. Ten of the sixteen countries surveyed by Martin Tracy (1988) in 1985 provided these spousal supplements to the basic coverage for employed husbands. Beside reinforcing the traditional view of the stay-at-home housewife dependent on her hus-

Table 1.1 Models of Family Relationships and Policy Choices

Policy Area	Model of Family Relationships		
	Traditional Hierarchy	Functional Equality	Domestic Partnership
Pension benefits	Derivative spousal benefits	Separate accounts	Equal shares of combined public and private accounts
Retirement age	Younger for wife than husband	Same age	Adjustable in relation to partner
Childcare	Wife's responsibility	Socialization of activity, with equal division of residual care	Socialization of daycare costs, with activity divided by partner choice and awarded pension credits
Cohabitation	No benefit rights	Separate coverage	Partner rights based on formal obligations

band for financial support, this policy is often criticized as inequitable on several counts.

In the United States a dependent's supplement equals 50 percent of the wage earner's retirement benefit. When a wage-earning wife looks at the size of the pension benefits that she would receive based on her contribution records compared with the dependent's supplement that she is entitled to based on her husband's earnings, it is often the case that she gains little or nothing from her own contributions beyond what she is eligible for simply as a dependent. As Table 1.2 illustrates, the employed wife in the Jones family, with average lifetime monthly earnings less than one-sixth her husband's, is eligible for the same total monthly benefit as the unemployed wife in the Smith family, who receives only a dependent's allowance. A wife's paycheck must account for at least one-third of the couple's lifetime indexed income before the retirement benefit based on her earnings is larger than the sum to which she is entitled as a dependent (Ross and Upp,

Table 1.2 Dependents' Allowances and Benefit Inequities

	Averaged Monthly Earnings	Benefit Received as Worker	Benefit Received as Spouse	Total Monthly Benefits
Jones Family				
Husband	$1,290	$626	$ 0	$626
Wife	200	180	133	313
Combined	1,490	—	—	939
Smith Family				
Husband	1,290	626	0	626
Wife	0	0	313	313
Combined	1,290	—	—	939
Green Family				
Husband	645	368	0	368
Wife	645	368	0	368
Combined	1,290	—	—	736

Source: Adapted from Social Security Administration data in Ross and Upp, 1988.

1988). According to one set of calculations (Iams, 1993), the proportion of wives whose earnings are so low relative to their husband's that they would receive higher benefits as a dependent than as a retired worker has declined from 66 percent (for women born in 1930) to 40 percent (for women born in 1959). Currently, about two-thirds of the women aged sixty-two or older are receiving social security benefits based partly or totally on their husband's contributions (Lingg, 1990).

Even when the wife's earnings account for close to half the couple's joint income, the dependent's benefit may still discriminate against two-earner couples. Compare, for example, the total benefits received by the Smith and Green families in Table 1.2. Both couples have the same total income. But for the Greens it represents the combined equal earnings of husband and wife, whereas for the Smith family it represents the total earnings of the husband. With the same family income, the one-earner couple's retirement benefit is higher than that of the two-earner couple.

The dependent's benefit not only creates inequities among married couples with different patterns of work and income; it also provides the one-earner married couple with a return on their social security contributions that is 50 percent higher than the return to a single worker at the same income level. Besides these inequities, concerns have been expressed that spousal allowances may encourage dependency and reduce the incentive for women to become economically self-sufficient (Tracy, 1988).

From the perspective of functional equality, wives are independent individuals who should earn their own income and accumulate their own pension benefits in separate accounts. The OECD (1991:28) advocates taking the individual as the unit of assessment for pension benefits because doing so not only promotes personal autonomy and economic independence but "also helps to reject the notion that women's incomes are supplementary to and therefore dispensable portions of overall family income."

The main difficulty with this approach as things currently stand is that women earn considerably less income than men. The reasons are well recognized; they involve limited opportunities, employment bias, childbirth, and women's assumption of a disproportionate share of household duties and caring functions. Although the intention is to advance functional equality, the establishment of separate pension accounts would result in highly unequal pension benefits for men and women. Thus, as the OECD Working Party on the Role of Women explains, the movement to secure equality through a system of individual pension rights for women "will have to go hand in hand with measures in other policy areas to improve women's position in the labor market" (OECD, 1985:148). The additional measures include market adjustments that eliminate wage and employment discrimination against women, the development of daycare and other public services to reduce the burdens of family maintenance, and an effort by men to share responsibility for caregiving and other domestic activities. It is evident from this list that in the drive toward functional equality, proposals for separate old-age pension accounts are closely connected to a broader movement for institutional change.

Instead of discouraging role differentiation, policies that foster domestic partnership enable husbands and wives to divide the chores of running the family enterprise according to their preferences and share equally in the benefits. With regard to retirement income, these family benefits would include all public and private pension assets and rights accumulated by both parties. Though not immediately liquid, pension entitlements represent major financial assets for most families. Thus, the principles of domestic partnership translate into old-age pension policies that dictate the splitting of benefit entitlements.

In 1977 both Canada and Germany enacted reforms that involved the splitting of pension credits between spouses. Credit sharing in Germany was enacted within the framework of family legislation, whereas the Canadian scheme was introduced under social security law. Compared to the Canadian provisions, which entail splitting only the entitlements to public pensions, the German provisions are broader in scope, encompassing all entitlements acquired in both public and private pension plans. Although spouses have legal rights to equal shares of their combined pension credits, in both countries the tangible division of old-age pension entitlements occurs only in cases of divorce (Reinhard, 1988). In the Canadian scheme, evidence from British Columbia indicates that among divorced couples there was initially a very low take-up rate (under 5 percent), attributed in part to the lack of public awareness about the formal application procedures for voluntary credit-sharing (Tracy, 1987).

The actual sharing of pensions need not be contingent upon divorce. I can imagine a credit-sharing arrangement based on joint accounts that combine both partners' pension credits. An exemplary policy for old-age pension reform in support of domestic partnership would include the establishment of joint accounts that cover all public and private pension entitlements and from which checks are issued in both parties' names upon their retirement. Pension benefits might also be allocated through separate checks for equal amounts issued to each party from the joint account. Indeed, some would argue that by conferring explicit recognition of the wife's contribution to the family enterprise, separate checks provide a psychological benefit to wives, which men, who are more accustomed to a breadwinner's role, might not entirely appreciate.[3]

3. I am indebted to Christoph Badelt for bringing this point to my attention (while taking me on a memorable hike in the Vienna woods).

Among the issues sometimes raised about credit sharing is the concern that it might dissuade people from marriage because it embodies an egalitarian approach to pension entitlements not fully accepted by society (Brocas, 1988). Yet there is no indication that marriage rates in Germany and Canada have suffered in comparison with those of other industrial countries where pensions include dependents' allowances or separate accounts.

Although Germany and Canada are the only countries with credit-sharing arrangements for social security, the Netherlands and the United States have evinced serious interest in such arrangements. In support of the basic tenets of domestic partnerships in the United States, the National Women's Conference of 1977 called for federal and state legislatures to base laws relating to property, inheritance, and domestic relations "on the principle that marriage is a partnership in which the contribution of each spouse is of equal importance and value" (Ross and Upp, 1988:83). In 1979 the Advisory Council on Social Security embraced this principle and recommended consideration of credit-sharing arrangements.

Many policy analysts considered the concept attractive, but efforts to reform social security stalled for various reasons, including the fact that credit sharing meant a reduction in benefits for the traditional one-earner family and for divorced men. Thus, substituting a credit-sharing scheme for the dependent's allowance would make social security benefits more equitable at the same time that it would diminish their adequacy for certain groups. This is a serious problem. If social security were redesigned along the lines of private insurance, with benefits directly related to contributions, one way to ensure adequate support in old age would entail increasing reliance on means-tested income maintenance schemes, such as the Supplementary Security Income program (Munnell, 1977). But many liberal interest groups and policy analysts oppose switching from universal to selective provisions, especially for the elderly (Schorr, 1986; Townsend, 1968). By the late 1980s the costs and conflicts attached to the various proposals seemed to have eliminated earning-sharing reforms from the political agenda (Ross and Upp, 1988). Although a proposal to split social security entitlements resurfaced in Title IV of the Economic Equity Act introduced in Congress in 1992, the immediate prospects for this type of reform remain faint.

The choice of individual versus shared credits for retirement benefits could be finessed by providing universal or means-tested public pensions that are disconnected from employment records. Australia, New Zealand, and several other countries have such uniform payment systems, under which benefits are extended to all elderly citizens. But these uniform pensions provide only a minimum level of support. The next tiers of support are provided by employment-based public schemes and occupational pensions—and with these, policymakers still must address the issue of separate accounts versus split credits.

Socialization of Child Care: Costs or Activities?

Under the traditional hierarchy of marital relationships, childcare is regarded as a private family responsibility. It is the mother's job, and no public provisions are needed. As a basis for social policy in this area, the traditional hierarchy thus begets a formula for public inaction.

But traditional relationships are in the midst of change. In the United States almost two-thirds of the mothers with school-age children are gainfully employed at least some of the time. Despite the rising number of two-earner families, the median income of married-couple families (adjusted for inflation) has remained almost constant since the early 1970s (U.S. Bureau of the Census, 1990). Given the increasing pressure on traditional-family-based arrangements, public provisions for childcare have expanded throughout the industrialized world. In 1987, for example, the U.S. Congress logged over seventy bills dealing with various aspects of childcare assistance (Meyers, 1990). The basic policy issue concerning childcare in the 1990s is not whether to take public action but what form the public initiatives should take. Here we encounter the classic debate over in-kind benefits versus cash: Should public aid be devoted to the socialization of childcare activities or costs? Should government provide for childcare services or give parents cash grants to assist in the payment for private care?

Supporters of the functional equality model of family relationships, for whom the labor force participation of women is the main avenue to independence and autonomy, favor in-kind policies that involve the socialization of childcare activities. The state may produce childcare services, contract with private providers for the services, and offer tax incentives for business enterprises to supply their employees with childcare services. In each case public funds are allocated to service producers rather than to individual consumers.

Social policy literature abounds with arguments about the alternative benefits of allocating welfare provisions either in cash or in kind (Gilbert, Specht, and Terrell, 1993). The case for the government's producing or purchasing in-kind provisions for childcare rests in part on the argument that this approach benefits from economies of scale and helps to create an adequate supply of services. Individual cash grants to parents, on the other hand, offer no guarantee that producers will emerge to meet the demand. In-kind assistance also allows greater control than cash grants over how tax dollars are being spent. If the objective is to ensure that children are supervised in certain types of group settings outside the home, public funds can be designated to support such supervision. Through income-testing measures, the allocation of both cash and in-kind childcare provisions can be designed so that the poorest families receive the largest public subsidies. This would require charging fees for services on a sliding scale according to family income; cash benefits could be similarly targeted—for example, through refundable tax credits that decline as income rises.

Furnishing childcare assistance in the form of publicly sponsored services affords both a practical convenience and a work incentive for two-earner families. Public services available free of charge (or on a sliding scale) would reduce the time and effort that working parents need to invest in shopping around for daycare and would promise a basic standard of health and safety. The daycare system in Sweden illustrates the way these provisions foster work incentives. Functional equality is an explicit objective of Swedish family policy, which, according to a parliamentary committee, "must take as a basic principle that both parents have the same right and duty to assume bread-winning as well as practical responsibility for home and children" (Popenoe, 1988:149).

In Sweden, 83 percent of the married women with children under seven work for pay, mainly because the average family cannot manage on the salary of one wage earner. The average production worker's wage is not so low; rather, almost 62 percent of it goes to pay direct and indirect taxes (1983 figures).[4] These taxes finance a host of social welfare services distributed freely by the state, including an elaborate network of daycare services. With trained staff, a supervisory ratio of two adults for every five children under three, and well-equipped facilities, daycare services in Sweden are subsidized by as much as $11,900 per child (Swedish Institute, 1992). But Swedish parents who might want to care for their children at home cannot choose between consuming this "free" daycare service and, for example, receiving a tax rebate equal to the cost of this service. By investing labor in domestic childcare they miss out on a huge public subsidy while continuing to pay the taxes that support it. This arrangement creates a financial inducement to shift responsibility for the care of children from the family to the state.

Although state-supported childcare services are popular in Sweden, there is some indication that many mothers would prefer having opportunities for other arrangements, particularly for the early years of childhood. A 1987 poll of Swedish women, for example, found that of those surveyed, 60 percent favored, not increasing public investment in state-run daycare centers, but putting the resources toward a childcare allowance that would assist parents who wanted to stay at home with their children or who wanted to purchase childcare privately (Svensson, 1987). Efforts to develop a childcare allowance for stay-at-home mothers in Sweden have been blocked by the Social Democrats, who claim that it would help preserve the traditional housewife system (Popenoe, 1988).

According to Gosta Esping-Andersen (1991), employment in the area of social welfare accounts for 75 percent of the net job creation in Sweden over the past twenty years; virtually all the jobs have been filled by women. These data suggest that for many women, emanci-

4. The tax rate is based on OECD Secretariat estimates reported in the *Wall Street Journal* ("Supply Side," 1987) and includes payroll taxes, social insurance contributions, personal income taxes, and general consumption and excise taxes. According to the Swedish Institute (1978), an "80/85 percent rule" was established in the late 1970s to ensure that the aggregate of national, local, and net-worth taxes did not exceed 80 percent of a taxpayer's income—85 percent for those with the highest earnings.

pation from household work has mainly involved a shift from performing caring activities for children and elderly people voluntarily, out of a personal commitment to family and friends, to performing social services for strangers for pay.

When the state seeks to help families meet the costs of caring for children, aid in the form of a cash subsidy for childcare is more consistent with the domestic partnership model of family relationships than are provisions in the form of in-kind services for out-of-home care. A policy of cash payments, whether through direct grants or through refundable tax credits to all families with young children, socializes the costs of childcare but not the activity. Cash payments allow parents to decide together how each can best contribute to the welfare of the family enterprise. If the average cost for the care of a preschool child is $5,000, for example, parents with young children could choose to purchase daycare services so that both might work or to keep all or part of the stipend to offset the loss of income from having one of the partners stay at home full-time or part-time to care for the children.[5] Finland is the only Western welfare state whose family policy offers parents a choice between subsidized daycare for those who work and cash benefits for those who wish to remain at home with their children during the early years (Kamerman and Kahn, 1987).

Both parents work for pay in most American families with children. They tend to divide their labor between childcare and wage earning in patterns of employment that are not always clearly reflected in the standard reporting of the Bureau of Labor Statistics on working mothers. In the mid-1980s, for example, 62 percent of mothers in the United States participated in the labor force, but only 41 percent were employed full-time; 16 percent worked part-time, and the remainder were actively seeking jobs. The bureau lists in the full-time category any mothers who worked full-time for any period during the calendar year; a breakdown of this category shows that only

5. The $5,000 figure represents the average annual per pupil cost of public elementary and secondary education in 1990. According to an estimate by Gill and Gill (1994), professionally approved daycare for preschool children of full-time working parents would cost around $10,000 a year (which is close to what Sweden spends).

29 percent worked full-time for an entire year. The 16 percent of mothers defined as part-time employees worked anywhere from a few hours a week during holiday periods to thirty-four hours a week for the year (Besharov and Dally, 1986). There is some indication that in recent years a growing proportion of American women are more inclined to stay at home and care for their family than to join the labor force. In the annual Virginia Slims survey of 3,000 women in the United States, the proportion of respondents who said that if free to choose, they would rather have a job than stay at home to take care of the family rose from 36 percent in 1974 to 52 percent in 1985 but then declined to 42 percent in 1989 (Glenn, 1992).

In advancing a policy of cash benefits over services, the domestic partnership model of family relationships permits parents to tailor arrangements for childcare to varying patterns of employment without being penalized by the loss of the subsidy when they wish to invest their labor in caring for children at home. What parents who stay at home to care for children often do lose are the credits toward public pension retirement benefits that would accrue if they were otherwise employed during that period. Among the several countries that provide pension credit for caregiving, the amounts differ, as does the eligibility of men and women for the credit. In Austria, for example, women receive one year of credit for each child, whereas Sweden awards credit to either spouse for each year they care for a child under three years of age. In Britain people who interrupt work careers to assume caregiving duties are compensated through the Home Responsibility Protection policy, under which both men and women are credited with a minimum level of contribution during the years they spend caring for children or disabled people (Barr and Coulter, 1990). In France pension benefits are increased by 10 percent for insured persons who have reared at least three children, and Hungary grants an increased benefit for three years of infant care (Tracy and Tracy, 1987).

If childcare assistance is provided in the form of cash benefits, the case can be made that parents who use these benefits to subsidize in-home care should be allowed to accrue contributory pension credits for this activity. Joan Green, for example, uses her $5,000 childcare subsidy to enroll her son and daughter in the Happy Meadows Day-care Center, where she also happens to work as a service provider. Her children's fees pay a substantial part of her salary, from which she contributes social security payments; the fees also help pay for the employer's portion of her social security contribution. If Joan Green elected instead to remain home with her children, using the childcare subsidy to compensate for the family income that would be lost by her withdrawal from the labor market, she would be unable to accrue pension coverage. From the domestic partnership perspective, equity is enhanced among families that choose to divide work and caregiving roles by linking cash subsidies for childcare with contributory pension credits for the periods when either spouse assumes the caregiving role.

Retirement Age: Fixed or Variable?

In the late 1980s the standard retirement ages for men and women with public pensions were the same in 60 percent of the twenty-four OECD member countries, including the United States, and were lower for women in 40 percent (OECD, 1988b). Pension schemes in which the retirement age is set lower for women than for men (usually by three to five years) tend to be justified on grounds that uphold the traditional hierarchy of family relationships. Wives are often younger than their husband, and the arrangement compensates for that fact, permitting spouses to retire at the same time. The assumption is that a wife's career is secondary to her husband's and that she is prepared to quit as soon as he retires. In addition, the earlier retirement age for women takes account of the fact that they often carry a double burden: household chores and outside employment (Brocas, 1988). Support for the five-year difference in qualifying ages for pensions in Austria, for example, was affirmed by a 1987 ruling of the Vienna provincial court, which notes that this double burden impairs women's capacity to work at an earlier age than the standard age of retirement for men (Peterka, 1988).

Advocates of functional equality regard differences in the pensionable age of men and women as "unjustifiable discrimination between the sexes. It is argued that women are treated unfairly by being expected to retire earlier than men and that in employment-based pension systems this practice makes it difficult for them to build up a long enough contribution record" (OECD, 1985:145). Men, too, are treated unfairly, because earlier retirement allows women to draw pensions for a longer period of time on the basis of similar contributions—a disparity compounded by women's greater life expectancy.

Where retirement age is concerned, the general trend in pension reform is toward measures that promote functional equality. This is evident in the social policy initiatives for the European Union. Efforts to harmonize European social policies decree equal treatment for men and women. Although the policies do not specify a common age of retirement for members of the European Union, they do mandate that both sexes become eligible for the basic public pension at the same age (Leibfried and Pierson, 1992).

Although policies that authorize a lower age of retirement for women are unfair on various social and actuarial grounds, those that require men and women to retire at the same age draw a rigid line between work and leisure and fail to accommodate different needs and preferences. Equalizing the pensionable age works against (1) spouses who wish to retire at the same time in cases when one partner is older than the other; (2) wives and husbands who postpone entering the labor force to stay at home with children and later wish to pursue a career beyond the time of their spouse's retirement; and (3) couples in which one partner carries a heavier burden or does more physically demanding work than the other and consequently seeks to retire at a younger age. In each case, the decision to retire at different times would not affect either partner's entitlement to an equal share of the couple's pension rights under a split-credit scheme like those in Canada and Germany.

Beyond efforts to equalize the age of retirement for men and women, the domestic partnership approach to social security policy focuses on the need for variable arrangements, which allows greater choice to suit diverse circumstances. A number of pension programs already contain some flexibility with regard to retirement age. In the United States, for instance, where the standard age of retirement is sixty-five, it is possible to retire at age sixty-two at a reduced level of benefit (80 percent of the full amount, which will drop to 70 percent by 2027) or to retire after sixty-five with a delayed retirement credit, which increases the benefit by 3 percent a year (rising to 8 percent per annum by 2027). Finland allows for retirement anytime during the decade beginning at age sixty; pension benefits are reduced by 4 percent to 6 percent a year until age sixty-five, after which benefits can be increased by a delayed-retirement increment of 12.5 percent per year until age seventy (Holzmann, 1988). Several European countries—Belgium and France among them—have special arrangements under which public pensions are provided for workers retiring prior to the standard age on condition that the employer replaces the worker with an unemployed person (Hart, 1984).

Cohabitation and Pension Rights

The growing rate of cohabitation outside marriage not only affects the legal edifice of traditional family life but also challenges the basis of entitlements for family-oriented social security policies. Sweden is among the world's leaders in the rate of nonmarital cohabitation. According to an 1985 study, the probability that Swedish women aged thirty have lived in a consensual union has mounted dramatically—from 34 percent of those born in 1936 to 83 percent of those born in 1955 (Hoem and Rennermalm, 1985). At the same time, the length of cohabitation has extended; what was often a prelude to marriage has become a permanent alternative (Popenoe, 1988; Etzler, 1987). The level of cohabitation in the United States, though considerably lower than in Sweden, has risen precipitously, too, from 0.5 million unmarried-couple households in 1970 to 2.5 million in 1988 (U.S. Bureau of the Census, 1990). The trend toward cohabitation lends social urgency to the question of whether men and women who enter into consensual unions should be entitled to the same social rights as married couples.

From the viewpoint of those who uphold the traditional hierarchy of family relationships, cohabitation should not qualify partners for the same rights as marriage because it does not manifest the same commitment and obligation as in a family bound together by the conventions of marriage. The weakness of the ties is evident in the Swedish experience, for example, which reveals that cohabiting couples with children are about three times more likely to separate than married couples with children (Popenoe, 1992). Evidence from the United States indicates that compared with married couples, cohabiting partners are more than twice as likely to abuse one another physically. One explanation for these findings, Jan Stets (1991) suggests, might be that the cost associated with aggressive behavior is not as great for cohabiting couples as for those who have invested in, and made the long-term commitment to, marriage.

The issue of whether cohabitation should entitle the partners to family benefits is largely bypassed by those who favor policies in support of functional equality. Because the individual is the basic unit, rights to benefits are perceived as appropriately organized in terms of separate accounts for everyone, as in the example of social security. From this perspective, marital status and living arrangements are irrelevant.

In contrast to the individualistic focus of functional equality, from the standpoint of the partnership model the nature of living arrangements and commitments that hold couples together *are* pertinent for defining benefit rights. Supporters seek a reasonable balance between rights and obligations, however; they would consider cohabitation per se an insufficient basis for entitlements to family benefits, because commitments associated with the partnership of family life are more than a matter of sharing the same residence.

This is not to say that supporters of the domestic partnership model maintain the traditional view that a marriage license is the only certification of a committed relationship. To qualify for social benefits as a family unit in the absence of a marriage license requires, they would argue, some formal expression of a mutual commitment to share the benefits and burdens of an enduring relationship, including social, emotional, legal, and economic dimensions of mutual care. Marriage is a formal covenant that embraces all these dimensions of mutual care, whereas cohabitation often involves a relationship of similar commitments, secured only by informal agreement. To obtain the same entitlement to family benefits as couples joined in wedlock, cohabiting couples should invest their relationship with an equivalent level of mutual obligation. Outside marriage, this can be achieved through formal compacts centered on the most explicit and tangible dimension of mutual support, which involves financial interdependence. Such measures might include formal agreements to treat assets as community property, to guarantee joint support of children, and to pool pension credits in a single account to be divided equally between the partners (as in the split-credit arrangements for social security described before).

Domestic partnerships that are founded on ties of affection and reinforced by formal agreements to share the costs and gains of an ongoing relationship embody the interpersonal commitments and conventional obligations of family life—in which case the partners should be entitled to the social benefits designed for the family unit. If domestic partnerships that function like families deserve to be accorded the rights of families, there is no reason that these rights should not be extended to consensual unions of both heterosexual and homosexual couples who demonstrate an equivalent degree of commitment.[6]

Employment or Family Policy?

The functional equality and the domestic partnership models of family relationships, which are vying to replace the traditional hierarchy of male dominance, form different templates for social policy. To judge the relative merits of these models, we must assess how they affect social choice, economic independence, self-realization, and family stability.

On the issue of choice, the domestic partnership model has an apparent advantage in that it does not prescribe how families should organize their labor between household and market. Policies that encourage domestic partnerships allow couples who want a relationship of complete functional equality to organize family life along those lines without any loss of social benefits. In contrast, policies that sup-

---

6. In recent years a number of localities have extended the definition of family to include domestic partnerships for some limited benefits, such as sick leave to care for an ailing partner, bereavement leave, and the right to a joint mortgage (Lewin, 1990; Hartman, 1992).

port functional equality prescribe a shift of women's labor from the household to the market so the family will benefit from separate social security accounts, for example, and state-subsidized childcare services.

Under policies associated with the domestic partnership all couples are treated the same regardless of the division of labor within their family units. Some would say, however, that neutrality toward the division of labor in family life perpetuates the traditional hierarchy of male dominance. That is, given men's reluctance to share in household chores, the socialization of women into traditional caregiving roles, and "glass ceilings" and other sorts of employment discrimination, the so-called choices promoted by domestic partnerships will inevitably result in traditional arrangements that leave women economically dependent on men.[7] The only way to avoid reinforcing the traditional division of labor, then, is through social policies that encourage women to join the labor force and that seek to obliterate gender distinctions. As Susan Okin (1992:171) explains, "Any just and fair solution to women's and children's vulnerability must encourage and facilitate the equal sharing by men and women of paid and unpaid work, of productive and reproductive labor." In her view, social policies should induce people to choose this mode of life, under which "a just future would be one without gender."

Creating a genderless future—that is a large order to fill. Okin's idealistic view raises a question about the ultimate pliability of gender roles and the limits of resocialization. Rhona Rapoport and Peter Moss (1990:1) contend that if some men and some women prefer "home activities more highly than employment activities, it is equitable as long as the choice is not involuntarily imposed." But to some extent, biology imposes predispositions, particularly in regard to childrearing (Popenoe, 1993). Thus, Mary Ann Mason (1990:48) maintains that "gender-neutral laws work to the disadvantage of women in two

7. Mohammadreza Hojat (1993) anticipates that radical feminists may challenge the United Nations Convention on the Rights of the Child, which affirms the "inalienable right of a child to be cared for by his or her parents in the home environment." Although the convention emphasizes the importance of childcare by "parents" in the home environment, it is likely to create more pressure on women than on men to assume traditional caring roles.

ways: they deny the biological and social reality of the importance of children in women's lives, and they hold mothers to a male model of competition when they are not in an equal position to compete." Moderate feminists would no doubt agree with Elizabeth Fox-Genovese's (1992:30) opinion that "sex is a difference that enlightened social policies cannot be expected to wipe away entirely."

Another reason that advocates of functional equality urge women to enter the labor force full-time involves Okin's (1992:150) claim that "in terms of the quality of work, there are considerable disadvantages to the role of housewife." In spite of findings that full-time and part-time housewives work fewer hours per week (on the average, 22 percent and 13 percent, respectively) than their employed husbands, Okin believes that women should prefer paid employment because much housework is monotonous and unpleasant. That relatively few men choose to be homemakers is offered as further evidence in support of this position.

Contrary to these claims, however, various polls indicate that large proportions of married women would prefer not to work outside the home—at least, not full-time. In response to a nationwide Gallup Organization survey in 1980, for example, 55 percent of the women who wanted to be married and have children did not wish to have a full-time job or career outside the home. And, as noted earlier, only 42 percent of the respondents in the 1989 Virginia Slims survey said that they would prefer to have jobs instead of staying home and caring for the family (Glenn, 1992).[8] A similar reluctance to engage in full-time paid employment when children are young is expressed by Danish mothers, even though public daycare is provided for children from the age of six months on and even though 90 percent of the mothers of young children are employed an average of thirty-four hours per week. When asked to describe the ideal arrangement for a nuclear family with children of nursery school age, only 3 percent of the mothers preferred to have both parents working full-time; 15 percent chose to have

8. These findings are supported by other surveys. Barbara Whitehead and David Blankenhorn (1991) cite a *Washington Post* poll and a survey by Mark Baldassare and Associates, according to which a majority of working mothers sampled in Washington, D.C., and Los Angeles would prefer to stay at home with young children if finances permitted.

the mother at home as a full-time housewife, 42 percent favored part-time employment for the mother, and 40 percent preferred to have both parents work part-time (Denmark, Ministry of Social Affairs, 1992). Christoph Badelt (1992:47) reports that in Austria, "opinion polls make clear that women do not see paid work and family work as mutually exclusive alternatives but wish to combine both options in the long run."

Whether these surveys reflect true preferences or choices shaped by social constraints encountered in the labor market is difficult to know. Critics of functional equality contend that respondents are expressing the natural desire to spend time at home with their children (Levin, 1986; Fox-Genovese, 1992; Kersten, 1991). Advocates of functional equality argue that the women's responses are influenced by social constraints (Kaminer, 1990; Faludi, 1991). Both claims may have some degree of validity. The extent to which many of the women surveyed are expressing an authentic preference for childcare and domestic activities over the full range of paid work that they are reasonably qualified to perform depends largely on how much they gain in the way of self-realization and economic independence, which are often attributed to participation in the labor force.

Unpaid family work may be described as shaping unformed personalities, nurturing relatives, and managing a household—in more pedestrian terms, caregiving, cooking, and cleaning. However portrayed, the work is less variable than the range of jobs in the paid labor force—which include, of course, caregiving, cooking, and cleaning. Participation in the labor force encompasses a vast array of activities from work that is low in status, boring, physically demanding, poorly rewarded, and dangerous to positions that are high in status, exciting, physically easy, well rewarded, and safe. We might expect those laboring at the more favorable end of this continuum—for example, artists, writers, professors, lawyers, politicians, and media personalities—to choose full-time careers over household activities. At the other end, given a choice of employment as a coal miner, factory worker, taxi driver, salesperson, clerk, guard, service worker, or mail carrier, a woman might prefer a combination of family work and part-time paid employment or a secondary career or not working in the labor force at all if she can afford it. (Some men might also make this choice.) Viewing participation in the labor force as the thoroughfare to self-realization idealizes paid employment as much as it impugns family work. The sense of challenge, achievement, and personal satisfaction often attributed to the world of paid work is, in Deborah Fallows's (1985:234) experience, "indeed compatible with the major commitment of spending time at home raising children."

With regard to economic independence, policies to achieve functional equality provide incentives for the development of two-earner families that reduce women's financial dependence on men. However, the immediate independence gained through employment and through contracting out domestic work is in a larger sense paradoxical (Gilbert, 1983). At the same time that a paycheck increases a wife's autonomy and economic independence within the family, it also heightens her susceptibility to the vagaries of the marketplace and the interpersonal constraints on wage labor. There are, of course, exceptions—typically, successful artists and writers, tenured professors, law partners, media personalities, and those at the top of the pyramid in their business firms. Still, for most men and women in the labor force, freedom from economic dependence on relatives has its own price. Employees are subject daily to the authority of supervisors, the normal discipline of the work environment, and the demands of customers—all of which may be said to exercise their own form of oppression. When spouses contract out domestic work, the autonomy that they may gain with regard to each other and the family unit they lose through increased social and economic dependence on the market economy for meeting many individual and family needs previously satisfied through the division of family labor.

If a major objective of social policy is to stabilize family life, it can be argued that policies designed to facilitate the domestic partnership model of family relationships will be more effective than those in support of functional equality. By prescribing an arrangement under which husbands and wives perform the same household tasks and divide their labor equally between housework and paid employment, the functional equality model strengthens the individual's ability to meet all of his or her social and economic needs independently. Individual autonomy reduces social and economic interdependence among family members, scraping away some of the adhesion of the family unit. What remains are emotional attachments—necessary but not always sufficient to hold the unit together over the rough patches of life. Many couples behave as an integral economic unit, pooling their resources for the common good, rather than acting as free agents joined for the advantageous exchange of goods and services.[9] Although social and economic interdependence are not the most desirable reasons for a family unit to stay together, they do thicken the glue. In any event, efforts to reinforce the stability of the family unit may involve sacrifices that do not always promote the individual happiness of adult members.

However we assess the merits of domestic partnership versus functional equality, it is clear that with the advancement in women's rights and the changing division of labor in family life, the traditional hierarchy of male dominance no longer serves as an adequate guide for family-oriented social policy. As guides to policy, the alternative models of family relationships have essential differences. The functional equality model rewards women for shifting their labor from the household to the market economy; this increases the labor supply as well as consumer demand for goods and services that were previously produced at home. At one level, the model is an employment strategy serving the needs of the marketplace. At another level, it constitutes a blueprint for structural change in society. The domestic partnership model emphasizes social choice more than structural change, focusing on the family unit and rewarding members for making mutual decisions on how best to allocate their labor between housework and paid employment. Rather than prescribing the wholesale transfer of household labor to the market, it enables varying patterns of paid and unpaid work to emerge in response to different family needs, life-cycle stages, and partners' preferences. In this sense, domestic partnership lends resiliency to family efforts to perform caretaking and domestic functions while regulating the movement of labor from the home to the market.

9. Income pooling is prevalent in American families: about two-thirds of married couples with bank accounts have only joint accounts. Couples are more likely to have separate accounts when either spouse had a previous divorce or when the wife is employed outside the home (Treas, 1993).

Chapter 2

Empowering Children and Teenage Mothers: The Presumption of Competence

The Great Society programs of the early 1960s launched almost two decades of expansion that transformed the American welfare state along several important dimensions. Measured by direct public expenditures between 1960 and 1980, the size of the welfare state almost doubled, from 10 percent to 19 percent of the gross national product. The rate of growth was remarkable compared with the relatively steady level of outlays between 1940 and 1960, when social welfare expenditures hovered at 10 percent of the GNP. Although a large part of the growth is attributable to the rising costs of social insurance for an aging population, between 1960 and 1980 every category of social welfare expenditure increased significantly as a proportion of the GNP (Social Security Administration, 1981).

As social spending climbed, a host of new programs offered benefits to many people with incomes above the poverty level. From 1973 to 1976, for example, federal expenditures for human service programs that were not earmarked for the poor increased from 47 percent to 54 percent of the total budget outlay (Aaron, 1978). In addition to an array of indirect social transfers for housing, health, retirement, and education, many welfare programs, such as daycare, community mental health, and services for elderly people, ministered to an increasingly middle-class clientele (Gilbert, 1977). The United States was not the only country affected by this trend; studies in England and Australia have documented what was coming to be called the middle-class capture of the welfare state (Le Grand, 1982; Jamrozik, 1983; Graycar, 1983).

The welfare state's accelerated growth between 1960 and 1980 was fueled by the distributive impulses of what Theodore Lowi (1969) has called interest-group liberalism. New claims to public care, protection, and support emerged as the needs of poor, elderly, and disabled people, single parents, minorities, women, children, veterans, and other groups were brought before legislators. Public officials and advocate planners encouraged these claims (Derthick, 1975; Davidoff, 1965). This brand of liberalism differed from the type practiced by the classic New Deal liberals, for whom public interests took precedence over private rights (Wolfe, 1993). From the early 1960s to the mid-1970s the number of federal domestic grant-in-aid programs soared from 200 to 1,100. With the initiation of new programs and the expansion of old ones, many groups were imbued with a growing sense of entitlement to social provisions. It was an era of burgeoning social rights, the magnitude of which was sometimes portrayed as revolutionary. But, as Mary Ann Glendon (1991:4) explains, "If there is any justification for using the overworked word 'revolution' to describe these developments, it is not that they have eliminated the ills at which they were aimed." One problem is that, lacking a finite character, social rights can be extended to cover a multitude of needs and interests, some of which conflict with, or may be more important than, others (Mishra, 1981). Joined to an ever-enlarging list, the most essential social rights may lose force and centrality.

But the growing emphasis on social rights was accompanied by a liberal mode of thought that inhibited discerning judgments. To question a beneficiary's right to public care and support was construed as "blaming the victim" of misfortune, social oppression, or capitalist exploitation (Ryan, 1971)—an accusation that discomforted people of liberal sympathies. Many social scientists were reluctant to examine the individual characteristics and behavior of those in need in order to understand their predicament. As Richard Felson (1991:19) points out, "The charge in the 1970s that certain causal arguments imply blame for victims was extremely influential in sociology." Norman Polansky (1987:42) recalls that "it was socially dangerous to focus on clients' dynamics. The fact that hard lives leave their traces on people's character was not to be discussed."[1] Thus, ardent claims to social rights by various groups and their advocates, together with views on the exercise of those rights, encountered limited opposition. Generally seen as an implicit good, social rights were not a subject for extensive critical thought. (By the 1990s this notion of unqualified rights to welfare came under reexamination, for various reasons discussed in the next chapter.)

In the absence of a critical perspective, few questions were raised that might have moderated and refined the expansion of social rights. Analyzing the haphazard proliferation of rights, Glendon (1991:177) identifies a variety of matters that deserve attention, such as "the relation a given right should have to other rights and interests; the responsibilities, if any, that should be correlative with a given right; the social costs of rights; and what effects a given right can be expected to have on the setting of conditions for the durable protection of freedom and human dignity." An important and related matter that has received little notice involves the presumption of competence to exercise social rights and their attendant responsibilities. The presumption of competence is particularly complicated in welfare efforts that address family life. Here, policy objectives are often muddled by the desire to extend parental rights while ensuring the well-being of children and to protect children's rights while encouraging parental responsibility—goals that are not always compatible. The programs of Aid to Families with Dependent Children (AFDC) and sexual abuse prevention training illustrate how the dilemma posed by these conflicting objectives is compounded by the presumption of competence. In one case the presumption of competence sustains the wrong rights for unwed teenage mothers, and in the other it promotes the wrong rights for children.

1. Relating an experience that was not uncommon at the time, Polansky (1987:42) notes, "When my coauthors and I published our book, *Roots of Futility*, describing the emotional problems of mothers implicated in substandard child care in the rural mountains, it was reviewed in *Social Work* with the borrowed title 'Blaming the Victim.'"

Parents' Rights Versus Children's Welfare: Assistance to Teenage Mothers

In 1991 the Aid to Families with Dependent Children (AFDC) program provided financial assistance to 4.3 million single-parent families at an annual cost of $20.3 billion. The average monthly AFDC payment to single-parent families is $388, ranging from $119 in Alabama to $688 in Alaska (U.S. House of Representatives, 1992). An overwhelming majority of families on AFDC are headed by women. Fifty-three percent were teenagers when their first child was born (Moore and Burt, 1982); 77 percent of all unwed teenage mothers are on the welfare rolls within five years of their first child's birth (Besharov and Gardiner, 1993). In matters of both size and composition, this caseload differs dramatically from the group that the program was originally intended to serve.

When Aid to Dependent Children (ADC, later retitled AFDC) was established in 1935, its planners conceived of the program mainly as a protective measure for deserving widows and their children, a small group who, it was believed, would shortly disappear from the public-assistance rolls through absorption into the social security system under the proviso for survivors' insurance. History, of course, proved the planners wrong. It would be unseemly to fault them for the inability to forecast the tremendous increases in divorces and out-of-wedlock births that swelled the AFDC roll to its current dimensions. Indeed, in the short run, the trends were not as precipitous as those that have emerged since 1960. Between 1940 and 1960 unmarried women gave birth at a low and fairly stable rate, rising from 3.8 percent to 5.3 percent of all births. From 1960 to 1989, however, the rate increased almost fivefold, climbing from 5.3 percent to 27 percent of all births (U.S. Bureau of the Census, 1981 and 1992). In 1989 teenage mothers accounted for about one-third of all out-of-wedlock births. But a dramatic change had taken place within this population. Although the birthrate for teenagers actually declined from ninety births per thousand women in 1960 to about sixty per thousand in 1989, the proportion of out-of-wedlock births soared, going from 15 percent of all births to teenagers in 1960 to 67 percent in 1989 (Testa, 1992; Luker, 1991).

Although the AFDC program strayed considerably from the original course envisioned by its planners, many programs evolve in unexpected directions, and such divergences are not necessarily objectionable. The changing demographic composition of AFDC recipients, however, raises a fundamental question about the presumption of competence that initially justified the provision of cash grants to single mothers in the program. In designing social welfare programs, policymakers have the option of providing benefits in various forms, such as cash, vouchers, and in-kind goods and services. As with daycare services (see Chapter 1), in-kind benefits give policymakers some control over the way tax dollars are consumed by welfare recipients; this imbues social welfare provisions with a paternalistic character which supports public choice over the exercise of individual responsibility. Cash benefits allow recipients the freedom to decide exactly what goods and services should be purchased to satisfy their needs. The recipients are presumed to be competent and responsible enough to exercise consumer choice in ways deemed socially desirable or at least inoffensive to public sensibilities. When AFDC began, it was taken for granted that the deserving widows for whom the program was designed were reasonably competent as parents and managers of family affairs. Few people imagined that a high proportion of the cash benefits provided under the program would be going to unwed teenage mothers, a group for whom the presumption of competence is open to question.

Although this question concerns only the teenage-mother segment of AFDC recipients, over half of all the women on AFDC started as teenage mothers, and the number of children of teenage mothers on AFDC (more than 213,000 in 1986) is not trivial at any time (U.S. House of Representatives, 1992). The well-being of these children deserves more attention than it has received in proposals for welfare reform.

Caring for a young child is normally a struggle, even with two parents at hand to share the physical and emotional demands. For a single parent the burden is truly formidable. If the single parent is a mother still in her teens, an unusually stormy period of human development, the demands of childrearing are often beyond her capability. The point is supported by bleak testimony: the group's excessive rates of child abuse and neglect, particularly among those who are poor (Kleiman, 1993). The American Humane Association reports that children in single-parent families are more than twice as much at risk of abuse as those in households where both parents are present, and the risk is even greater when the single parent is a teenager. Even more unsettling are the findings that the incidence of Sudden Infant Death Syndrome is 68 percent higher among children of teenage mothers than in the general population ("Baby Death," 1985). Teenage mothers have proportionately more babies with a low weight at birth than the general population does, and the percentage of low-birth-weight babies born to unmarried teenagers is even higher than for their married counterparts (Eberstadt, 1990). And children of poor teenage mothers are more likely to experience deficiencies in cognitive development, although these deficiencies are alleviated when the responsibility for childrearing is shared with an adult (Baldwin and Cain, 1980).

The formal distinction between adolescence and the age of maturity is largely one of normative judgment. The line may be fuzzy, but it is drawn by many public bodies. Federal and state governments impose constraints on youths between fourteen and twenty-one with regard to voting, qualifying for a driver's license, consuming alcoholic beverages, securing parental consent for medical treatment, and enlisting in the armed forces, to note activities that immediately come to mind. Limits are fixed because the community is not fully convinced that teenagers are able to perform responsibly in areas of social life where incompetence or lack of impulse control can have serious consequences.

In sharp contrast to the qualms about normal teenage behavior that underlie age-specific regulation of drinking, driving, voting, and the like is the remarkably lax attitude toward teenage parents that public policymakers assume when it comes to caring for their children. Adolescents presumed insufficiently mature to drive an automobile safely (not, by the way, an irrational belief in light of the unusually high accident rate among teenage drivers) are given public support under AFDC to nurture and socialize helpless infants, with virtually no conditions attached. Why is the parental competence of teenage recipients disregarded by AFDC policy despite compelling evidence of calamity?

Given the alarming rates of child abuse, neglect, and Sudden Infant Death Syndrome in this group, public officials surely must question the parental competence of unwed teenagers on AFDC. Rather than ill-placed confidence in their maternal abilities, it is more likely the dread of state intrusion into the sacred realm of parent-child relationships that deflects critical judgments on this matter. Indeed, if AFDC policy is any indication, parental competence may be a more delicate issue than the question of general competence to deal with the ordinary affairs of daily life. Up to the early 1970s everyone on public assistance was required to accept periodic home visits from caseworkers, who provided advice and counseling. The social services were linked to financial aid, the assumption being that poor people were in some manner deficient, suffering from personal pathologies that could be alleviated through casework intervention. The assumption grossly exaggerated both the curative powers of social casework and the pathology of the poor. Poor people are a diverse lot, some of whom no doubt would benefit from social services. But there is little evidence that most people on public assistance, let alone everyone—the group includes elderly, disabled, and blind people and single-parent families—need these services.

Critics charged that the obligation to accept social services in order to obtain financial aid humiliated clients and spread caseworkers so thin that their efforts could not be concentrated on those most in need. A more effective and efficient system, it was argued, would allow for the provision of services only when specifically requested by clients (Piliavin and Gross, 1977). This view eventually prevailed because, among other things, the public-assistance rolls increased by over a million recipients in the four years after funds were made available to expand casework services under the Social Security amendments of 1962.

The shift from a system of mandatory social services for all to a system of voluntary services upon request took no account of the special needs of different groups. To admit that not every public-assistance recipient requires social services simply by virtue of their economic status is not to say that no one should be obliged to accept these services. The turnabout from mandatory to voluntary provisions forfeited the opportunity to mold the service component of AFDC around factors like risk and vulnerability. Although the move to a voluntary system released AFDC parents from the infrequent but continual supervision and implicit social control of the family caseworker, it has left the children of teenage mothers exposed to care by those whom the community deems in many cases too imprudent to drive, drink, and vote. Children are rearing infants without supervision, and the public is supporting that practice. Because these children are parents, much of the common sense exercised in age-related regulatory social policies is suspended in deference to parental rights and the sanctity of family life.

What can be done? It would be best, of course, to prevent the problem of out-of-wedlock teenage births. Toward this end, various programs, such as sex education, abortion services, the distribution of contraceptives in high schools, and family-planning services, have been widely implemented over the past several decades. Evidence from national surveys in the mid-1970s suggests, however, that there are limits to what sex education alone can accomplish (Zelnick, Kanter, and Ford, 1981). Not only does it appear to have little impact on behavior, but, according to Douglas Besharov (1993b:56), "the unavoidable conclusion is that many young people who have had sex education still seem abysmally ignorant about their own bodies and reproductive processes." Moving from education to incentives, Planned Parenthood in Denver has gone so far as to experiment with paying high-risk adolescents aged sixteen and younger a dollar a day not to get pregnant.[2]

Because men contribute to the risk of pregnancy, some incentives have been honed to reckon with them, too. Men cannot be paid to avoid getting pregnant, but they can be held responsible for the support of children they sire. Under the Child Support Enforcement

2. To receive this payment, the participants—teenagers who had been pregnant before the age of sixteen—had to attend a weekly meeting and to avoid a second pregnancy (Kates, 1990).

amendments of 1984, efforts have been introduced to hold absent fathers increasingly accountable for child-support payments. The provisions were reinforced in the Family Support Act of 1988.[3]

But the extent to which education and incentives will prevent out-of-wedlock births among minors awaits the verdict of human experience. Reducing the pregnancy rate of unwed teenagers is an exquisitely complex problem, wrought of adolescent sexuality, the spontaneity and emotional exuberance of youth, deep-seated needs for acceptance and affection, and perceptions of limited opportunities for self-realization—all operating in a highly permissive social context. These psychological, biological, and cultural forces exert a powerful influence on teenage behavior, one that often transcends the preventive efforts and weak incentives of social policy.

Those young people who respond least to policies that aim to prevent illegitimacy through remedial services or incentives are the group most lacking in the judgment and self-control required to be competent parents. To the extent that preventive efforts are successful, they will reduce the incidence of illegitimate births among teenagers, leaving the AFDC rolls with a smaller but more intensely problematic group of adolescent mothers.

Ultimately, the question of what can be done must lead us to address ways to protect the vulnerable infants of unwed teenage parents. Framing the question in this manner challenges the presumption of competence under which the right to public support for unwed teenage mothers is provided without assuring their qualifications to discharge parental duties. It raises doubts about the current balance between freedom and social control for unwed teenage parents receiving AFDC and directs our attention to the unfinished business of welfare reform.

In the Interest of Children

Much of the current debate on the reform of AFDC centers on how to encourage and prepare welfare recipients for entry into the labor

---

3. Much of the credit for the renewed development of child-support enforcement schemes belongs to the research and demonstration efforts of Irwin Garfinkel and his colleagues (Garfinkel and Uhr, 1984; Oellerich and Garfinkel, 1983; Garfinkel, 1992).

force. Taking perhaps the most conservative stand held by a Democratic candidate since the inception of the welfare state, Bill Clinton proposed during the 1992 presidential campaign that recipients be allowed to collect AFDC payments for no more than two years, after which they would be expected to find employment.[4] With middle-class mothers going to work in unprecedented numbers, AFDC's original mission of providing public relief for families headed by women who are outside the labor force is not as compelling as it was half a century ago. The shift of women's labor from the household to the market economy has left less time and energy for rearing children; never an easy process, childrearing has become more complicated as families struggle to balance workplace demands with parental responsibilities. Nowadays two-paycheck families earning well above the median income often experience uncomfortable strains in managing the daily chores of domestic life. Although the domestic burdens of a two-earner family shrink in comparison with those of the employed mother in a single-parent family, public sympathies for the special conditions of the latter have contracted under the increasing pressures on family life felt throughout society.

The consensus of liberal and conservative thought on welfare reform that generated the Family Support Act of 1988 derived in part from the entrance into the labor force of a majority of mothers with school-age children; the trend makes it awkward for even the most sympathetic welfare advocates to hold AFDC recipients exempt from the obligation to seek employment.[5] There was also an emerging con-

4. A tremendous cost is attached to this proposal. Christopher Jencks (1992:36) estimates that to close the gap between what single mothers in minimum-wage jobs can earn and what they need to support their families would require annual supplements, including free medical care and at least $5,000 worth of additional resources. Otherwise, he notes, "we will end up with more abandoned children, recreating the very problem we invented AFDC to solve in the 1930s."

5. A few dissenting opinions have been voiced. George Gilder (1987:21), for example, argues that "by lending government authority to the idea that the mother's prime role is earning money rather than raising children, and by implying that government is remotely competent in child-care and job creation, a national workfare scheme would subvert the foundations of both capitalism and the family." Hardly known for his advocacy of welfare rights, Gilder centers his criticism on the extent to which reforms embodied in the Family Support Act encourage a shift in childrearing responsibility from family to government.

cern (see Chapter 3) about the moral symmetry of welfare—the stipulation that the social rights to various forms of public aid should be squared with the civic responsibility to be self-supporting (Mead, 1985).

Although the Family Support Act did not limit the allowable time on welfare to two years, it introduced the most substantial reform of AFDC since its establishment in 1935. AFDC was revised along several lines. The most important of the new provisions constitute a program generically labeled workfare; they include requiring states to operate a Job Opportunities and Basic Skills (JOBS) training program; requiring AFDC recipients with children over three years old to participate in the JOBS program (states can, at their discretion, lower the age of exemption to mothers with one-year-old children); and providing childcare services and Medicaid health coverage not only during participation in the program but also for twelve months after a family is no longer eligible to receive AFDC owing to increased income from employment.

Workfare conveys an audible message about the link between the welfare recipient's right to aid and the social responsibility to be self-supporting. It is rather mute, however, on the topic of maternal obligations and the presumption of competence for unwed teenage mothers. Focusing on parents' rights and obligations related to financial support, workfare reforms fail to take into consideration the health and safety of the children of teenage mothers on AFDC. To ensure the social protection of this high-risk group requires broadening AFDC policy concerns beyond the economic issues. In this regard, we may contemplate the feasibility of several measures, ranging from the simple extension of current reforms to the imposition of a more exacting system of AFDC program requirements for teenage parents.

Beginning with the extension of current reforms, we could make a case for requiring teenage mothers with children under three to participate in workfare programs. The implementation of President Clinton's proposal to limit the time on AFDC to two years would effectively bring a move in this direction, but for reasons connected more with the employment of AFDC mothers than with the care of their children. Taking the children's welfare as a primary objective, we could argue that they will be safer and will receive better care in all-day preschool programs than at home. From this perspective, daycare for young children would be seen as a benign experience. The interpretation of findings from a substantial body of research seems at first to support this view. The corpus of research on the effects of daycare has been summarized with such firm assurances as "It typically does no harm," "Children of working mothers do as well in school as those of mothers who stay at home," and "Children of employed and non-employed mothers do not differ on various child-adjustment measures."[6]

Upon attending more closely to the data, however, we find that the assurances are muffled by a host of qualifications acknowledging the inconsistency of findings, the lack of data on long-term effects, the inability to measure subtle characteristics, and the significant, if undetermined, influences by numerous "mediating variables"—quality of care, number of hours in daycare each day, mother's satisfaction, child's temperament, social class, age of child, father's involvement, mother's work schedule, child's sex, and number of children in the family, to mention the most obvious. Filtered through all these qualifications, summary statements equating the consequences of daycare and homecare emerge as empty generalizations.

Some argue that the generalizations are not simply meaningless but dead wrong when it comes to most full-time care for children under four. It is widely believed that the bond of love formed between mother and child in these early years affects the child's future capacity for human attachments and the regulation of aggression. As Selma Fraiberg reads the evidence, the bond is seriously impaired by placing youngsters in childcare facilities for eight to ten hours daily, Monday through Friday—the schedule that would apply to their preschool children if AFDC mothers were employed thirty to forty hours a week. At the time in life when love, trust, and self-valuation are shaped through human interaction, children in daycare may learn only the

---

6. These similar conclusions are drawn from three independent reviews of the literature: Moore and Hofferth, 1979; Heyns, 1982; and Lerner and Galambos, 1986.

churlish manners and rough justice of the preschool playground. Or they may learn "that all adults are interchangeable, that love is capricious, that human attachment is a perilous investment, and that love should be hoarded for the self in the service of survival" (Fraiberg, 1977:111).

These concerns are echoed by Deborah Fallows, whose long-standing sympathies for the women's movement were shaken by visceral reactions to the cheerless, desultory milieu of most of the daycare facilities that she observed around the country. (There were exceptional facilities, of course, the best of which charged parents from $5,000 to $8,000 a year.) Ruminating on the everyday experience of a typical child in these settings, Fallows (1985:73) depicts an ordeal marked less by outright abuse than by benign neglect: "He didn't do badly—he roamed independently, joining in when he felt like it, taking off when he didn't. He got no individual attention, because he didn't demand any. He got no special instruction, because none was offered. No one talked to him or hugged him, because there weren't enough adults to go around." It was a familiar scene of life at many centers where the main activity was filling time. If Fallows's observations are accurate, whatever the long-term effects of institutional childcare, the daily existence afforded to young children in these facilities rarely celebrates the joys of childhood.

But these kinds of evidence do not entirely dispose of the argument for full-time daycare. Even those who believe that daycare rarely provides the optimal experience for young children must address the question of its impact on highly vulnerable groups, such as the children of unwed teenage mothers, with an eye to the alternatives. Consider, for example, the statement by a child-development specialist at the University of Virginia that "children are usually better off with satisfied substitute care-givers and a happy part-time mother than with an angry frustrated full-time mother" (quoted in Krucoff, 1985:31). Though scarcely a scientific endorsement for the benefits of daycare, this claim is a reminder that, as elsewhere in life, the care of children can descend to choices between unsatisfactory alternatives. Given the high rates of abuse and neglect by teenage mothers and the teenagers' generally deficient parenting skills, it is not illusory to see daycare as a refuge from a potentially harmful home and even an asset to child development. In some cases, full-time daycare at an early age might serve this positive function reasonably well.

With regard to the effects of early daycare on child development, no one has analyzed the evidence more carefully than Jay Belsky. Psychologists find that the security of the mother-child bond exerts a measurable influence on the child's future emotional development, particularly feelings about self and others and the capacity to form relationships. In initial reviews of the research literature, Belsky and his colleagues detected little evidence that daycare for infants had any detrimental effects on the mother-child bond (Belsky and Steinberg, 1978; Belsky, Steinberg, and Walker, 1982). In the mid-1980s, however, concerns raised by findings from other studies led Belsky to reexamine the earlier research in this area (Belsky, 1988). He concluded, in cautious terms, "that if one does not feel compelled to draw only irrefutable conclusions, a relatively persuasive *circumstantial* case can be made that early infant care *may* be associated with the increased avoidance of mother, *possibly* to the point of greater insecurity in the attachment relationship, and that such care *may* also be associated with diminished compliance and cooperation with adults, increased aggressiveness, and possibly even greater social maladjustment in the preschool and early school-age years" (Belsky, 1986:6, emphasis in original).

Although this reappraisal of the data raises a serious question about the benefits of full-time daycare for young children, a new wave of research lends an intriguing twist that is particularly relevant for the infants of unmarried teenage mothers. Studies of children with extensive early daycare experiences indicate that it is not their attachment to their mothers that predicts emotional development but the security of their attachment to alternative caregivers. These findings raise the possibility that, as Belsky (1990:897) points out, "the influence that parents would otherwise exert on their children is 'lost' to or, at least assumed by, nonparental caregivers." High-quality alternative care could, then, be an asset to child development in the early years, particularly for such at-risk cases as infants of unmarried teenage mothers on AFDC.

In this light, extending workfare requirements to teenage mothers with youngsters under the age of three can be seen as beneficial to children when high-quality daycare is available. But good daycare for that age-group is very expensive, more so than most estimates suggest (Gill and Gill, 1994; Fallows, 1985). The extension of workfare would reduce the demands on teenage AFDC recipients to tend to their children in the early years and would increase their obligation to provide financial support through employment in the marketplace. This tradeoff avoids the difficult question of how to improve teenage mothering in those early years that are so critical to children's social and intellectual development.

Although workfare combined with full-time high-quality daycare for children under three sidesteps the issue, we can imagine several reform measures that would affirm the importance of early mothering and seek to influence parental behavior directly. In particular, three AFDC program changes likely to improve the quality of parental care by teenage mothers involve mandatory parent education, home-health visitors, and in-kind provision of welfare assistance. These measures differ markedly from the extension of workfare in that they invoke social controls leveled at the parent-child relationship.

Mandatory parent education is a simple, unobtrusive reform measure under which teenage mothers on AFDC would be required to take a course in childcare and to demonstrate mastery of its content. Such courses are widely available to young mothers, although at the moment they are unconnected to eligibility for AFDC benefits. No one seriously questions the unwed teenage mother's right to state support when she is unable to provide for her family. But should the community not expect that this right be accompanied by an obligation to acquire the skills and knowledge necessary to achieve an adequate standard of performance in the parenting role for which she is being subsidized? Although parent education might well be required of all AFDC recipients, it is especially germane to teenage parents, for whom the presumption of competence is most in question and the record of childcare least assuring.

What happens if a mother either refuses to attend the course or is unable to demonstrate mastery of its content? To disqualify such a parent for AFDC support leaves her children in double jeopardy, with a mother who is both destitute and inept. In the circumstances, denial of eligibility for support would be highly undesirable. The essential point of the requirement can be reinforced, however, by combining it with other reform measures. The few who, through lack of attendance or ability, are unable to pass a parenting course might be obliged, for example, to participate in a more intensive home-health visiting service than those who can demonstrate adequate knowledge of parenting skills. Enrollment in workfare is another option that could be adopted in such cases, on the assumption that children, for most of their waking hours during the week, would be better cared for in daycare centers than by a mother who cannot pass a course in the basics of good parenting.

Home-health visiting is a more intrusive measure than parent education. Although this function is routinely performed by the National Health Service for all families with babies in Britain, many Americans would probably object to having state employees regularly enter their homes to check on how well their children are doing. Even in England the practice is changing. As Robert Dingwall (1992:70) explains, "This method of total population surveillance by unannounced visits to all families by public health nurses was a key innovation in the development of tutelary thinking in the English welfare state." But in 1990 the practice was abandoned by the conservative government in favor of a contractual relationship between health visitor and parents. In the United States, loss of a certain degree of privacy has been one of the personal costs typically associated with the receipt of public aid.

As I mentioned previously, home visiting by social workers was a fundamental condition of eligibility for all AFDC recipients through the mid-1970s, but the practice was discontinued—in part because it proved ineffective in reducing economic dependency. Compared to these earlier social-casework services, home-health visiting would be more limited in both purpose and coverage. Whereas caseworkers sought to treat and rehabilitate all those on public assistance, home-health visitors would concentrate on the physical well-being of the children of teenage mothers on public aid. The weekly or biweekly visitors would offer advice and support to young mothers, as well as professional supervision of their childcare practices. At the same time that it is an attempt to enhance the parenting skills of teenage welfare mothers, this intense periodic monitoring is perhaps the best form of protection that the state can offer against abuse and neglect, short of high-quality institutional care.[7]

A move beyond incremental reforms like parent education and home visiting, the provision of in-kind assistance is a sweeping measure that would substitute residential facilities providing board and care for existing cash grants to teenage mothers on AFDC. This shift to in-kind benefits challenges the presumption of competence that justifies awarding public assistance in the form of cash to minors.

The argument, plainly stated, is that along with inadequate parenting skills, many unwed teenage mothers lack the good judgment necessary to handle cash grants and manage household affairs on their own. In accordance with this train of thought, the Family Support Act of 1988 gives the option of requiring unmarried mothers under eighteen to live with their parents or other adult relatives or to reside in a foster home or some other adult-supervised living arrangement. In fact, the majority of first-time AFDC recipients do remain at home with their parents, at least during their first year of motherhood (Jencks, 1985).

Ongoing adult supervision is generally beneficial, but not in every case. We must assess the probable quality of that supervision of minors on AFDC and the living conditions in which it occurs. Among the teenage mothers who stay with their parents, many bring the newborn child into a poor, tense, already crowded household—the same place where parental supervision, such as it was, did not impede the daughter from becoming pregnant out of wedlock. Even in the best of circumstances, teenage mothers who remain at home are likely to

7. The home visitor's role would be similar to that of the family-support workers in the Healthy Start program in Hawaii, which provides services to high-risk families with newborn children. Among the 1,204 high-risk families enrolled in this program from 1987 to 1989, only one case of child abuse and six cases of neglect were reported. Interpretation of these successful results, however, must take into account that participation in the program is voluntary (Breakey and Pratt, 1991).

experience the normal conflicts between adolescents and their parents (Musick, 1990). Among those who leave home, some are fleeing, no doubt, from an environment that would be detrimental to their children's well-being. In any event, teenage mothers might find a residential facility along the lines of a college dormitory with a variety of childcare and educational services to be an agreeable alternative to living at home with their parents.

Group homes for teenage mothers have both tight-fisted and generous renditions, depending on their primary purpose. If this approach to welfare provision is designed mainly to have a deterrent effect on potential AFDC recipients who contemplate pregnancy or single parenthood or who neglect their children, the group home will surely resemble—as Charles Murray (1985:30) observes—"a good correctional half-way house," where regulations are stern and amenities meager but where the children are at least safe and well nourished. The setting conjures visions of the nineteenth-century poorhouse, an institution rarely distinguished by humanitarian tendencies. In a short-lived 1983 revival of the poorhouse, California's Sacramento County Welfare Department introduced a program under which people eligible for General Assistance were given room and board at the Banyon Street Shelter in lieu of cash grants. Banyon Street was a squalid affair, attesting to the conventional opinion that facilities of this sort are a punitive device intended to discourage application for public assistance (Segal and Specht, 1983).

What if deterrence is not the main objective?[8] It is possible to imagine a residential facility designed to help mothers care for their children in a secure, congenial setting, where the physical environment and social temper are in closer affinity to a college dormitory than to a correctional halfway house. Such a facility would have professional staff on hand to counsel the mothers on childcare practices

---

8. If implemented, the home for unwed mothers would be likely to have some deterrent effect. A teenager may view the AFDC grant as a source of independence, as George Leibmann (1993) argues, "since it enables her to set up her own household free of parental control and supervision." He thinks that bringing back the home for unwed mothers would send a clear signal that having a child out of wedlock is no longer a means to an independent household.

and to organize cooperative efforts around the preparation of meals, babysitting, and other work needed to keep the residence running smoothly. These communal arrangements would present an opportunity to gain experience in household management and childcare while allowing sufficient time for residents to enroll in educational programs that would prepare them for future employment. Denmark has "collective houses" for single parents. One resident describes the institution as "an apartment house for mothers. We like it. We help each other, babysit for each other—we think it's great for students" (Wagner and Wagner, 1976:155).

The analogy with a college dormitory, however, should not be carried too far. Differences between a correctional halfway house and a college dormitory can be attributed as much to the character of their respective residents as to any pattern in institutional life. A group home for unwed teenagers, whatever its planned affinity with a college dormitory, would certainly possess a distinct social complexion and generate its own special problems of management.

The types of supportive services and basic amenities envisioned in a well-designed group home would be expensive, probably costing more than the average AFDC grant in many states. And the immediate benefits of a secure, nurturing environment in the early years of life are experienced only by the children served. The public benefits of such an investment are many years down the road, and even then they are not easy to measure. Some, too, might caution that the facilities not be made too agreeable lest they create an incentive for teenage pregnancy. For the moment, the danger of public spending to produce a residential environment quite that attractive to teenagers would seem highly remote.

Neither liberals nor conservatives are likely to support the coupling of a teenage mother's right to welfare with services that reinforce parental obligations to socialize, nurture, and protect children. They would object not so much to the idea of balancing parental rights and responsibilities as to the specific policy measures proposed to achieve this balance, such as parent education, home-health visiting, and residential facilities. Although many liberals might find parent education and home-health visiting generally agreeable, the selective focus and compulsory nature of these requirements for teenage AFDC mothers run counter to the conventional liberal view that government programs should be universal and voluntary—universal so that services do not discriminate in ways that might label certain groups as less worthy or competent than others, and voluntary so that they do not impose any kind of social control.[9] The standard conservative view is that the government should meddle in people's lives as little as possible, because there are limits to what federal programs can achieve. Brigitte Berger (1987:26) voices this opinion, instructing us to mind the "unintended negative by-products of scores of well-intended social programs that we have learned of in bitter past experiences."

These critiques from the left (interventions are too narrow) and right (interventions are too intrusive) are not without merit. Liberals argue that targeting services and introducing an element of social control may create discomfort for young welfare mothers. Even though children most in need of home-health visiting are found disproportionately in the households of teenage mothers on AFDC, why not provide this service to all families, they ask? To be sure, some children outside AFDC families would benefit from a universal approach to service delivery. However, to the extent that one sees home visitors from a public agency as meddling in family life, targeted services touch fewer households and are less intrusive for the general population. Also, to the extent that need is disproportionate among teenage AFDC families, targeting is more efficient than the universal approach. Even with targeted services, conservatives would complain that a healthy skepticism is in order when estimating the extent to which government programs can modify behavior to achieve socially desirable ends (for examples, see the discussion of unanticipated consequences in Chapter 3).

Yet if our concern is to invest a teenage mother's right to welfare with the obligation to care for children, measures such as parent education, home visiting, and residential facilities should be aimed toward

9. The potentially negative effects of labeling is an issue long debated in the social sciences (Rains, 1975).

this group. And if these interventions do not substantially change a teenage mother's behavior, at least they offer additional protection to children. None of the measures is entirely new. They are old schemes, adapted to accommodate the needs of the children of unwed teenage mothers. Such fine-tuning of social policy, by its very nature, offers only partial solutions to the stubborn problems of AFDC mothers. As a package, the reforms present an opportunity for a flexible, yet more exacting, policy response in the delicate realm of family relationships—a response that focuses on the early years of life. That is the best time to start caring for children.

Children's Rights Magnified: Training to Prevent Sexual Abuse

The AFDC program affords teenage mothers the right to receive aid but pays scant attention to the question of their competence to exercise the obligations of parenthood. The connections among rights, obligations, and competence take a different twist in certain programs aimed at empowering children. Sexual-abuse-prevention training programs for preschoolers epitomize the case in which children's rights are emphasized without careful evaluation of their ability to exercise these rights or of a possible conflict with parental obligations.

Programs to prevent child sexual abuse emerged in response to a serious and growing problem, the exact depths of which are difficult to gauge. Suspected incidents of child sexual abuse have multiplied at an alarming rate, climbing from 7,559 reported cases in 1976 to 155,000 in 1986 to almost half a million in 1992 (Finkelhor, 1986; U.S. Department of Health and Human Services, 1988; McCurdy and Daro, 1993). A large part of this increase reflects the framing and enlargement of mandatory reporting laws (Besharov, 1990). In spite of the expansion of these laws, experts say that many, if not most, incidents of child sexual abuse are never reported to the authorities.[10]

10. Various attempts have been made to determine the prevalence of child sexual abuse through self-reports from victims. Among fifteen surveys conducted between 1976 and 1985 (discussed in Chapter 4), estimates of the proportion of females sexually abused in the course of their childhood ranged from 6 percent to 62 percent of the population (Finkelhor, 1986).

Although rearing young children has never exactly been trouble free, today parents are engulfed by anxiety, as the most lurid cases of child rape, molestation, and kidnapping are documented in the news media with chilling frequency. The surge of reports in recent years has awakened parental fears and sparked a proliferation of initiatives throughout the United States to prevent sexual abuse of young children. Over the past decade a virtual industry has sprung up around courses in sexual abuse prevention for young children; books, curricula, videos, and an array of educational paraphernalia, such as puppets, anatomically correct dolls, and posters, have been produced for use in numerous programs supported by public funds. Most of these programs are geared for classroom training. According to one estimate, almost half the school districts across the nation provide classroom presentations on sexual abuse prevention (Daro, Casey, and Abraham, 1990).

California led the way in 1984, implementing the largest and most comprehensive classroom-based program in the country. Under the Child Abuse Prevention Training Act the state awarded $10.4 million annually for special instruction in preschool, kindergarten, elementary, and high school classes. A political juggernaut, the bill sailed through the state assembly with a seventy to two margin and won unanimous approval in the senate. The overwhelming support surely reflected a desire to protect young children. But it is difficult to form a picture of exactly what legislators thought might be transmitted in the classroom to three-, four-, and five-year-old children that could help them prevent sexual abuse. If opposition to the bill was absent, so was a critical assessment of its merits, particularly in regard to preschool children. One reason has to do with the claim by dozens of preschool children in southern California that they were sexually molested by staff at the McMartin Daycare Center. With the highly publicized McMartin case breaking just as the child abuse prevention bill was introduced in the legislature, the time was not auspicious for lawmakers to question well-intentioned prevention schemes (Berrick and Gilbert, 1991).

Although California initiated the most extensive effort in early education, sexual-abuse-prevention training programs for young children have been introduced in virtually every state. Since the early 1980s these classroom-based programs have been delivered to millions of children in thousands of schools throughout the country. Assorted titles aside—Bubbylonian Encounter (Kansas City), You're in Charge (Salt Lake City), Red Flag, Green Flag People (Fargo, North Dakota), and Talking About Touching (Seattle)—the vast majority of these programs are remarkably similar in orientation and basic content, particularly for the early grades. Beginning at the preschool level, with youngsters three to five, the majority of the programs are built around the idea that children have personal rights and should be psychologically empowered to exercise them. A content analysis of forty-one sexual abuse prevention programs across the United States identifies the "empowerment" model as the guiding framework in 61 percent of the cases and reveals that some aspects of this model were present in almost every program (Tharinger et al., 1988).

The empowerment model originated in one of the oldest and most widely used curricula, the Child Assault Prevention Program (CAPP), developed by Women Against Rape in Columbus, Ohio, in the late 1970s. Based on a philosophy drawn in part from rape-prevention programs for women, CAPP emphasizes the objectives of individual empowerment and self-protection. Underlying this approach is a feminist perspective on "powerlessness," plainly expressed in the text of a CAPP preschool training manual: "Women and children share a similar victim status in that both groups are dependent upon another group of people from whom rapists, or abusers, are drawn. Just as women have traditionally been dependent upon men, children are dependent on adults for economic support, for social identity, for protection. In addition to this dependence, children are vulnerable in other ways. Like women, children are physically smaller and muscularly weaker than their attackers" (Child Abuse Prevention Training Center of Northern California, 1983:8).

The conventional metaphor used to describe prevention programs is that they "inoculate" children with knowledge and skills, empowering them to exercise their rights and to ward off sexual abuse. What knowledge and skills are being taught by these programs? What rights are children being empowered to exercise? Although the programs employ varied instructional techniques, such as puppet shows, parrots repeating catchphrases, contests, role-playing, videotapes, songs, and stories, they usually deliver the same messages. There are, after all, certain fundamental constraints in working with preschool children: they have a brief attention span and limited ability to grasp complex ideas, so only a few simple messages can be conveyed in one to three sessions of thirty to forty minutes. Most programs try to convey basic information about touching, feeling, telling, fighting back, and dealing with strangers. At first glance, lessons like "good touch, bad touch," "no, go tell," and "stranger danger" seem to offer sound advice that might actually help to prevent the sexual abuse of young children. On closer examination the messages that these programs transmit are neither as simple nor as sound as they may appear.

The presumption is that preschool children are competent to absorb much of what is being taught and can then put the knowledge to use outside the classroom. The evidence on how much children learn from these programs is not encouraging. Among the several studies done, a two-year evaluation of seven preschool programs in California contains one of the largest samples and most detailed results (Gilbert et al., 1989). Testing 118 children before and after participation in sexual-abuse-prevention training courses, the researchers examined what the subjects—who ranged in age from three and one-half to five—learned from lessons about feelings associated with being touched and how to react to them, when not to keep secrets, and how to deal with strangers. The researchers found that preschoolers had only a rudimentary grasp of the connection between the physical act of being touched and the emotions it might generate; many of the subjects could not absorb the central lessons of prevention training, which rely on children's feelings to interpret "good touch, bad touch" experiences. Many children were also confused by the idea that they should report to adults when other grown-ups told them secrets that made them feel uncomfortable. Finally, they made only limited gains in dealing with strangers, which left about half the children ill equipped to face potentially threatening situations. At the same time, there was some indication that the programs may have heightened children's sensitivity to negative feelings about physical contact. Overall, the researchers conclude that under the most conservative assumptions (that is, ignoring increases in knowledge that might be due only to the effect of being tested and ignoring the possible erosion of learning over time), the best that can be said is that these programs yield very limited gains in knowledge.

This general conclusion is corroborated by findings from several smaller studies on prevention programs in preschool and the early grades of elementary school (Melton, 1991). Joyce Borkin and Lesley Frank (1986), for example, carried out a study in which a group of eighty-four preschoolers were asked, after they received prevention training: What should you do if someone tries to touch you in a way that does not feel good? In response, only 4 percent of the three-year-olds and 43 percent of the four- and five-year-olds spontaneously offered one of the safety rules that they had been taught—say no, run away, tell someone. Because this study involved a post-test-only design with no control group, it is not possible to determine what proportion of the children who responded correctly would have done so even without the training. Whatever learning may have taken place, two-thirds of the children were apparently unable to absorb the simple lessons.

Findings from a study of 183 children participating in the Talking About Touching program are similar: the subjects achieved an average score of 47 percent on the curriculum content for which they were tested (Liddell, Young, and Yamagishi, 1988). Unlike the average prevention-training curriculum for preschoolers, which covers the material in two or three sessions, the Talking About Touching program involves over twenty lessons. The findings from this study are particularly interesting because they suggest that after more than twenty lessons the children were still unable to answer correctly more than half the items on a small test (which ranged from 0 to 13 points). Moreover, it is unclear to what extent the correct responses were learned from the program, because these researchers also employed a post-test-only design; there was no measure of how much children knew before they took the prevention training.

If none of the social research on sexual abuse prevention training for three- to five-year-olds is methodologically flawless, well, the subject matter is elusive, and the trainees are very young. To understand just how young, consider the classic findings of the development theorist Jean Piaget (1954): When water in a flat dish is poured into a tall, narrow cylinder, most four-year-olds will observe that the cylinder contains more liquid than the dish from which it came, mistaking a change in shape for a change in mass. Is the four-year-old who cannot grasp what Piaget calls the conservation of quantity likely to seize the meaning of lessons that try to convey the far more subtle change of emotions aroused by a soft touch that at first feels good, then becomes confusing, and finally feels bad?

Whatever is learned in prevention training, answering the question of how well that knowledge will be put to work outside school is extremely difficult for both practical and ethical reasons. Testing how children might employ classroom instructions about "good touch, bad touch," "no, go tell," "yelling for help," and "physical self-defense" would require placing them in threatening or seductive situations, and doing so is beyond the pale of acceptable social experimentation. Lessons on coping with "stranger danger" are easier and less controversial to simulate (although the deception required for such research remains open to serious criticism). Evidence drawn from several studies using simulations suggests that training techniques can increase the degree of stranger avoidance in particular circumstances (Fryer, Kraizer, and Miyoshi, 1987; Peterson, 1984; Poche, Yoder, and Miltenberger, 1988). As Gary Melton (1991) points out, however, it is unclear whether what is learned can be applied to social contexts in which a stranger's approach is more subtle or threatening than approaches simulated for research purposes.

Altogether, the empirical evidence on preschool programs shows that even though the participants' scores went up, the actual increase in learning was usually quite limited, even when the changes were statistically significant. We would hardly expect these small gains to materially influence behavior in ways that would prevent sexual abuse.[11]

---

11. Research on other forms of prevention training with much older children than preschoolers (programs for adolescents to reduce pregnancy, alcohol abuse, and drug

The programs might be improved if training curricula were revised in light of the developmental abilities of preschool children and if more classroom time was devoted to their presentation. It is not at all clear, however, whether such awful and mysterious adult behavior can be explained in ways that are comprehensible to small children. Definitiveness and simplicity are required to convey ideas to young children, but training to prevent sexual abuse must deal with behaviors and emotions that are relative and complex.

Six years after the California legislature had hastily passed the Child Abuse Prevention Training Act of 1984, the presumption of competence underlying preschool training came under critical scrutiny. In the face of a budget deficit and a critical report by the Legislative Analyst's Office, state funding for the programs was withdrawn. The report had concluded: "It is, in general, unclear whether the knowledge imparted by the program helps children to change their behavior and thereby prevents abuse. Moreover, researchers and experts disagree over how to interpret the information gains that the program has demonstrated. Finally, a large body of evidence, summarized in the department's own task force report, indicates that much of the preschool curricula is beyond the cognitive ability of preschoolers" (Berrick and Gilbert, 1991:123). Sexual abuse prevention training for preschoolers, however, continues to be offered in many schools throughout the country.

Undermining Parental Authority

Even if preschool children could learn the material and put it to use as instructed in the sexual abuse prevention programs, there remains a fundamental normative issue: Are the lessons on children's rights and behaviors ones that preschoolers *should* be learning? The question of what is learned can be answered with varying degrees of precision by empirical research, but the normative issue cannot be settled so neatly. It deals with questions like What are the acceptable bounds of physical

---

abuse, for example) indicates that although gains in knowledge usually follow program participation, knowledge about prevention is rarely related to changes in behavior (Kirby, 1984; Moskowitz, 1989).

intimacy? What are appropriate parent-child relationships? What are the social expectations for childhood? To understand the normative implications of prevention programs, we must examine their curricula.

A content analysis of five widely used preschool curricula reveals that a considerable amount of material in every program is devoted to discussions about physical contact, the feelings aroused by being touched on different parts of the body, and the appropriate reaction for young children.[12] Both assaultive and sexually related behaviors are addressed as forms of touching. Of the two, assaultive behavior is the easier to describe to children. But, even here, complications arise. Hitting, pinching, kicking, and biting are painful to those on the receiving end. It is not difficult to convey the idea that a bad touch is one that hurts. In virtually every curriculum the uniform response to a bad touch is "no, go tell." Children are taught to demand that the touching stop and then to tell their parents, the police, a teacher, or some other adult. The lesson is reinforced by explaining to children that they own their bodies and that no one has a right to touch them in ways that do not feel good.

This emphasis on children's rights and feelings affirms the philosophical position that underlies much of the training in prevention programs. The position takes little account of parental rights and responsibilities in family life. One curriculum, for example, begins with a skit in which three-year-old Vivian tells her mother and father that she feels hungry and asks for something to eat. When the parents refuse, this is presented as a violation of Vivian's "right to eat." By no means atypical, this example illustrates the unconditional view of children's rights that is expressed in many programs.

By contrast, parental rights—indeed, parental obligations—to

12. The material discussed here is based on a content analysis of the following five curricula: Children's Self-Help Project, *Preschool Curriculum* (San Francisco, 1985); *Child Sexual Abuse Prevention Education Program* (San Luis Obispo, Calif., mimeo, n.d.); Child Assault Prevention Training Center of Northern California, *Preschool Project Training Manual* (Berkeley, 1983); Carol Grimm and Beck Montgomery, *Red Flag, Green Flag People Program Guide*, rev. ed. (Fargo, N.Dak.: Rape and Abuse Crisis Center, 1985); and *Talking About Touching with Preschoolers: A Personal Safety Curriculum* (Seattle, Wash.: Seattle Institute for Child Advocacy, 1985), adapted by Margaret Schonfield from the Talking About Touching elementary curriculum by Ruth Harms and Donna James.

deny some of a child's requests are given little recognition. Often parents exercise discretion about feeding their children; they may refuse a child's request for food because the child just had lunch, is having dinner in a little while, is overweight, or is asking for junk food. Do children really have a right to eat whenever they feel hungry? Do they have a right to eat whatever tastes good to them? The answers are not quite so simple as the message that children receive in these programs. We could say that a child has a right to a balanced nutritious diet, but such a concept is well beyond the grasp of three-year-olds. Obviously, there is a need to simplify ideas for presentation to young children.

Simplifying the material, however, overlooks the complicated issue of balancing the rights of parents and children. A case in point is the way these lessons treat corporal punishment. Does spanking qualify as a bad touch? Is it a violation of a child's rights? Should children report this parental behavior to other adults or authorities? Among the five curricula analyzed, only one program guide addresses the distinction between a spanking given by parents and "bad touches." Here teachers are explicitly instructed to point out that a bad touch is different from a spanking and to suggest that children may deserve to be spanked by parents if they do something naughty or dangerous. The instructions go on to draw a line between a simple spanking and a beating that results in bruises, bleeding, or broken bones: if children are hit so hard as to suffer physical injury, they are encouraged to report the incident. Most prevention programs not only fail to distinguish spankings from assaultive behavior; they also quietly but directly advance the view that spanking is a form of child abuse.

The view is not uncommon. In Sweden, for example, it is illegal to spank children. Although the law carries no penalties for violations, it does embody a symbolic consensus concerning proper childrearing behavior. Many people in the United States also oppose corporal punishment for children, but public opinion is substantially divided. Studying 364 mothers from six ethnic groups (African Americans, Cambodians, Caucasians, Hispanics, Koreans, and Vietnamese), for example, Helen Ahn (1994) found that 70 percent thought that spanking was an effective punishment for children, and 40 percent reported that it was one of the ways they usually disciplined their own children. The responses to both questions revealed significant differences among ethnic groups.

If opposition to corporal punishment was all that good touch, bad touch lessons promoted, then those with dissenting views might register a mild objection and leave it at that. To spank or not to spank is not, after all, an issue over which most people get terribly exercised. But more profound matters of social and physical intimacy are at stake, particularly when the lessons on touching move from physically assaultive to sexually related behaviors.

What exactly constitutes a bad touch? In most cases children are told that how they feel about a touch is what makes it good or bad. One curriculum guide includes wet or yucky kisses, tight hugs, and spankings that children receive from parents and grandparents among the typical negative or "Red Flag" touches. These touches are put into the same Red Flag category as incest, genital fondling, and other sexual abuses. At several points the curriculum guide reminds teachers to emphasize "that it is how the person receiving the touch feels that makes it a Red Flag or Green Flag touch." When children feel they have received a Red Flag touch, they are instructed to tell their parents, a police officer, or their teacher.

In introducing bad touches that are sexual, many programs begin by teaching children to identify their private parts. But there is disagreement about what these private parts include. The minimalists define them as the genitals or the body parts covered by underwear. A more expansive view includes the mouth and chest. And in some programs physical contact on any part of the body that does not "feel good" is a bad touch. One curriculum, for example, explicitly acknowledges that the hair is not a private part, whereas another uses role-playing in which a four-year-old girl is congratulated for informing her teacher about the next-door neighbor who sometimes invites her into his house for milk and cookies and then touches her hair. Thus, in the most inclusive view of bad touching, children are taught that even a pat on the head should be reported to the authorities if it feels funny. From this perspective (all-embracing in every sense), how a child feels about gentle physical contact anywhere is the essential determinant for separating good and bad touches. Reliance on children's intuition is a dominant feature in preschool curricula for sexual abuse prevention training. This is true even though the designers of one program do not trust entirely in children's feelings; the class is told that if "someone touches them very gently on their private parts and it feels nice," the touch is still a bad one. According to another program, however, "no one should touch you in private parts of your body *if it feels funny or you don't like it*" (emphasis added). In this case, presumably, if it feels nice, it is all right.

Talking About Touching is among the most popular curricula in the country. The 1985 revision of the program guide includes a simple rule on safe and unsafe touching to supplement the conventional reliance on children's feelings. The rule is that no part of the body covered by a bathing suit (with tops for girls) should ever be touched by another person except while one is being bathed or being examined by a doctor. If the rule is broken, children are encouraged to report the touch to parents or teachers. It is no doubt physically possible for mothers and fathers to pick up their four-year-old-daughters for a hug or hold them on their laps without touching the child's chest—if the parents' hands are carefully placed under the children's arms and their fingers do not stray an inch. But if anyone took the rule seriously, it would certainly induce the avoidance of such physical contact.

In 1986 the superintendent of the Waukegan (Illinois) School District warned his 700 teachers not to touch any of the 12,000 students in any way, fearing that a hug or a pat on the back might bring accusations of sexual abuse in the classroom. This advice met with sharp criticism from childcare experts and community leaders. "Touching and hugging," in the words of a PTA leader, are "an indication that love is present" (Olmstead, 1986:22). But children are being taught that a hug from a teacher whom they do not like, a hug that feels too tight or that they are not in the mood for, is not an expression of affection but a bad touch. The school superintendent's warning, which at first appears recklessly insensitive, seems merely prudent when placed in the context of good touch, bad touch lessons.

If children are expected to cope with bad touches, they must be made aware of the possible sources of sexual abuse. Whom should children be on guard against? In the words of one curriculum guide, "There are two kinds of people who touch children on parts of their bodies when they don't like it or it feels funny: strangers (or people you don't know), and people you do know." Stranger danger is one of the themes widely communicated in child-abuse-prevention programs. Children are instructed not to speak to strangers, not to take anything from them, and not to accompany them anywhere. One rule often cited is to stand at least an arm's distance away when strangers approach, which presumably gives children room to run if the stranger tries to grab them. This kind of simple rule appears precise, sounds almost scientific, and gives the impression that a practical lesson is being taught. It is highly unlikely, however, that a four-year-old could outrun a determined adult with a mere arm's distance between them at the outset. By recommending such a strategy, instructors may impart a false sense of security to their pupils.[13]

But strangers are not the only potential offenders discussed in the training programs. Family members, particularly fathers, stepfathers, and uncles, are more quietly but no less clearly identified as examples of people who may sexually abuse children.[14] Three- and four-year-old children are unlikely to imagine spontaneously that their parents might sexually abuse them. To place the thought in their minds is

13. Nobody knows how many children are sexually abused by strangers. Most estimates indicate that 80–90 percent of the cases of sexual abuse involve offenders known to the child. The actual rate of abuse by strangers is probably lower than those estimates suggest, because molestation by strangers is more likely to be reported than instances involving family members. Why, then, do programs devote such attention to stranger danger? Because many parents find the lesson reassuring. More important, we would not expect most parents to harbor much enthusiasm for programs that teach their children about protecting themselves against "daddy danger" or sexual assault by other family members.

14. There is some evidence that communicating the possibility of intrafamilial sexual abuse is one of the lessons that older children can learn rather quickly. A study of sixty-three children aged eight to eleven, for example, found that after taking a course that included information on family members as potential sexual offenders, there was a significant increase in the extent to which subjects contemplated the possibility of interfamilial sexual abuse. Indeed, among twelve measures of change, the largest difference was registered on the question of whether a family member could inflict violent sexual abuse; the proportion of affirmative responses more than doubled, from 39 percent to 88 percent (Swan, Press, and Briggs, 1985).

risky. As one curriculum guide notes: "This point needs to be made in a sensitive way that will not overly concern children about responsible parental figures." The example offered in the guide tells the story of a father who touches his daughter's private parts while tucking her into bed. Exactly how to present this story in a way that is not overly disturbing, however, is left to the teacher's imagination.

In addition to dealing with good and bad touches, when children are unable to avoid a threatening situation—being cornered or grabbed by an assailant—the programs inform them to scream as loudly as possible. The *Child Assault Prevention Training Preschool Training Manual*, one of the most frequently used, also teaches children to fight back: "You can kick them. Even if they try to pick you up you can kick them. But, you have to remember not to kick them too high or you can fall over. (Dolls demonstrate kick.) You can stomp on their foot. (Demonstrate stomp.) And you can bite, scratch, pinch. You can do anything you can to get away." By creating a dangerously false impression of a four-year-old's ability to defend herself against an adult, this lesson exemplifies the shallowness of the presumption of competence underlying much of preschool training. It is hard to imagine how a ten-minute lesson teaching little children to fight can increase their safety.

At the end of the day, what are children and their parents to make of these ideas? True, touching can be good, bad, or confusing depending on which parts of the body are touched, by whom, and in what circumstances. Intuition may be helpful, but even adults have a hard time sorting all this out. How many adults are seduced every day by false promises, candy, flowers, and gentle touches? Perhaps the children, in their innocence, have intuition that is more penetrating than adults'. However, the evidence on this score is hardly compelling.

Because of the need for simplicity, these curricula promote the importance of children's rights and feelings at the expense of adults' rights and feelings. Hence the programs teach that the yucky kiss from Uncle Bill, the tight hug from Grandma, and the unwanted caress from Dad, none of which may feel good, are therefore bad touches. The touches are seen as infringing on the child's rights; they should be automatically resisted and perhaps even reported. At best, this view disregards the deep affection from which these physical expressions usually arise; at worst, it implies that something insidious lurks behind simple physical contact. Relying heavily on the intuitive powers of three- to five-year-old children, the lessons cultivate self-centeredness and place unwarranted confidence in children's abilities to sort out complex emotional responses.

It is true that most seductions of young children start with a touch, a pat on the head or the behind, a kiss, an offer of candy, or the like; but most touches, pats, kisses, and offers of candy do not lead to the seduction of young children. They are, instead, warm, sincere, and nurturing expressions of familial love. But through numerous examples of bad touches and "uh-oh feelings" the lessons transmit a sense of touching as perilous. Even strong advocates of sexual abuse prevention training have voiced serious concerns about the unanticipated consequences of these lessons, noting, for example: "If children have already had peer sexual experiences (playing doctor, etc.) what sense do they make of it after all the discussion about good and bad touching? Are they apt to feel guilty or confused, especially since the programs are unlikely to give such sex play specific endorsement? How many children exposed to these programs get the idea that sexual touching is always or almost always bad or dangerous or exploitive? . . . These are important issues that have not been considered very thoroughly by the educators themselves, not to mention researchers" (Finkelhor and Strapko, 1991:163).

What children learn in school carries the implicit weight of public authority. And preschoolers are highly impressionable. The few groups who design and deliver child-abuse-prevention training throughout the country have come to exercise an undue influence in defining appropriate behavior for parents and children. Under the presumptive authority of the schools in which these programs are offered, the curriculum planners prescribe narrow boundaries for children's responses to physical intimacy in family life. But physical intimacy between parents and children is intensely private and quite diverse in its expression. The lessons of child-abuse-prevention training set normative boundaries that do not take into account the diverse patterns of acceptable behavior in American family life (Ahn and Gilbert, 1992). To a four-year-old child, depending on the curriculum, a parent's affectionate pat on the behind may appear to violate the dictum against touching private parts or to require conscious appraisal to determine its momentary goodness or badness.

Whether or not the cognitive development of preschoolers allows them to make sense of prevention training, these programs raise fundamental questions about children's and parents' rights and responsibilities. Preschool children need care and security. At a time in their life when it is important for them to feel that their parents will nurture and protect them, should children be taught to evaluate the boundaries of appropriate adult behavior? The underlying message in the empowerment of four-year-olds is that they must try to control the dangerous outside world; they have not only the rights to privacy, to restricting access to their bodies, and to saying no to unwanted touches but the obligation to exercise these rights. In the course of emphasizing the empowerment of children, sexual abuse prevention programs discount both parental rights to set boundaries in family life and parental responsibilities for protecting their children.

Real dangers do, of course, exist. A distressing number of children are at risk of physical and emotional injury from adults whose touches are not innocent expressions of affection. To criticize sexual abuse prevention training for preschoolers is not to deny the serious problems that these programs attempt to alleviate. But empowering four-year-olds, whom adults normally forbid to cross the street alone, defies common sense. Viewed most positively, these lessons are a social placebo that may bewilder children while soothing parental anxieties. At worst, the training experience may leave youngsters psychologically on edge—a little less able to enjoy the innocence of childhood. The resources consumed by training preschool children might be used more constructively for programs designed to sharpen the vigilance of parents, teachers, and other responsible caretakers in children's lives. This approach would place the duty for protecting children closer to family and community, where it belongs. Thus, after reviewing the research evidence and critical assumptions underlying these programs, Reppucci and Haugaard (1993:307) conclude "that the targeting of children as their own protectors may be misguided, and that advocates' faith in these programs may actually retard the development of other programs targeting parents, other adults, and the community that might be more effective."

In recent years the expansion of social rights has come under increasing scrutiny. Without challenging their importance, questions are being raised about the need to balance rights and responsibilities, to consider how one group's rights and interests relate to another group's, and to measure the growing cost of social rights (Glendon, 1991; Wolfe, 1991; Etzioni, 1991). Teenage mothers on AFDC and preschoolers in training programs to prevent sexual abuse are cases in point. Beyond the need to examine the different and sometimes competing rights and interests of parents and children, these cases draw attention to a more difficult issue: the presumption of competence. Policymakers and program planners who confer and reinforce social rights must come to grips with the question of how well beneficiaries are able not only to exercise the rights but to discharge the accompanying responsibilities. As the philosophy of social protection shifts from emphasizing rights to clarifying responsibilities, the presumption of competence to fulfill social obligations will carry an increasing burden of proof where the weakest and most vulnerable are concerned.

Chapter 3

Changing the Philosophy of Welfare: From Entitlements to Incentives

Entitlements to social benefits increased with the development of modern welfare systems not only in the United States but in most industrialized democracies as well. The rise is reflected in the growth of social expenditures, the average volume of which doubled, from 12.3 percent to 24.6 percent of the gross domestic product (GDP), among twenty-one member nations of the Organization for Economic Cooperation and Development between 1960 and 1985 (OECD, 1988).[1] Although direct social expenditures are just a crude estimate of total welfare spending (see Chapter 5), these figures convey a sense of the powerful tides of expansion that buoyed social policy initiatives between 1960 and 1980, when most of the increases took place.

During that period the fundamental problems of social welfare allocation were framed by two questions: How much can society afford to spend (usually expressed as a percentage of the GDP) on the different needs of various groups? and How will policymakers identify the people in these groups who are entitled to benefits? (Berkowitz, 1981). The logic of rational planning dictates answering the first question, which poses a global constraint, before addressing the second, which formulates the rules of entitlement for allocating resources under that constraint. In practice, things tend to work the other way around: the amount to be spent is derived from decisions about the nature of entitlement.

1. The average represents a scale of expenditures in 1985, which ranged from 15 percent to 36 percent of the GDP, and rates of growth, which ranged from 50 percent to 360 percent over the span of twenty-five years.

Thus, in analyzing disability insurance, Monroe Berkowitz (1981:1) points out "that in almost all nations, it is the entitlement to benefits questions that are asked and answered first." In fact, his observation applies to most areas of social provision and reflects the perennial concern with extending entitlements that exemplified the policy orientation of welfare states until the early 1980s.

Philosophically, welfare-state entitlements are often interpreted as the "social rights of citizenship." As T. H. Marshall (1950) has explained, in the transition from traditional to industrial society these rights not only offered social protection against the vicissitudes of the market economy but also served as a means for social integration, forming a bond that joined the individual and the state. The exact package of social rights to which citizens are entitled is indeterminate, however, allowing considerable leeway for the proliferation of welfare benefits.

From the social-rights perspective, the criteria for entitlement to welfare benefits usually include one's status as a citizen and one's membership in a group vulnerable to some form of risk, such as disabled, elderly, poor, or unemployed people or sole parents. The focus of concern is neither the worthiness of recipients nor their behavior; rather, it is the range of benefits to which citizens may lay claim. As a guide to policy over the past several decades, the social-rights perspective has provided a beacon illuminating problems and dangers against which citizens were entitled to a wide array of protections.

In recent years there has been a marked shift in philosophical orientation toward welfare entitlements—a shift accompanied by a new class of practical issues with which policymakers are just now coming to grips. The social-rights perspective has been inverted as analyses concerning the nature of entitlements have turned from expanding social claims to delineating the responsibilities associated with these claims. The question now being asked is, If social welfare benefits are the rights of citizenship, what civic responsibilities attend these rights? Although social rights are manifest in tangible benefits to which individuals are legally entitled, social responsibilities are more difficult to identify. They rest more on a normative consensus about how people are expected to behave and what they owe each other than on a set of prescribed legal duties. Alan Wolfe (1989:2) explains the difficulty of defining a moral code that specifies people's obligations to one another: "Neither the liberal market nor the democratic state is comfortable with explicit discussions of the obligations such codes ought to impose. . . . Both emphasize rights rather than obligations. Both value procedure over purpose. When capitalism and liberal democracy combine, people are given the potential to determine for themselves what their obligations to others ought to be, but are then given few satisfactory guidelines on how to fulfill them."

Current philosophical deliberations about the nature of social responsibilities that accompany entitlements to social welfare benefits have been more explicit and vigorous in the United States than in Europe. Lawrence Mead's (1986) analysis of social obligations in the mid-1980s launched the American debate over the extent to which entitlement to public aid should be conditioned on the recipients' performance of expected behaviors, such as working in available jobs, contributing to the support of their families, learning enough in school to be employable, and respecting the law. The debate was broadened by the Communitarian movement, which started a few years after the debate was under way (Etzioni, 1991b; Glendon, 1991). The movement has attracted members from both liberal and conservative camps with an agenda dedicated to forging a new middle ground between Reagan-Bush conservatism and New Deal–Great Society liberalism and bringing questions of the appropriate balance between social rights and responsibilities to the forefront of public discourse on social policy.[2] One measure of its progress is reflected in the support for Communitarian themes frequently expressed by both Clinton and Gore during the 1992 presidential campaign (Galston, 1992).

Centrist intentions to carve the middle ground notwithstanding, discussions of social responsibilities tend to echo conservative thinking

2. Communitarian principles for improving the moral symmetry between individual rights and civic obligations are outlined in the *Responsive Communitarian Platform* (1992), whose initial signatories include such thinkers as Robert Bellah, Amitai Etzioni, William Galston, Mary Ann Glendon, Albert O. Hirschman, Richard John Neuhaus, David Reisman, Alice Rossi, Isabel Sawhill, and Lester Thurow.

about welfare, which recalls earlier distinctions between the "deserving" (socially responsible) and "undeserving" (irresponsible) poor. If the general inquiry into how social rights to welfare are related to individual responsibilities is less vigorously pursued by social policy analysts in Europe, this may reflect the fact that the liberal tradition among European supporters of the welfare state is stronger than in the United States and perhaps more sensitive to the peal of conservative thought in these questions. Some might see raising philosophical questions about the balance of social rights and responsibilities as challenging the basic tenets of social rights to welfare. In policy analyses conducted by the Organization for Economic Cooperation and Development, for example, we find that advice to limit or redefine entitlements is often qualified by an affirmation of social rights, as in the following: "This logic, therefore, equally suggests that *within a framework which respects individual rights* some form of training could be a mandatory part of any income support package" (OECD, 1988a:27, emphasis added). Here is another such reassuring phrase: "*Without calling into question its central tenets*, the welfare system should be refocused and made less generous in terms of eligibility and benefits" (OECD, 1991:89, emphasis added).

Whatever hesitancy may exist about entering the philosophical debate, practically speaking, the questions of how welfare policy may influence social behavior, particularly in connection with participation in the labor force, are very much on the agenda of modern welfare states. Although this development is not uniform across industrial countries, it is strong enough to be noticeable. The International Social Security Association's (1989:258) review of major trends in social security between 1978 and 1989, for example, takes note of an increasing realization that "social policies should be designed in such a way that they do not hinder the development of the economy by their absorption of resources, but on the contrary support it by reinforcing the social factors that underlie productivity." In a similar vein, the Organization for Economic Cooperation and Development (1988a:24) suggests in a report entitled *The Future of Social Protection* that social policies should be more attuned to the improvement of economic performance and "concerned with the effective functioning of the supply side of the economy as one way to achieve important social aims." In the diplomatic language of international organizations, both of these statements are saying that social welfare efforts should be directed toward putting more people to work.

Encouraging the development of an "active society," the OECD favors replacing welfare policies that offer "passive" income supports with measures designed to stimulate employment and other responsible activities (OECD, 1989; Kalisch, 1991). Commenting on this development in Sweden, Marklund (1992:10) finds that "the move towards market-oriented social security structures in Sweden includes an effort to increase the productivity and competitiveness of the economy. But it also includes stronger pressures on the individual worker. The idea of welfare according to need has at least partly been replaced by incentive-oriented policies." In the United States such incentive-oriented measures have been labeled the new paternalism (Besharov, 1992). Whether policy initiatives are identified as promoting the active society or presented in the less sanguine nomenclature of the new paternalism, in both Europe and the United States we see a growing interest in the formulation of measures that encourage labor-force participation and facilitate economic independence.

Linking Benefits and Incentives

Modern welfare states are built on a foundation of income-maintenance programs, including public assistance, unemployment insurance, disability insurance, and public pensions. Since the mid-1980s policymakers have introduced a wide range of laws and regulations to link welfare benefits in each of these areas with incentives to work.

In the United States the most extensive reforms have dealt with public assistance, starting with the Family Support Act of 1988. Representing what many herald as the new public consensus on welfare reform, the act requires welfare mothers with children over three years old to enroll in work-training or educational programs, at the completion of which they must seek employment. To facilitate the transition from welfare to work, eligibility for daycare services and Medicaid health insurance is continued during the first year of employment (Novak, 1987). Mothers applying for welfare are obliged to help establish paternity so that their children's fathers can be held accountable for child-support payments. Behind the carrot of extended services and benefits hovers the stick of threatened grant reduction for those who do not comply with the work-training and job-search requirements (though the sanction is rarely applied).

In 1991 a new wave of reforms rolled in as a number of states implemented various incentives to encourage self-sufficiency (Greenstein, 1992; Mead, 1992). New Jersey, for example, tied benefits to the requirement that recipients show progress toward a high-school-equivalency diploma, allowed welfare mothers to keep a portion of their benefits if they married, and denied benefit increases to mothers who had additional children while on the welfare rolls (Florio, 1992). Other states were also experimenting with rewards and penalties that would induce teenage mothers to attend school, secure preventive health care for their children, and require their children's attendance at school. By 1993 Congress was proposing ways to implement President Clinton's promise to put a two-year limit on welfare dependency (a reform discussed in Chapter 6).

Out of concerns similar to those that have prompted welfare reforms in the United States, public assistance in the United Kingdom is under review; policymakers have misgivings about the extent to which income support benefits create employment disincentives for single parents. Here, too, many noncustodial parents are remiss in meeting the financial obligation to support their families. Recognizing that the financial support of single parents is a legitimate function of public assistance, Jonathan Bradshaw and Jane Millar (1990:458) caution: "If it is to avoid providing 'enforced dependency,' action will be needed to enable lone parents to work."

France is also engaged in crafting work-oriented reforms. In 1988 the Revenu Minimum d'Insertion was introduced by Prime Minister Michel Rocard as a "veritable revolution in welfare entitlement" (Collins, 1990:121). Designed to aid the poor, the program provides allowances ranging from 53 percent of the national minimum wage for a single claimant to 86 percent for a couple with two children— amounts that are reduced franc for franc by income from any other sources. To receive these benefits, however, participants are obliged to sign a contract of rehabilitation, negotiated with a local committee, that contains a timetable for specific steps toward vocational reintegration. The allowances are reviewed quarterly and can be revoked if recipients fail to discharge their contractual obligations.

Just as public-assistance reforms are incorporating incentives to work, a number of initiatives have been undertaken to forge closer ties between unemployment-compensation benefits and measures to promote employment. These changes are more evident in Europe than in the United States because European unemployment schemes tend to offer benefits that are comparatively higher, last longer, and are often available to teenagers with no employment record. These more generous arrangements provide less incentive for recipients to seek work. To stimulate greater efforts in that direction, New Zealand, Sweden, and the United Kingdom, for example, now make a teenager's receipt of unemployment benefits conditional on participation in an employment-related activity (OECD, 1989). In Spain unemployed persons are faced with the loss of entitlements if they refuse to accept a suitable job offer or refuse to participate in training programs or public-utility work. Germany also imposes penalties for beneficiaries who refuse to take approved job-training courses. In Australia the payment of unemployment benefits under the Newstart program, introduced in 1989, is contingent upon the claimant's engaging in various job-training activities. As David Kalisch (1991:8) describes it, the program "builds in a balance of supportive assistance and client obligations to encourage and facilitate re-employment." (Expressed in terms of balancing assistance and obligations, the program can be seen within the broader philosophical context of promoting moral symmetry between rights and responsibilities in social policy.)

Other incentives have been fashioned that do not involve the possible forfeiture of benefits; examples are the provision of grants for traveling expenses incurred in quest of employment in other regions and lump-sum grants for unemployed persons seeking to create new enterprises. With such measures pointing the way, Alain Euzeby (1988:18) advises that unemployment insurance be designed to help the unemployed person adjust to the changing requirements of the labor market. Instead of making income maintenance the most immediate form of aid provided, he recommends that "payment of benefits to the unemployed should be considered as a last resort."

Disability insurance is also being reshaped by proposals for change and by reforms currently under way, which couple the right to benefits with incentives for economic independence. In 1991 policy reforms in the Netherlands, for example, were activated in response to the alarming level reached by entitlement claims. Between 1980 and 1990 the number of people receiving disability payments increased from 12 percent to 14 percent of the Dutch labor force. As the number rose, the average age of beneficiaries declined, and the proportion who qualified on the basis of psychological hardship expanded from 21 percent to 27 percent. Absences due to illness claimed another 6 percent of the labor force. Altogether, disability benefits and spending on sick leave amounted to 7 percent of the Dutch GDP in 1990. When other welfare spending is included, every one hundred employed Dutch people supported eighty-six recipients on social aid (OECD, 1991).

Comparative studies indicate that the incidence of sickness and disability claims in the Netherlands is considerably higher than in other western European countries. The Netherlands is not an unhealthy place. On the contrary, the Dutch live longer, consume less alcohol, have fewer traffic accidents, and visit doctors less often than their neighbors in Belgium and Germany (Prins, 1990; Prins, Veerman, and Andriessen, 1992). Recognizing the favorable health status of the Dutch, analysts at the OECD attribute the soaring rate of disability claims to social and economic factors.[3] First is the high replacement rate of benefits, which goes up to 70 percent of the last gross wage. (Replacement rates for disabled workers and their spouses in the United States range from 47 percent up to 77 percent for those

3. The trend is evident outside the Netherlands. According to a comparative study of six industrial nations, the rising rates of disability do not appear to be related to changes in the health of the local populations. Susan Lonsdale (1993:25) has observed that the increase "is rather more likely a consequence of changes in economic and social policy." One change that she notes is the growing tendency for disability benefits to be awarded to people who otherwise might be defined as unemployed, facilitating an early withdrawal from the labor force as an alternative to unemployment.

with current annual earnings of $42,000 to $12,000, respectively.) Second, employers are apparently using disability insurance as an early retirement scheme for superfluous labor. Finally, Dutch officials have noticed the rise of a permissive cultural climate in their country, where it has become increasingly acceptable to stay away from work for "vague physical and psychological complaints" (OECD, 1991:95).

In response to disability and sickness claims that are approaching an insupportable level, the Dutch cabinet agreed on a series of eighteen corrective reforms designed to lower financial disincentives to work while activating social encouragement to reenter the labor force and broadening opportunities for employment. Disincentives to work are curtailed by tightening eligibility requirements and limiting the length of payment at the 70 percent replacement level to a defined period of one to five years, after which benefits decline to 70 percent of the minimum wage plus a supplement that increases with age. (Unlike in the United States, the Dutch minimum wage is quite high, so the decline in benefits is not as draconian as it might sound.) Reentry into the labor force is advanced through an improved system of guidance that involves the development of return-to-work plans, assistance in retraining, and "reintegration talks" with disability counselors. Employment opportunities are broadened by a system of subsidies to reward firms for hiring and retaining disabled workers (OECD, 1991; The Netherlands, Ministry of Social Affairs and Employment, 1991). It is too early to judge whether these reforms will mitigate the social and economic forces that have given rise to the increasing disability claims, which are coming to bear in the Netherlands and elsewhere.

Since benefits for invalids were introduced in the United Kingdom in 1971, claims have grown beyond expectation. Between 1975 and 1985 the number of claimants rose from 479,000 to 850,000, an increase related more to the longer duration of benefits than to a rising inflow of claims (Holmes, Lynch, and Molho, 1991). To encourage labor-force participation among disabled people who might be able to work, the Disability Working Allowance was inaugurated in 1992. By permitting recipients to supplement their disability benefits through earned income, this scheme provides a financial incentive for disabled people to maximize their employment potential. Because the allowance slowly declines as earnings increase, a single person could earn up to £110 a week (roughly $165, equivalent to the U.S. minimum wage) and still remain entitled to some disability benefit (ISSA, 1991).

The disability insurance program in the United States has undergone trends similar to those reported in the United Kingdom and the Netherlands. The program has grown dramatically in recent years: the number of beneficiaries increased by 13 percent between 1985 and 1990. Actuarial estimates indicate that the number of disabled people will double, accounting for more than six million workers by the year 2015. Beyond escalating in size, the population being served has changed in ways that raise daunting social and economic questions. Over the past decade, for example, the age of new disability insurance beneficiaries declined (even as the median age of the U.S. population rose); the proportion awarded benefits on the basis of mental disorders more than doubled, rising from 11 percent to 23 percent; and the length of stay on the disability rolls increased as the termination rate of recipients fell, dropping 50 percent (Board of Trustees, Federal Old-Age and Survivors Insurance and Disability Insurance Trust Fund, 1991; Hennessey and Dykacz, 1989).

Given these and other trends, government figures reveal that by the year 2001 the Disability Insurance Trust Fund will probably fail to satisfy the short-range test of financial adequacy, which requires a reserve amounting to one year's expenditure. That will occur if the number of workers becoming disabled climbs as it is projected to, based on a prudent set of assumptions. According to more pessimistic assumptions, the Trust Fund will be exhausted by 1997. In either case, the problem is serious enough for the Disability Insurance Trust Fund Board of Trustees to recommend a reallocation of contribution rates that would increase payments for disability insurance and lower those for Old-Age and Survivors Insurance. A cost-neutral measure, the proposed shift would not jeopardize the fiscal integrity of the latter, which has a burgeoning surplus (Board of Trustees, Federal Old-Age and Survivors Insurance and Disability Insurance Trust Fund, 1991).

This immediate solution to the problem of meeting the rising costs of disability insurance, which are expected to go from $28 billion in 1990 to $54 billion in the year 2000, does not address the fundamental problem of how to trim program expenditures. Various recommendations have been put forth about ways to reduce program costs by converting from an income-support model of disability benefits to a program based on incentives and probabilities. One popular proposal, resembling the British Disability Working Allowance, would allow beneficiaries to receive Medicare and partial cash payments while employed. This plan is similar to the current arrangement authorized for disabled poor people under the Supplemental Security Income program. Taking another tack, Carolyn Weaver (1992) suggests privatizing disability insurance for routine risks. As she sees it, private insurers, prodded by the forces of competition, would be strongly inclined to employ cost-effective incentives, such as risk-grading premiums, that might be politically difficult for a public agency to implement.

In line with other income-maintenance policy reforms to boost labor-force participation, there is considerable pressure to raise the normal age of retirement in public pension plans. Since the mid-1960s the average retirement age has generally declined because the take-up rates of various pension options for early retirement have often exceeded government expectations (Tracy and Adams, 1989). According to the OECD (1988b:103), a reversal of this trend "appears necessary in the decades to come as a response to increasing life expectancy and as a means to curb expenditures." The organization suggests that incentives be built into the benefit structure of public pensions to increase the labor-force participation of elderly people.

Policy efforts in this direction are already being signaled in the United States, where the standard pensionable age will rise from sixty-five to sixty-seven in 2026; the rise is coupled with an incentive to withdraw from the labor force even later, for the delayed retirement credit will increase from 3 percent to 8 percent per year of delay (Hardy, 1988). In Sweden several initiatives are also under way. Widows' pensions are being gradually phased out, to be replaced with a readjustment pension that provides temporary aid to survivors for one year or until their youngest child reaches the age of twelve (Smedmark, 1992).[4] A report from the Swedish National Social Insurance Board (1992) suggested, among other pension-reform measures, raising the retirement age from sixty-five to sixty-seven and extending the qualifying period for supplementary pension benefits from thirty to forty years. Following this report, the Swedish parliament passed legislation in 1993 to increase the normal pensionable age from sixty-five to sixty-six but shelved plans to implement the change when it became evident that cost savings would be offset by additional expenditures for unemployment benefits. Whereas the normal pensionable age is sixty-five, the actual average pensionable age of Swedish workers has decreased to 59 or so, a consequence of early pension provisions. In light of this pattern, Swedish policymakers now think that the way to reduce program costs is not to increase the normal pensionable age but to eliminate early pension provisions (Haanes-Olsen, 1993).

Since 1985 financial aid under the basic income-maintenance programs has been increasingly linked with incentives to work. The International Social Security Association (1989:254) notes that this trend may signify "an over-all move towards reassessing social protection policies." Before we examine the nature and implications of incentive-oriented policies, it is worth considering why this move has occurred and what direction it may take.

Incentive Thinking: Impetus and Directions
The idea of using incentives in social policy is hardly new. Almost a quarter-century ago, the 1967 amendments to the U.S. Social Security Act established the Work Incentive Program (whose title formed an unfortunate acronym that was quickly converted to WIN). WIN provided job training and discounted the first thirty dollars of monthly earnings plus one-third of the remainder in calculating the participants' continued eligibility for assistance payments. The positive

---

4. The assumption underlying the repeal of the widows' pension plan was that survivors could become self-sufficient through gainful activity after a period of adjustment to their loss. Another concern was that a grant might be paid irrespective of a widow's real need for it (Smedmark, 1992).

incentive of earnings exemptions was reinforced by the negative incentive of threatened benefit termination for those who refused to accept work training without "good cause"—a sanction rarely evoked. Even before work incentives, some programs offering a children's allowance were seen as providing an incentive for pro-natalist tendencies (Schorr, 1965). Further back in time, Edward Bellamy's nineteenth-century classic, *Looking Backward*, describes utopia as a place where all citizens are entitled to an equal share of the goods and services produced by the nation, with work roles structured to make every task dignified and to allow for a wide choice of occupations. But Bellamy evidently thought that even under these ideal conditions, an extreme inducement was required. In his utopia all those who were able to work but refused were sentenced to solitary imprisonment on bread and water.

If efforts to design social policy incentives have been around for as long as people have thought about the provision of welfare benefits, current interest in this idea is distinguished by the remarkable convergence of liberal and conservative opinion that the right to benefits be firmly connected to the responsibility of each citizen to work and become self-sufficient. The idea that welfare policy should not only confer social rights but also promote the discharge of social obligations has spurred the use of incentives to increase labor-force participation in a range of programs. These efforts rest on the conviction that the proper incentives will produce the desired results. This turn of events results from a powerful combination of necessity, ideology, and unanticipated consequences.

Fiscal and Demographic Necessities   Although the level of welfare expenditures may not have reached its final ceiling, few modern welfare systems can continue the fiscal rate of growth experienced from 1960 to 1980, when welfare spending in OECD countries doubled as a percentage of the GDP. As mature systems of social provision have emerged covering large segments of the population, they now face increasing pressures from demographic changes. The current birthrate is below the replacement level in most OECD countries; thus, by 2040 the proportion of people over the age of sixty-five is expected to double, to 20–25 percent of their populations, and about half of those elderly will be over seventy-five (OECD, 1988a). The rising number of older people will intensify demand for retirement pensions, health services, and social care. Other changes between 1960 and the mid-1980s, such as the proliferation of two-income households and the climbing divorce rate, have created new pressures for social and financial assistance. Thus, as welfare systems approach the limits of social spending, there are near-future forecasts of sociodemographic changes that "give rise to new needs and eliminate practically no previous ones" (Cantillon 1990:399). In this context, the emphasis on social obligations and the introduction of work incentives can be seen as a practical response to fiscal and demographic necessity. By increasing labor-force participation, work-oriented policies may help to shrink existing program commitments, which would give welfare systems more flexibility in redirecting available resources to meet new demands.

Market Ideology Writing in 1942, Joseph Schumpeter found that the public mind had grown so thoroughly "out of humor" with capitalism "as to make condemnation of [it] and all its works a foregone conclusion—almost a requirement of the etiquette of discussion." No enemy of capitalism, Schumpeter ([1942] 1950:63) nevertheless believed that its days were numbered. Granted the benefit of hindsight, we can now say that his verdict on the imminent demise of capitalism was premature. Propelled by events in Russia and eastern Europe, capitalism's stock has risen to record heights of public acceptance. The renewed faith in the virtues of capitalism has brought the values and methods of the market economy into social welfare transactions. The results are most evident in the widely documented movement toward the privatization of many social-welfare functions, which started in the 1980s (Chapter 5; Kahn and Kamerman, 1989; Gilbert, 1983; Abramovitz, 1986). But public contracting with private enterprise for the delivery of diverse social services represents only part of a larger configuration of ideas and policies being shaped by an infusion of the capitalist ethos into the welfare state. Contemporary social-welfare policies are increasingly oriented toward stimulating competition in service delivery and introducing incentives to promote the work ethic. The press of fiscal and demographic requirements to increase labor-force participation among the beneficiaries of various social-welfare programs is thus reinforced by the ideology of market capitalism.

Unanticipated Consequences The current interest in work incentives also comes as a corrective to the unanticipated consequences of past social-welfare policies, particularly those that may have created disincentives to work. The "corrective measures" being proposed by the Dutch government, for example, result largely from "clear indications that the generosity of social benefits and high effective marginal tax rates implicit in income-dependent subsidies create strong disincentives to work and underlie the exceptionally high dependency ratio in the Netherlands, where one employed person supports almost one person on social benefits" (OECD, 1991:90). As this analysis of the Dutch experience reflects, references to the possibility that welfare benefits might produce "poverty traps" or "enforced dependency" have become commonplace (OECD, 1988a; Bradshaw and Millar, 1990; Euzeby, 1988). One report goes so far as to say that "dependency traps are an unintended outcome of most social security systems" (OECD, 1991b:27). Prime Minister Carl Bildt of Sweden has admitted that "if you look at the levels of benefits, they had become so high that they reduced the incentives to work" (Stevenson, 1993:10). Indeed, I am tempted to conclude, though it may stretch the point a bit, that Charles Murray's (1984) conservative analysis of public welfare as a strong disincentive to work, once viewed as heresy by social welfare advocates, has achieved the status of conventional wisdom in the field.

If it is reasonably evident that fiscal and demographic necessity, market ideology, and unanticipated consequences have contributed to the resurgence of incentive thinking in social welfare policy circles, it is less clear exactly where this development is headed. The introduction of incentive-oriented policy is a delicate matter, the description of which is often couched in equivocal terms that exude good intentions. According to the OECD (1989, 1990), the new policy drive should be "to 'enable' people to participate actively in society, and in particular in the labour market." The active society moves away from reliance on merely passive income support as the principal approach to ameliorating social disadvantage. In describing the active measures to increase labor-force participation, the language of positive incentives that "enhance," "encourage," "facilitate," and "enable" behavior is preferred over the language of rules and sanctions, which conveys a more punitive attitude and the readiness to employ coercive measures. When we examine the recent work-oriented policy initiatives in disability insurance, public assistance, public pensions, and unemployment insurance, however, the pattern is not quite that clear. In most of the cases discussed so far, the structure of incentives involves a combination of rules and penalties, along with the more positive type of enabling benefits, such as training, daycare, health services, and earnings disregards.[5]

Social Policy and Human Behavior

Incentive-oriented policies may influence behavior through both symbolic and substantive processes. Symbolically, policies send signals that shape normative expectations (Glazer, 1988). For example, public welfare in the United States was originally seen as a program of financial support for single mothers who stayed at home and cared for their children. This view changed with the Family Support Act of 1988, which sends the message that society now expects single mothers to work and be self-supporting. As the message gains credence, young women who in the past might have become single mothers in the anticipation of receiving public assistance to remain home with their children may reevaluate their plans in light of the new social expectations. This line of influence usually takes time to

5. Nathan Glazer (1988) analyzes the shift away from the use of positive economic incentives in the AFDC program in 1981, when the earnings disregard was substantially reduced. Harsher administration and reduced benefits were used to reinforce the normative expectation that AFDC recipients should return to work. By the early 1990s, when AFDC grants were lowered in many states, other benefits, such as daycare and transitional medical insurance, were extended to welfare mothers who found employment. Various localities also experimented with positive economic incentives, such as grants for attending school and new earnings disregards.

appear and is difficult to gauge because social policies constitute only one of the many forces that mold normative behavior.

The substantive influence that incentives have on behavior involves the allocation of material benefits, which have a more immediate and direct impact than the symbolic messages. That is, mothers now on welfare who enroll in training programs and seek employment are rewarded with extended daycare and health insurance; those who do not try to become gainfully employed risk a reduction in their benefits.

However, just as social welfare policies underwriting passive income supports had unanticipated consequences, so, too, may active policies endorsing behavioral incentives produce their share of unexpected results. For example, although the Dutch cabinet's proposal to have employees surrender one day of their holiday allowance each time they report sick aims to lower the absence rate due to illness, it could provide as much an incentive for those reporting ill to stay away from work a day or two longer as to take fewer sick leaves (The Netherlands, Ministry of Social Affairs, 1991). In the United States, some states have initiated reforms that allow an AFDC mother to retain the portion of the public-assistance grant that is meant to provide for her child if she marries a person who is not the child's father (Florio, 1992). This provision is an incentive for AFDC mothers to get married, but not to the father of their children.

Whether incentives are derived from rewards or penalties, then, the efforts to reduce public costs and increase labor-force participation may not always go as planned. Let me list the most obvious possibilities for unintended outcomes.

Measures that penalize beneficiaries of various welfare programs for failing to do what is expected of them (such as attend training courses, search for jobs, and participate in public-works projects) may necessitate high administrative costs to ensure compliance and manage procedures for appeal. This is particularly true when diagnostic judgments are required for those unable to comply because of claims involving physical ailments, psychological disorders, family emergencies, and the like. The more severe the penalty for noncompliance (for instance, large reductions or full denial of benefits), the less likely the social-service staff are to enforce it in ambiguous cases. At least, experience with the implementation of the Family Support Act in the United States seems to bear this out; for various reasons, a large proportion of welfare mothers drop out of job training and other required activities without loss of benefits (Family Welfare Research Group, 1992). Small penalties can be as expensive to administer as large ones while presenting a weaker incentive to work and achieving lower savings on the costs of program benefits.

Measures that encourage and enable positive behavior, such as the provision of training and daycare services, often increase program costs initially and may even raise costs over long periods. This is because the measures are vulnerable to the familiar problem of "creaming," whereby additional benefits are delivered to those who are already highly motivated, most of whom would be likely to find a job in the absence of these incentives. In public-assistance and unemployment programs and programs for people who are disabled, there are always some beneficiaries who exit the rolls through their own efforts. If these motivated recipients constitute a large proportion of those who are drawn to take advantage of the new enabling benefits, program costs are likely to increase. Sar Levitan and Robert Taggart (1971) found in evaluating the Work Incentive Program, for example, that most of 25,000 enrollees who had found jobs by 1970 were among the applicants best prepared to work—those who would probably have found employment sooner or later without WIN.

Measures that impose large penalties can reduce immediate costs in one program area only to have these costs reappear in another area. The unintended shift in the public burden may even exacerbate the problems of those in need, raising the long-run costs of support and reintegration. An initiative on the 1992 ballot in California proposed to cut public-assistance benefits to families with dependent children by 10 percent and impose an additional 15 percent reduction after aid had been received for six months. The measure provided a strong incentive to find a job but ignored the fact that most public-assistance recipients on the rolls for longer than six months are single parents with a poor education and few marketable skills. Developing the skills and attitudes necessary to find a job may not be within their reach over a six-month period, especially during periods of recession. Although the measure would have saved a considerable sum for the public-assistance program, the 25 percent reduction in grants was certain to create serious dislocations among the recipient families, many of whom would find it difficult to continue paying their rent. The measure failed. But if it had passed, the declining cost of public assistance would eventually have been met with rising public expenditures for homeless shelters, child-protective services, and food stamps (Gilbert, 1992).

Measures that substantially reward beneficiaries of various programs for returning to paid employment run the risk of creating a moral hazard. The problem, as Carolyn Weaver (1992:120) points out, is that these measures "deal with only half of the work incentive issue, ignoring entirely the incentives created for people still at work." Among disabled people, she suggests, incentives that would allow beneficiaries who returned to work to continue receiving medical insurance as well as partial grant payments might well tempt people now at work despite impairments to leave their jobs long enough to establish eligibility for these benefits. A similar risk is posed by public-assistance workfare reforms that provide childcare services and medical insurance for recipients entering the labor force. A case in point is a workfare graduate who was publicized as a model of program success until it was revealed that she had left a job to go on welfare in order to receive health and childcare benefits when returning to work (Kaus, 1986b).

Finally, we should not overlook the obvious point that the success of incentive-oriented policies rests in part on the availability of jobs for those whom these policies intend to motivate. A strong demand for laborers, as Walter Heller (1964) notes, is itself an incentive for people to undertake training or retraining. In periods of high unemployment, incentive-oriented measures may squeeze a few more workers into the labor market. At the same time, however, many social welfare beneficiaries will experience increasing frustration given the social pressure to work created by behavioral incentives and the limited opportunities for employment. Incentive-oriented policies may wind up demoralizing those they are designed to encourage.

To recall the possibility of unintended consequences is not to deny the promise of incentive-oriented policies but to emphasize the need for careful monitoring to understand what is taking place and how people are responding to the policy initiatives. This means being forthright about the design of incentives and the extent to which they incorporate penalties and rewards. Caution is also in order, as Douglas Besharov (1992) advises, for the policymakers are often "tinkering with the lives of the most deprived and least powerful among us."

State and Market: The Diminishing Counterforce

Beyond the uncertainty of behavioral responses to work-oriented incentives, the changing philosophy of social protection has profound implications for the individual's dependence on the market economy. That is, as measures for social protection move away from being policies designed for support and income maintenance toward being policies formulated to reintegrate people into the labor force, the market economy becomes increasingly important for the satisfaction of basic human needs. Since the industrial revolution, market exchanges have been the major vehicle for meeting these needs. At the same time, state and family have stood as alternative arrangements for protecting those most vulnerable to the vicissitudes of the market and for assisting those incapable of fulfilling their needs through market participation. By providing rights to income outside market exchanges, social welfare transfers contribute to the decommodification of labor, making labor less like a commodity bought and sold purely in response to market forces. In this sense, to the extent that welfare transfers reduce the compulsion to take paid employment in order to meet basic needs, they afford workers a certain degree of control and autonomy over their labor. There is, of course, a delicate balance between providing welfare transfers that meet a minimally acceptable standard of living and offering an amount so high that it impedes economic incentives to work.

Critics of the welfare state on the right and the left have argued that social transfers provide either too much or too little in the way of meeting basic needs divorced from the compulsion to work. From the right, welfare benefits are seen as far too generous a substitute for

earned income, eroding the work ethic and the
From the left, they are seen as cunning handout
offering just enough relief from the hardships
the masses in check without really altering their exploitau̲ᴄ̲

Supporters of welfare assistance in capitalist societies argue that it
neither corrupts the work ethic nor buttresses capitalist exploitation.
Instead, they see the welfare system as a social counterforce that
employs state aid to mitigate the hazards and potential coerciveness of
the market without inhibiting its productive energies. From this centrist perspective, as social welfare policies place greater emphasis on
the encouragement of labor-force participation, the welfare system
moves toward serving the market economy and away from acting as a
protective counterforce. "Before, the top priority was protecting
people," says an official in the Dutch Ministry of Social Affairs. "Now
it is avoiding fraud, getting people back to work as fast as possible, and
encouraging citizens to supplement national insurance with private
insurance policies" (Cohen, 1993:1).

As new policies aim for a fairer balance between the right to welfare and the responsibility for self-sufficiency, the danger is that they
will rely too heavily on the presumption of competence. Owing to
personal incompetence, as well as to social forces beyond personal
control, some people are temporarily or permanently unable to support themselves and meet other responsibilities of citizenship. Policies
devised to enable people to meet their needs through publicly supported private efforts raise serious questions: Can all welfare mothers
become self-supporting? Can they earn enough to offset the costs of
publicly subsidized daycare services? Should elderly people be encouraged to work? Underlying these and similar questions is the fundamental issue of whether the changing philosophy of social protection
will lead to a society that is not only fairer but also gentle enough to
permit an honorable dependence for its frailest members.

Chapter 4

Miscounting Social Ills: Sexual Assault and Advocacy Research

To establish a fairer system of social protection involves not only balancing the social rights and responsibilities of AFDC mothers, elderly people, disabled people, and other needy groups but also achieving an equitable distribution of public resources among them. This is a complicated process that requires more than the calibration of benefits to empirical measures of need. Beyond assessing levels of deprivation, policymakers' appraisals of what constitutes an equitable distribution are influenced by the characteristics of the groups in need and by estimates of the effectiveness of public aid in helping them to solve their problems. Policymakers rarely ignore the relative voting strength of different groups, either.

Although empirical data on the size of needy groups and the nature of their problems cannot fully answer the question of what constitutes an equitable distribution, they give deliberations on social welfare policy a sense of proportion about the scope of need and its rate of growth. In recent years, however, advocates for different groups have muddled policy deliberations by generating vast and often questionable estimates of the social ills afflicting their clients.

Advocacy research has not always been that way. Beginning with Charles Booth's (1892) large-scale survey of poverty in London during the 1880s, the development of social welfare policy in industrial society has benefited from a long and honorable tradition of advocacy research —studies that seek to measure social problems, heighten public awareness of them, and recommend possible solutions. At the start of the twentieth century, studies intended to spur social reform in the United States focused on the problem of poverty and its related miseries of slum housing, poor health, hunger, and child labor. Robert Hunter's book *Poverty*, first published in 1904, was an early classic in the advocacy research genre. Taking $460 a year as the poverty index for an average family of five in the northern states and $300 a year in the South, Hunter estimated that at least ten million Americans (13 percent of the population) lived in poverty. Noting that these poverty indexes were arbitrary but not unreasonable, he proposed an agenda of social reforms that included increased public health measures, minimum wages, unemployment compensation, workers' disability insurance, and old-age pensions (Hunter, 1965).

More than half a century later, in an era of relative prosperity, public concerns about poverty were revived by another study, Michael Harrington's (1962) classic *The Other America*. Harrington reviewed estimates that showed between forty million and fifty million Americans (20 percent to 25 percent of the population) living in poverty. He concluded that an attack on poverty was necessary. "All that is lacking," he observed, "is political will." Harrington's work is often credited with furnishing the moral impetus, along with an empirical case, for the Johnson administration's war on poverty (Schlesinger, 1965).[1] Michael Harrington and Robert Hunter were the same breed of advocacy researchers. Both had spent time on the front lines as social workers, both were drawn to socialism, and, though well versed in the social sciences, both wrote a felicitous combination of reportage and analysis that was highly accessible to the general public. Indeed, it might be said that their prose was as persuasive as their statistics.

Harrington (1962:176), reflecting on his approach to the study of poverty, offers a candid account of the style and nature of advocacy research: "If my interpretation is bleak and grim, and even if it overstates the case slightly, that is intentional. My moral point of departure

---

1. Harrington's study also sparked the production of literature on the characteristics and conditions of poverty in the United States. Within several years of his work two large anthologies were published, both entitled *Poverty in America*. Other collections, *New Perspectives on Poverty*, *Poverty as a Public Issue*, and *Poverty in Affluence* came out, followed by *Poverty amid Affluence*, to name just a few.

is a sense of outrage, a feeling that it would be better to describe it in dark tones than to minimize it." This is not to say that his statistics were invented or misrepresented. Harrington explicitly identifies the assumptions and definitions that underlie his reading of the numbers. He readily admits that legitimate differences in point of view give rise to other definitions and interpretations, which yield different counts. And he reviews these alternative estimates of poverty in a balanced manner. Harrington explains that two principles guided his efforts to study the Other America: "to be as honest and objective as possible about the figures; to speak emotionally in the name of the common humanity of those who dwell in the culture of poverty" (177). Joining unbiased measurement with committed expression of concern, these principles reflected a standard of advocacy research at its best—a standard that has eroded with the proliferation of such research since the 1960s.

After Harrington's study of poverty in the early 1960s, there was a notable rise in the production of advocacy research, accompanied by changes in the style and focus of these efforts. As social rights for different interest groups expanded and public expenditures for new social programs climbed, an unprecedented amount of federal funding became available to study the problems addressed by these programs and the groups affected by them. With millions in research funds distributed among such federal agencies as the Administration on Aging, the National Institute of Mental Health, the National Center on Child Abuse and Neglect, the Department of Housing and Urban Development, and the Children's Bureau, the research focus shifted from the poor to diverse constituencies of the oppressed and deprived who claimed entitlements to social protection; included were women, gays and lesbians, ethnic minorities, children, and people who were elderly, homeless, disabled, or suffering from various addictions.

Along with an infusion of research funds that began with the Great Society programs in the early 1960s, the expansion of social research gained impetus from computer technology and new analytic tools that promised to inform policy debates with useful data. These developments were accelerated by the tremendous growth in the number of people professionally trained to conduct social science research (Aaron, 1978). By the late 1960s social scientists had come to play an important role as advocates for social welfare policies, gaining—in Daniel Patrick Moynihan's (1969:177) words—"quite extraordinary access to power."

With more voluminous output, advocacy researchers' efforts to identify and measure the problems of those in need became more dubious and their prose less elegant. Estimates of need were questionable in part because some of the emerging problems were harder to gauge than poverty. The measurement of homelessness does not lend itself to conventional social-science sampling methods using telephone interviews or door-to-door surveys; unlike poverty, racial and gender discrimination, child abuse, elder abuse, and drug abuse involve criminal behaviors, which are difficult to uncover with surveys. The expansion of social welfare benefits for various groups produced competition, increasing the temptation to inflate evidence of the need for program support. Competition with other groups is less an issue in measuring the more inclusive problem of poverty. Figuring the national incidence of poverty, for example, Harrington was not concerned if an error in his calculations showed that the number of poor people was ten million lower than he estimated. After all, he insisted, "give or take 10,000,000, the American poor are one of the greatest scandals of a society that has the ability to provide a decent life for every man, woman, and child" (1962:177). But as advocacy research has turned to problems that are more limited in scope than poverty, its function of promoting public awareness is being compromised by the growing tendency to magnify needs while asserting the scientific validity of large numbers.

Emotive Statistics: Kidnapping, Sexual Abuse of Children, and Homelessness

In recent years the rising volume and declining quality of advocacy research have generated the increasing use of emotive statistics—startling figures that purport to uncover hidden crises and silent epidemics. These figures are regularly broadcast not only by Oprah, Geraldo, and the *National Enquirer* but also in steadier sources, such as *Time*, the *New York Times*, and network newscasts. A story in the *Los*

Angeles Times, for example, cites a study in which 25 percent of 32,000 California children reported that "they had gotten away from someone trying to kidnap them" (Trombley, 1990). Is it conceivable that one in four children, or almost one child in every other family, was a victim of attempted kidnapping? On a little reflection, most people would find it difficult to take the figure seriously. But not the University of Chicago professor of social work who conducted the study; in his view, the survey results indicate that California's extensive statewide program to provide children with training to prevent sexual abuse (see Chapter 2) "is effective in teaching youngsters how to deal with the threat of physical and sexual abuse."

In the mid-1980s fear of kidnappings was intensified by the widely publicized estimate that 50,000 children were being abducted by strangers each year. According to Child Find, an organization devoted to the plight of missing children, only 10 percent of these children were recovered by their parents; another 10 percent were found dead, and the remaining 40,000 cases per year continued to be missing. Prominently reported by the media, these figures first provided sensational headlines proclaiming a national crisis and later became the grist for a Pulitzer Prize–winning analysis of the problem in the *Denver Post*. The *Post* reporters criticized the risk of child abduction as wildly inflated and revealed the astonishing discrepancy between the 50,000 estimate put forth by the crusaders for missing children and the official number of FBI investigations of children abducted by strangers, which totaled sixty-seven cases in 1984.

A closer analysis of these figures by Joel Best (1988) shows that if the advocates' estimate of 50,000 was too high, the FBI count was too low. The FBI's jurisdiction in kidnapping cases is limited to offenses that violate a federal statute, such as transporting a victim across state lines; only a fraction of the cases reported to local law-enforcement authorities come under the Federal Kidnapping Statute. Best, who examines data from a study by the National Center for Missing and Exploited Children (NCMEC), which included police records on every crime reported in 1984 that involved the kidnapping or attempted kidnapping of children in Jacksonville, Florida, and Houston, Texas, demonstrates that a reasonable extrapolation of serious incidents would yield a nationwide estimate of 550 cases annually—a figure eight times higher than the FBI count but still ninety times lower than the rate claimed by advocates.

In defining the serious incidents of stranger abductions, Best considered only those cases in which a child was either missing for more than one day or murdered. This definition coincides with the image of child abduction originally portrayed by the advocates who promulgated the 50,000 figure, which was widely publicized by ABC News and other media sources. Researchers at NCMEC employed a broader definition, which included attempted kidnappings and cases in which the victim was missing for less than twenty-four hours. Using the NCMEC definition to extrapolate a nationwide rate from the Jacksonville and Houston data yields an annual figure of 15,000 cases of stranger abduction. But, as Best points out, in the enlarged definition to which NCMEC researchers subscribed, a child was missing for less than twenty-four hours in 97 percent of the cases, and a child was molested in more than 60 percent of the cases (short-term abductions in which the victim was moved to a different place). Indeed, local police classified only 15 percent of the cases as kidnappings or abductions. Sexual molestations are tragic for the victims but are not kidnappings, as advocates initially portrayed them; advocates claimed that 80 percent of abducted children are never found.

By including cases in which most victims are missing for less than one day, the broader definition of kidnapping advanced by the NCMEC and other missing-children advocates generates a high incidence rate, which suggests an urgent need for new policies to address the problem. Proposals for these policies typically focus on efforts to increase education, prevention, and social control.

Currently parents can choose among dozens of anti-kidnapping books, games, videotapes, ID kits, and other commercial products designed to educate children about the dangers of abduction. Most are reasonably priced, but it is more difficult to calculate the social costs of encouraging both children and adults to believe that terrifying crimes are commonplace. The missing-children movement also emphasizes the need for greater social control: schools should require detailed identification records for every student; police should have the power to hold runaways. . . . The unspeakable threat posed by the stranger abduction epidemic justifies these changes; the new policies' potential costs and dangers receive little attention. (Best, 1988:91)

As advocates for missing children seek to expand the definition of this terrible offense to include incidents of sexual molestation, they enter the realm of what is widely perceived as a much larger problem. Estimates of missing children shrivel in comparison with those advanced by the movement to prevent child sexual abuse; the most frequently reported forecast is that one girl in three or four will be sexually molested before leaving high school, most often by a relative (Gilbert et al., 1989; Berrick and Gilbert, 1991).[2] John Briere and Marsha Runtz (1989:65) offer a typical statement of the problem: "Sexual victimization of children by adults is now acknowledged to be a significant social problem in the United States. Most modern surveys of the prevalence of sexual abuse in the general population, for instance, indicate that 22% to 45% of adult women experienced some form of contact sexual victimization as children."

But unlike missing children, who are almost always reported to the authorities, sexually abused children are difficult to document. The estimated prevalence is considerably higher than we would infer from official figures on the number of reports of child sexual abuse substantiated annually. In 1992, for example, an estimated 499,120 cases of child sexual abuse were reported to child protective services, of which approximately 40 percent were substantiated (McCurdy and Daro, 1993). An annual incidence rate of about 200,000 substantiated cases (or 3 in 1,000 children), though extremely serious, does not begin to yield a 25–33 percent prevalence rate over the course of childhood. Because many, if not most, incidents of child sexual abuse

2. The figure is constantly recited by authorities in the field of child sexual abuse prevention, and there is some evidence that it has made an impact on how the public perceives the magnitude of the problem. According to surveys, a huge majority of parents in California believe that 25 percent or more of all children are victims of sexual abuse (Gilbert et al., 1989; Berrick and Gilbert, 1991).

are never reported to the authorities, however, the official annual rates yield a fairly conservative estimate of the problem.[3]

Although the official reports underestimate the full extent of the problem, the highly publicized prevalence rates go to the other extreme. These figures of 25–33 percent come from surveys of adult women who were asked to recall if they had experienced any episodes of sexual abuse during childhood. In spite of advocacy groups' claims about the enormous prevalence of child sexual abuse in the United States, an analysis of these surveys discloses more about the ambiguities of this problem than its magnitude.

Definitions of child sexual abuse include misbehaviors ranging from despicable violations that everyone would condemn to mild acts that many might find inappropriate or irritating but would not necessarily label sexually abusive (Ahn and Gilbert 1992; Giovannoni and Becerra, 1979). Different views of the full range of offenses that constitute child sexual abuse come to light in the fifteen surveys conducted since 1976 to estimate the prevalence of this problem. According to these surveys, the proportion of females sexually molested as children ranges from 6 percent to 62 percent of the population (for males, from 3 percent to 31 percent). In half the studies the rate for females is a much lower 6 percent to 15 percent. Discrepancies among these findings are due in large part to differences in the researchers' operational definitions of sexual abuse, which include sexual propositions, exposure to an exhibitionist, unwanted touches and kisses, fondling, sexual intercourse, and other physical contact (Finkelhor and Associates, 1986).

Two of the largest and most widely cited surveys of the prevalence of child sexual abuse illustrate how broadly the problem is usually defined by advocacy researchers (and by sexual abuse prevention pro-

3. The substantiation of a case does not always mean that behavior deemed sexually abusive by the investigating authorities was motivated by sexual impulses on the part of the perpetrator and experienced by the child as emotionally or physically harmful. In some cultures it is considered generally permissible for family members to touch, even fondle, the sexual organs of babies and young children. Individuals from these groups have been charged with sexual abuse for behavior—like touching a grandson's genitals—which they regard as an expression of pride rather than salaciousness (Ahn and Gilbert, 1992).

grams, as noted in Chapter 2). Diana Russell (1984) reports that 54 percent of the respondents in a survey of 930 women in San Francisco were victims of incestuous or extrafamilial sexual abuse at least once before the age of eighteen. This prevalence rate reflects her definition of sexual abuse, under which children who received unwanted hugs and kisses and others who had not been touched at all (for example, children who encountered exhibitionists) were classified as victims. Russell calculated a lower rate of 38 percent using a slightly narrower definition that eliminated cases not involving physical contact. This narrower measure included "unwanted sexual experiences ranging from attempted petting to rape" by persons outside the family and "any kind of exploitive sexual contact or attempted contact" by relatives. The information used to determine an episode of sexual abuse comprised the responses to fourteen screening questions, such as "Did anyone ever try or succeed in touching your breasts or genitals against your wishes before you turned 14?" "Did anyone ever feel you, grab you, or kiss you in a way you felt was threatening?" "At any time in your life has an uncle, brother, father, grandfather or female relative ever had any kind of sexual contact with you?"

The supposedly more stringent definition of child sexual abuse actually stretches to cover everything from attempted petting and threatening kisses to any exploitive contact, like touches on the leg or other body part, all the way to forced vaginal intercourse, fellatio, and other forms of penetration. Claiming that Russell's study is one of the most accurate to date, Lloyd Demause argues that it nevertheless substantially underestimates the true rate because many people do not consciously recall traumatic events before the age of five. According to Demause's (1991:136) calculations, "the corrected incidence rates are at least 60 percent for girls and 45 percent for boys." His appraisal of the problem would have a sexually abused child in almost every family in the United States (or two abused children in every other family).

In another major survey of child sexual abuse, more than 2,600 men and women were interviewed. David Finkelhor and his colleagues (1990) registered a prevalence rate somewhat lower than Russell's; they found that 27 percent of women (and 16 percent of men) were sexually abused as children. The four screening questions used to detect abuse in this study are fewer in number than those employed by Russell but as conceptually indiscriminate. To illustrate the range of experiences merged under the definition of child sexual abuse, it is worth reporting these questions verbatim.

> When you were a child can you remember having any experience you would now consider as sexual abuse—like someone trying or succeeding in having any kind of sexual intercourse with you or anything like that?
>
> When you were a child can you remember having any experience you would now consider as sexual abuse involving someone touching you or grabbing you, or kissing you, or rubbing up against your body either in a public place or private—anything like that?
>
> When you were a child can you remember any kind of experience that you would now consider sexual abuse involving someone taking nude photographs of you, or someone exhibiting parts of their body to you or someone performing some sex act in your presence—or anything like that?
>
> When you were a child can you remember any kind of experience that you would now consider sexual abuse involving oral sex or sodomy—or anything like that?

Positive responses to the first two questions—about someone trying to have or succeeding in having any kind of sexual intercourse or anything like that, or any kind of touching, grabbing, or kissing, or anything like that—accounted for nearly 90 percent of the acts defined as sexual abuse, with the remaining 10 percent involving exhibitionism.[4]

4. On the vague wording and the judgments required by these questions Finkelhor and colleagues (1990:20) note: "Experiences *some* researchers might define as abuse could be left out because the respondents did not consider them as abuse. Other experiences of a minor nature that *many* researchers would exclude could have been counted because of a respondent's broad interpretation of the phrase 'anything like that.' Unfortunately, no subsequent questions were asked about the sexual acts that could have been used to exclude experiences that did not meet researchers' criteria" (emphasis added). The qualifications "some" and "many" offer the only hint as to whether the researchers believed that the questions were more likely to exaggerate or undercount rates of sexual abuse. About two-thirds of these incidents occurred only once, and more than three-quarters did not involve the use of force.

As these studies demonstrate, the most widely cited prevalence rates of child sexual abuse rest on responses to woolly questions like Were you ever the victim of *attempted* petting? Did someone *try* to have or succeed in having *any kind* of sexual intercourse or *anything like that*? Did a relative ever have *any kind of sexual contact* with you? Did you receive a threatening kiss or an uncomfortable touch? The basic problem with this research is that when we think of child sexual abuse, a single incident of attempted petting, a touch on the leg, a disagreeable kiss, or an unwanted pat on the buttock (or anything like that) is hardly what comes to mind. By designing research that lumps together possibly harmless behavior with the trauma of child rape, advocates have inflated the estimates of child sexual abuse to critical proportions. Examining the prevalence surveys, one scholar "cannot help wondering why no attempt was made in these studies to single out the serious cases we are all interested in, the ones that are similar to those we see in the clinics or courts; those in which children have been victims of prolonged incest committed by a parent or a parent figure, or are forcibly molested, or abducted and abused, and so on" (Kutchinsky, 1994:12).[5]

Following the approach of earlier surveys, research by advocates who indiscriminately link trivial, annoying, and impertinent acts with serious and terribly damaging sex crimes has recently taken a new twist. Redefining programs to prevent child sexual abuse as programs to prevent "victimization," Finkelhor, Asdigian, and Dziuba-Leatherman (1993) surveyed 2,000 children to assess the prevalence of this problem and the effectiveness of prevention training. They report a 42 percent prevalence rate of "victimization" among the children surveyed. These victimizations included fights and attempted assaults by peers, gangs, or family members, kidnapping, and sexual abuse. Measures of sexual abuse involved positive responses to broadly worded questions: "Has there ever been a time when an older person tried to feel you, grab you, or kiss you in a sexual way that made you

5. According to Kutchinsky (1994:12), "The prevalence of single or episodic relatively serious events [is] in the neighborhood of 1%; and . . . prototype incest cases with small children being abused over several years by a parent run into a few cases per thousand."

feel bad or afraid?" By equating schoolyard scraps, attempted fights, unwanted squeezes, and unpleasant kisses with kidnapping and rape, the researchers assemble a 42 percent victimization rate to construct a problem that has an impact on almost every family in the country (a rate that also suggests a pressing need for more prevention programs). In fact, when sexual abuse is separated from other forms of victimization, the prevalence rate drops to 6 percent. And half of these responses involve attempted cases. Thus, the findings show an actual sexual-abuse prevalence rate of 3 percent, which includes kisses and touches that felt bad. Curiously, the discrepancy between this finding and the 27 percent prevalence rate of female child sexual abuse found in the 1990 survey (Finkelhor et al., 1990) seems to have gone unnoticed.

As the problems of child sexual abuse gained public notice and elicited new policies from state and federal government, advocates for the elderly discovered that children were not the only victims of mal-treatment. *A National Disgrace* was the title of the 1985 report issued by the Aging Committee's Subcommittee on Health and Long-Term Care. Citing evidence that an estimated 4 percent of the elderly, or one million older citizens, are victims of abuse each year, the subcommittee maintained that "abuse of the elderly by their loved ones and caretakers existed with a frequency and rate only slightly less than child abuse" (Crystal, 1987:56).

One million victims is the kind of figure that attracts media attention, and the estimated incidence rate of 4 percent gained authority with frequent citation. But on closer inspection the figure evaporates into a haze of fuzzy calculations. The estimate is based on a survey of 433 elderly residents of Washington, D.C., of whom only 73 people (16 percent of the sample) responded. Such a low response rate immediately disqualifies any generalizations drawn from the results. As it turned out, three of the 73 respondents, or 4 percent, reported experiencing some form of psychological, physical, or material abuse. Advocates extrapolated from this small and unreliable sample to show that one million elderly people are victims of abuse, thereby constructing a national epidemic out of three incidents. In a review of these "mythical numbers," Stephen Crystal (1987) points out that such findings stem from the strong interest among advocates for the elderly in keeping the victimization rate high—and from little interest in keeping it correct.[6]

In advocacy research, keeping the number high is often only part of the agenda. Beyond magnifying the size of a client group's problem to draw public attention, advocates habitually seek to define its essential characteristics. They tend not only to see their client group's problem as approaching epidemic proportions but to attribute the underlying causes to oppressive social conditions—such as sexism, racism, ageism, and capitalism—which can be corrected only through fundamental changes in society. Of course, there is a relation between the magnitude of a problem and the extent to which its cause is attributable to social forces or personal factors. If 4 percent of the labor force is unemployed, the workers without jobs are unskilled, unmotivated, or temporarily down on their luck; if the unemployment rate rises to 24 percent, they are victims of a depression. If 5 percent of females are sexually abused as children, the offenders are sick deviants; if 50 percent of females are sexually abused as children, the problem is the way that males are regularly socialized to take advantage of females.

Along these lines, advocacy research on homelessness has been concerned not only with inflating the estimates of the number of homeless people but also with defining the nature of their problem. Advocates' estimates of the number of homeless in Chicago are nine times higher than the figures produced by repeated, carefully designed scientific surveys (Rossi, Fisher, and Willis, 1986). Similarly, the National Coalition of the Homeless has calculated that there are 500,000 homeless children in the United States, a number more than ten times higher than the 35,000 calculated from the Urban Institute's national sample and the 40,000 calculated by the U.S. Department of Housing and Urban Development (U.S. House of Representatives, Committee on Ways and Means, 1992). In assessing the cause of

6. According to Crystal (1987:59), the claims that "abuse of the elderly by their children or other family caretakers is increasing with epidemic proportions is particularly striking since fewer and fewer of the elderly are living with family at all. . . . Available evidence suggests that lack of a caretaker is a far more widespread problem than abuse by a caretaker."

homelessness, advocates take the large numbers as confirmation that the homeless are essentially victims of structural flaws and economic forces rather than personal deficiencies.[7] Examining the history of homelessness in America, Henry Miller, for example, concludes that causes of the current problem "can be found in the risks attendant on the wage labor system." As he sees it, "Many members of the establishment would prefer to ignore a basic structural flaw in our socio-economic system, whose correction would require a rethinking and reconstruction of the American system, and shift the blame for homelessness to the much smaller arena of mental health and care for the mentally ill" (1991:162). The solution to the problem is employment. "Today's homeless," Miller explains, "need good jobs that pay decent wages. The homeless will work if they can find work" (170).

This view of the homeless as people just like you and me who, for lack of a job, find themselves on the street ignores compelling evidence to the contrary. Considerable information shows that between 40 percent and 66 percent of homeless adults suffer from significant alcohol problems (Fischer and Breakey, 1991; Wright, 1988; Rossi, Fisher, and Willis, 1986); research findings also agree that between 33 percent and 50 percent of homeless adults suffer from severe psychiatric disorders, such as schizophrenia (Burt and Cohen, 1989; Fischer and Breakey, 1991);[8] and between 10 percent and 25 percent of homeless people are addicted to drugs (Wright, 1988; Lubran, 1990). Recognizing that alcoholism, mental illness, and drug abuse are not mutually exclusive problems, Alice Baum and Donald Burnes (1993)

7. In 1982 the Community for Creative Non-Violence estimated that 2.2 million people (about 1 percent of the U.S. population) were homeless. The empirical basis for this highly publicized figure was never specified (Proch and Taber, 1987).

8. As a result of deinstitutionalization, the resident population in state hospitals declined from 475,000 in 1965 to 137,000 in 1980, and the rate is still falling (Applebaum, 1987). Not only have a vast number of people with serious mental illnesses been discharged over the past thirty years, but many others who would have been institutionalized during this period have remained in the community. Some are in board and care facilities; others have drifted away to live on the streets. In an ironic conversion, the Keener Building on Wards Island in New York City, originally a psychiatric hospital, has become a men's shelter; it provides refuge to some of the same people who previously would have received professional treatment and care at the same facility.

estimate that 65 percent to 85 percent of homeless adults suffer from at least one of these disabling conditions. Advocates, who wish to avoid blaming the victim, present the issue in terms of social and economic forces, which denies the personal nature of the problems afflicting most homeless people. Instead of solutions that emphasize employment and subsidized housing, Baum and Burnes's reading of the data shows that above all, most homeless people require access to professional treatment and humane care.

Over the past decade, problems like stranger abduction, child abuse, elder abuse, and homelessness have been magnified by advocacy research. But these efforts are modest in comparison with the remarkably powerful campaign of advocacy research inspired by the rape crisis movement of the early 1990s.[9] According to the alarming accounts routinely voiced by radical feminist groups, about one in every two women will be a victim of rape or attempted rape an average of two times in her life, and many more will suffer other forms of sexual molestation. These claims are based on figures from several studies, among which the *Ms. Magazine* Campus Project on Sexual Assault, directed by Mary Koss, and Diana Russell's survey of sexual exploitation are the largest, most widely disseminated, and frequently cited. Both studies were funded by the National Institute of Mental Health, which gave them the imprimatur of a respected federal agency. Often quoted in newspapers and journals, on television, and in the 1991 and 1993 Senate reports on the Violence Against Women Bill, the findings from these studies have gained authority through repetition. Most of the time, however, those who cite the findings take them at face value, understanding neither where the numbers come from nor what they actually represent. A critical analysis of the studies will demonstrate how social scientists practice the craft of advocacy

9. Some advocates deny the existence of the rape crisis movement, but as Barbara Collins and Mary Whalen (1989:61) explain it, "The rape crisis movement was a radical feminist social issue that emerged in the early 1970s—feminist because the movement was conceived by women whose primary concerns focused on women's experiences, radical because it sought to dismantle the existing social order." By 1979 there were about 1,000 rape crisis centers forming the organizational core of the movement (Amir and Amir, 1979).

research and why the media and the public are often deceived by their studies.

Rape Research: Examining the Facts

Advocacy research on rape benefits from a powerful aura of "scientific" inquiry. The findings are prefaced by sophisticated discussions of the intricate research methods employed and presented in a virtual blizzard of data, along with a few convincing case examples and numerous references to lesser-known studies. But footnotes do not a scholar make, and the value of quantitative findings depends on the accuracy with which the research variables are measured, the reliability with which the sample is drawn, and the rigor with which the data are analyzed. In spite of the respected funding source, frequent acknowledgments in the media, and the air of scientific respectability, the two most prominent studies on rape have serious flaws that cast grave doubt on their credibility.

The *Ms.* study directed by Koss involved a survey of 6,159 students at thirty-two colleges. As Koss defines the problem, 27 percent of the female college students in her study had been victims of rape (15 percent) or attempted rape (12 percent) *an average of two times* between the ages of fourteen and twenty-one. Using the same survey questions, which she claims represent a strict legal description of the crime of rape, Koss calculates that during a twelve-month period 17 percent of college women were victims of rape or attempted rape and that more than half of the victims were assaulted twice (Koss, 1988; Koss, Gidycz, and Wisniewski, 1987; Warshaw, 1988). If victimization continued at this annual rate, we would expect well over half of all college women to suffer an incident of rape or attempted rape over the course of four years and more than one-quarter of them to be victimized twice.

There are several reasons for serious researchers to question the magnitude of sexual assault conveyed by the *Ms.* findings. To begin with, there is a notable discrepancy between Koss's definition of rape and the way most of the women whom she labeled as victims interpreted their experiences. When asked directly, 73 percent of the students whom Koss categorized as victims of rape did not think that they had been raped. This discrepancy is underscored by the subsequent behavior of a high proportion of those identified as victims: 42 percent had sex again with the man who supposedly raped them. Of those categorized as victims of attempted rape, 35 percent later had sex with the purported offender (Koss, 1988; Koss, Gidycz, and Wisniewski, 1987).

Although the exact legal definition of rape varies by state, most definitions involve sexual penetration accomplished against a person's will by means of physical force or threat of bodily harm or when the victim is incapable of giving consent; the latter condition usually involves cases in which the victim is mentally ill, developmentally disabled, or intentionally incapacitated through the administration of intoxicating or anesthetic substances.

Rape and attempted rape were operationally defined in the *Ms.* study by five questions, three of which referred to the threat or use of "some degree of physical force." The other two questions asked: "Have you had a man attempt sexual intercourse (get on top of you, attempt to insert his penis) when you didn't want to by giving you alcohol or drugs, but intercourse did not occur? Have you had sexual intercourse when you didn't want to because a man gave you alcohol or drugs?" (Koss, 1988; Koss, Gidycz, and Wisniewski, 1987). Forty-four percent of all the women identified as victims of rape and attempted rape in the previous year were so labeled because they responded positively to these awkward and vaguely worded questions. What does it mean to have sex "because" a man gives you drugs or alcohol? A positive response does not indicate whether duress, intoxication, force, or the threat of force was present; whether the woman's judgment or control was substantially impaired; or whether the man purposefully got the woman drunk to prevent her from resisting his sexual advances. Perhaps the woman was trading sex for drugs; or perhaps a few drinks lowered her inhibitions so that she consented to an act that she later regretted.[10] Koss assumes that a positive answer sig-

10. In Prince George County, Maryland, where more than one in four allegations of rape in 1990–91 was unfounded (that is, the women admitted that their charges were false, or the police found no evidence that a rape had occurred), the former head of criminal investigations concluded that the high rate of false reports was due in part "to frequent cases of sex-for-drug transactions gone sour" (Buckley, 1992:81).

nifies that the respondent engaged in sexual intercourse against her will because she was intoxicated to the point of being unable to deny consent (and that the man had administered the alcohol for this purpose). Although the question could have been clearly worded to denote "intentional incapacitation of the victim," only a mind reader could detect whether an affirmative response to the question as it stands corresponds to the legal definition of rape.

In an attempt to resolve this problem, Koss and Cook (1993a:3) first take the question as originally reported, "Have you had sexual intercourse with a man when you didn't want to because he gave you drugs or alcohol?" and claim that it included the words "to make you cooperate." Rather than helping the case, this revised version suggests that instead of being too drunk to deny consent, the woman actually cooperated in the act of intercourse after taking drugs and alcohol. After noting this criticism of their attempt to clarify the case by altering the original definition, Koss and Cook (1993b:106) concede that "for the sake of discussion it is helpful to examine what happens to the prevalence figures when these instances are removed."[11] According to Koss and Cook's revised estimates, when the item dealing with drugs and alcohol is removed, the prevalence rate of rape and attempted rape declines by one-third.[12]

During Koss's (1990) testimony in the Senate Judiciary Committee Hearings on the Violence Against Women Act, it emerged that three-quarters of the respondents classified as victims in the *Ms.* study did not think they had been raped. The committee chair, Joseph Biden, said: "My daughter is not going to have any doubt." But no one asked why all these other young college women did not know that they had experienced the brutal and terrifying crime of rape. On how they interpreted the event, Koss (1990:40) reported to the committee: "Among college women who had an experience that met legal require-

11. Later, in an interview with Nara Schoenberg and Sam Roe (1993), Koss acknowledged that the drug and alcohol questions, two of the five items used to define victims of rape and attempted rape, were ambiguous.

12. From the form in which the data are reported in Koss's earlier studies it is not possible to verify the new estimate. But, as noted earlier, calculations that can be made from the original data show that the one-year incidence rate declines by 44 percent when the item dealing with intercourse under the influence of drugs or alcohol is removed.

ments for rape, only a quarter labeled their experience as rape. Another quarter thought their experience was some kind of crime, but not rape. The remaining half did not think their experience qualified as any type of crime."

A different account of how the students interpreted their experience had been published several years earlier by Koss and her colleagues (Koss et al., 1988). According to that report, 11 percent of the students said they "don't feel victimized," 49 percent labeled the experience "miscommunication," 14 percent labeled it "crime, but not rape," and 27 percent said it was "rape." Although there was no indication that other data might have been available on this question, three years later a surprisingly different distribution of responses was put forth. In answer to questions raised about the fact that most of the victims did not think they had been raped (Gilbert, 1991a,b), Koss offered four new versions of the students' responses; in none did she mention that 49 percent thought it a matter of miscommunication. First, in a breathtaking disregard for the data that she had originally published, Koss (1991c:6) wrote that the students labeled as victims viewed the incident as follows: "One quarter thought it was rape, one quarter thought it was some kind of crime but did not believe it qualified as rape, one quarter thought it was sexual abuse but did not think it qualified as a crime, and one quarter did not feel victimized." In a later paper, Koss (1991b:9) revised the gist of these new findings: "One quarter thought it was some kind of crime, but did not *realize* it qualified as rape; one quarter thought it was *serious* sexual abuse, but did not *know* it qualified as a crime" (emphasis added). Two years later, yet another revision of these findings was published. Koss (1993) continued to deny that virtually half of the students labeled their experience a case of miscommunication; she claimed instead that "only one in ten victims said she felt unvictimized by the experience. The remaining nine who felt victimized were split between those who thought their experience was rape (the 27% fraction Mr. Gilbert quotes), those who thought their experience was a crime but might not be called rape, and *those who thought their incident was extremely traumatic* but was not a crime" (emphasis added). Finally, in a fourth effort, Koss and Cook (1993b:107) explain: "In fact, half the rape victims identified in the national survey considered their experience as rape or some crime similar to rape."

These inconsistencies aside, the additional data are difficult to interpret. If one-quarter thought the incidents involved a crime but not rape, what kind of crime did they have in mind? Were they referring to an illegal activity like drinking under age or taking drugs?[13] Despite Koss's elaboration of the data originally reported, in the first version of the findings 60 percent of the students either did not feel victimized or thought the incident was a case of miscommunication. Although in the second, third, and fourth versions Koss claims that many more of the students assessed the sexual encounter in negative terms, the fact remains that 73 percent did not think they had been raped.

Koss did not mention in her testimony to the Senate committee that 42 percent of students classified as victims in the *Ms.* survey had sex again with the man who supposedly raped them. But in response to questions raised elsewhere about this statistic, she again offers different accounts of her data. Originally she (1988:16) reported: "Surprisingly, 42% of the women indicated that they had sex again with the offender on a later occasion, *but it is not known if this was forced or voluntary*; most relationships (87%) did *eventually* break up subsequent to the victimization" (emphasis added). Three years later, in a letter to the *Wall Street Journal*, Koss was no longer surprised by this finding and claimed to know that the next instance of sexual intercourse with the same offender was likewise rape and that the relationship broke

13. In reviewing the research methodology for the *Ms.* study, Koss (1988; Koss, Gidycz, and Wisniewski, 1987) explains that previous reliability and validity studies conducted on the ten-item Sexual Experience Survey (SES) instrument showed that few of the female respondents misinterpreted the questions on rape. Examining the earlier studies, however, we find that the original SES instrument (Koss and Oros, 1982) differed from the version used in the *Ms.* study in at least one important respect: the original instrument contained neither of the questions dealing with rape or attempted rape that happened "because a man gave you alcohol or drugs." In a brief report on the assessment of validity Koss and Gidycz (1985:423) note: "To explore the veracity of the self-reported sexual experiences, the Sexual Experiences Survey (original wording) was administered to approximately 4,000 students." This suggests that the findings on validity would not include the vague items on "intentional incapacitation" absent from the original version of the SES instrument.

up, not eventually (as do most college relationships), but immediately after the second rape. In this revised version of the findings Koss (1991a:21) explains: "Many victims reacted to the first rape with self-blame and thought that if they tried harder to be clear they could influence the man's behavior. Only after the second rape did they realize the problem was the man, not themselves. Afterwards, 87% of the women ended the relationship with the man who raped them." Koss goes on to suggest that the students did not know that they had been raped because they were sexually inexperienced and "lacked familiarity with what consensual intercourse should be like."

These explanations are highly speculative. They also demean the judgment, functioning, and self-possession of young women. It is hard to imagine that so many college women, even if sexually inexperienced, are unable to judge whether their sexual encounters were consensual. As for the victims blaming themselves and believing that they might influence the man's behavior if they tried harder the second time, Koss offers no data from her survey to substantiate this reasoning. Although research indicates that victims of rape tend to blame themselves (Craig, 1990), there is no evidence that a sense of culpability induces them to have sex again with their assailant. Some battered wives do stay with their husbands in intolerable circumstances. But it is not apparent that the battered wife syndrome applies to a large proportion of female college students.

In a final attempt to explain the findings, Koss (1991a) asserts that most college women who are sexually violated by an acquaintance do not recognize themselves to be victims of rape. She argues that "many people do not realize that legal definitions of rape make no distinctions about the relationship between victim and offender." Contrary to this claim, findings from the Bureau of Justice Statistics (1989, 1991) suggest that the crime of acquaintance rape may not be so difficult to comprehend; in recent years 33 percent to 45 percent of the women who said that they had been raped identified their assailant as an acquaintance.

Moving beyond the experience of college students, Diana Russell's study is another source often quoted as evidence that rape has reached, as she describes it, "epidemic proportions throughout society"

(1984, 1991). In addition to reporting a prevalence rate of 38 percent to 54 percent for child sexual abuse, she (1984) found that 44 percent of the women in her sample were victims of rape (26 percent) or attempted rape (18 percent) an average of twice in their life and that many other women suffered experiences in marriage that, if not rape, were very close to it. If mutually desired intercourse and rape are placed at the ends of a continuum, Russell (1982:356) explains, "our study suggests that a considerable amount of marital sex is probably closer to the rape end of the continuum." Indeed, beyond marital sex, Russell (1984:121, 1975:261) suggests that, according to this view, "much of what passes for normal heterosexual intercourse would be seen as close to rape." Although this analysis of sex relations is not as censorious as that of Andrea Dworkin (1988), for whom all hetero-sexual sex is rape, it leans in that direction.

There are several fundamental problems with Russell's survey, which is based on interviews with a group of women in San Francisco. Although serious efforts were made to achieve a random sample of participants, the researchers were able to complete their interviews with only 930 people of the original sample of 2,000; 36 percent of those contacted refused outright to participate in the study. Russell offers two somewhat different accounts of the inaccessibility of the other nonparticipants. In *Rape in Marriage* (1982:31), she says, "Because of a high incidence of not-at-homes during the summer months when the interviews were conducted, and because of an unex-pectedly large number of households in which no eligible women resided, the original sample of two thousand drawn by the methods described proved insufficient for obtaining one thousand completed interviews." Later it appears that Russell did not know the (unexpect-edly large) number of households in which no eligible women resided. As she describes the sampling difficulties in *Sexual Exploitation*: "Many of the households that were inaccessible or where no one was at home *might have been* households in which no eligible women lived (for example, there are a large number of male households in San Fran-cisco)" (1984:38, emphasis added).

For whatever reasons, more than 50 percent of the women in the sample did not participate in the interview survey. Properly executed interview surveys, according to the standard textbook criterion, should achieve a completion rate of 80–85 percent, which is the range usually required of surveys by federal agencies (Rubin and Babbie, 1989). It is very doubtful that the 930 participants who agreed to be interviewed for Russell's study can be considered a representative random sample of the women in San Francisco.

There is a more basic problem, however. After starting with a questionable sample, Russell goes on to claim that her respondents' sexual experiences reflect those of not only all the women in San Francisco but the entire female population of the United States. A brief disclaimer to the effect that generalizing from the San Francisco sample "would be highly speculative" is quickly forgotten as, after adjusting her findings for age-specific probabilities, Russell (1984:50) concludes: "It is indeed shocking that 46% of American women are likely to be victims of attempted rape or completed rape sometimes in their lives." She continues to share this national estimate with the media (Freedburg, 1991). She also notes that victims are likely to be attacked an average of two times. Only 31 percent of the women in Russell's sample were married, compared with 63 percent nationally, one of many reasons that drawing the national estimate from the sexual experiences of the San Francisco sample is not just highly speculative but scientifically groundless.

Beyond sampling bias there is the question of how rates of rape and attempted rape were measured. Russell's estimates are derived from responses to thirty-eight questions. Only one question asked respondents whether they had been a victim of rape or attempted rape at any time in their life. Twenty-two percent of the sample, or one-half of the women defined as victims by Russell, gave an affirmative answer to this question. Although the entire questionnaire is not reported, Russell offers an example of a typical question that was repeated several times in reference to strangers, acquaintances, and dates or lovers: Have you ever had any unwanted sexual experiences, including kissing, petting or intercourse with a date because you felt physically threatened? If yes: did he either try to have or succeed in having any kind of sexual intercourse with you? A considerable proportion of the cases counted as rape and attempted rape in this study are based on the researcher's interpretation of experiences described by respondents. In assessing the standards applied in these cases we might bear in mind that it was even before Russell did this study that she claimed that "much of what passes for normal heterosexual intercourse would be seen as close to rape" (Russell, 1975:261).

Using her San Francisco findings, Russell offers a detailed analysis to extrapolate not only the lifetime probability but also the national incidence of rape and attempted rape in 1978. She explains: "The incidence figure for rape in the Russell survey . . . was 35 per 1000 females. (This includes cases of rape and attempted rape that occurred to residents of San Francisco, both inside and outside the city.) This is *24 times higher* than the 1.71 per 1000 females [in San Francisco] reported by the Uniform Crime Reports" (1984:46, emphasis in original). On the basis of this calculation, Russell takes the 1978 *Uniform Crime Report*'s figure of 67,131 for all the cases of rape and attempted rape in the United States and multiplies it by 24, which yields her estimate of 1.6 million incidents that year nationwide.

Faulty logic and poor arithmetic invalidate this analysis. First, the initial calculation (ironically, italicized) is incorrect. The San Francisco rate of 35 per 1,000 is 20.5 times (not 24 times) higher than the 1.71 per 1,000 in the *Uniform Crime Report*. Ignoring for a moment this arithmetic error, let us look at the logic of the second calculation, where Russell assumes a correspondence between the Uniform Crime Report rates for San Francisco and the nation. If Russell's sample had an incidence rate twenty-four times higher than the report's rate for San Francisco, we need only multiply by twenty-four the national rate given in the report to project the local difference on a national scale. However, those who study this subject know very well that the reported rates of rape are considerably higher for metropolitan areas than for the national population (Johnson, 1980). Indeed, the *Uniform Crime Report*'s total of 67,131 cases of rape and attempted rape in 1978 amounted to a national rate of 0.6 per 1,000 females, which was about one-third the rate of 1.7 per 1,000 females that the report showed for San Francisco (U.S. Bureau of the Census, 1986). Thus, if we include the initial arithmetic error, Russell's national estimate of the incidence of sexual assault exaggerates by about 350 percent the figure that would result from simply an accurate reading of her own data.

How Advocacy Research Is Done and Why It Sells

Russell's survey of sexual exploitation and the *Ms.* study by Koss are highly sophisticated examples of advocacy research. Behind the veil of social science, elaborate research methods are employed to persuade policymakers and the public that a problem is vastly larger than is commonly recognized. This is done in several ways:

1. by defining a problem so broadly that it forms a vessel into which almost any human difficulty can be poured;

2. by measuring a group highly impacted by the problem and then projecting the findings to society at large;

3. by asserting that a variety of smaller studies and reports that have different definitions of the problem, methodologies of diverse quality, and varying results form a cumulative block of evidence in support of current findings;

4. by claiming that the publication of findings in professional journals attests to their veracity;

5. by employing what Joel Best (1990) describes as "atrocity tales"—painfully detailed anecdotes that typify the human suffering caused by the problem but fail to give the slightest hint of its incidence in the population;[14]

6. by changing definitions and revising data in response to criticism in the hope that no one will examine the facts as originally reported; and, when all else fails,

7. by regressing to ad hominem argument.[15]

---

14. Russell introduces her book *Sexual Exploitation* (1984) with a series of case studies of sexual abuse; her work *Rape in Marriage* (1982) also contains detailed descriptions of sexual molestations. Warshaw, in her 1988 book (which reports Koss's findings), uses numerous vignettes to illustrate acquaintance rape.

15. Koss (1993), for example, unable to answer the questions that I raised or to resolve the discrepancies that I documented in her research, takes the offensive: "I don't understand what Mr. Gilbert's academic affiliation as a professor of 'social welfare' means. All we have heard is what he is against. When is he going to share with us how he proposes to meet the legitimate needs for healing of sexually victimized women and children?"

Initially, the findings of advocacy research often receive a favorable reception from the media. With a lack of critical scrutiny, the reporters at first rush to embrace advocates' claims about the magnitude and character of such problems as child abuse, homelessness, kidnapping, elder abuse, and rape. The various reasons for this willingness to suspend disbelief have to do with journalists, their public readership, and social scientists. As documented in *The Media Elite* (Lichter, Rothman, and Lichter, 1986), the majority of journalists hold distinctly liberal positions on political and social issues, and their ideology often translates into concerns about victims of oppression and social ills. "Afflict the comfortable and comfort the afflicted!"—the edict of a distinguished professor of journalism at Columbia University—"could have been the school slogan," notes Stephanie Gutmann (1993:51). The message at Columbia was that a viable story assignment for students "could combine any three from this list: Bronx, babies, community activist, crack, homelessness, social program that's losing its funding, single mothers, the Lower East Side, and AIDS— always AIDS." As a rule, journalists are quicker to report about experiences that are painful and sensational than about those that are comfortable and ordinary. One reason besides the liberal tendency to publicize the plight of victims is that murder and mayhem attract public attention, for which the media compete.

On the one hand, advocacy research benefits from a felicitous union between journalists' inclination to discover victims and their readers' curiosity about the horrors of modern life. On the other hand, it benefits from journalists' general inability to evaluate the data that advocates for causes and groups feed to the press. Most journalists are not well versed in social-science research methods. They gather and cross-check information by interviewing experts. And because advocates are frequently among the first to uncover and publicize information about emerging problems, they are the ones interviewed in the initial stages of problem discovery, and their data frame the issue.

A common tactic of advocacy researchers is to declare that their estimates are not only accurate but well replicated in many other studies. In support of the *Ms.* survey findings, for example, Koss often adduces additional studies as sources of independent verification. But if we take a close look at the studies that she usually cites, we find very little replication. Some of the studies (Ageton, 1983) use different definitions of forced sexual behavior (including verbal persuasion and psychological coercion) and involve small or nonrepresentative samples that are inadmissible as a basis for serious estimates of the size of the problem. Other studies are referred to without explanation or critical examination. Thus, for example, Koss and Cook (1993b) cite two studies using representative samples that show the prevalence rate of rape for college students in the 12 percent range, a figure not far from the 15 percent reported in the *Ms.* findings. One of these studies, conducted by Koss and Oros (1982), used the original version of the Sexual Experience Survey instrument to measure rape, which excluded items dealing with unwanted intercourse when "a man gives you drugs or alcohol." The second study defined rape as forced oral sex or intercourse, where force included verbal persuasion: "This study showed that most of the sexual encounters were forced through verbal persuasion-protestations by the male to 'go further' because of sexual need, arousal, or love." According to this definition, the conventional script of nagging and pleading—"Everyone does it," "If you really loved me, you'd do it," "I need it," "You will like it"—is transformed into a version of rape. After verbal persuasion, the form of force experienced most frequently by students was "use of alcohol or drugs," though the researcher neither elaborates on this category nor claims that it reflects intentional incapacitation of the victim (Yegidis, 1986:53).

As further evidence that the study results are verified by other research, Koss and Cook (1993b:110) refer to the National Victim Center (1992) study: "In a just released telephone survey of more than 4,000 women in a nationally representative sample, the rate of rape was reported to be 14%, although this rate excluded rapes of women unable to consent." This figure is close to the 15 percent rate reported in the *Ms.* study. What Koss and Cook fail to tell the reader is that approximately 40 percent of the rapes reported in the National Victim Center study occurred to women between the ages of fourteen and twenty-four, resulting in an estimated rate of 5 percent for that age-group.[16] According to Koss's findings in the *Ms.* study, 15 percent of college women are victims of rape between the ages of fourteen and twenty-one. Thus, for almost the same age cohort, Koss found a rate of rape three times higher than that detected in the National Victim Center survey.

Some critical issues have also been raised about the National Victim Center survey. One of the four questions used to define rape in this study includes sexual penetration by a man's fingers, which does not reflect the legal definition of rape in most states.[17] Christina Sommers (1994:216) suggests that such rapes might include "cases in which a boy penetrated a girl with his finger against her will in a heavy petting situation. Certainly the boy behaved badly. But is he a rapist? Probably neither he nor his date would say so. Yet the survey seems to classify him as a rapist." Although the study director assured Sommers that responses to the item did not significantly affect the outcome, she wondered about that because the study had found a large percentage of rapes among young people in the age-group most likely to find themselves in a heavy petting situation. Further questions about the nature of the experiences defined as rape in the center's study are raised by the fact that almost half (49 percent) of those defined as rape victims said that they had not been afraid of being seriously injured or killed during the incident.

Beyond knowing that half of the victims were not afraid of being seriously injured, we do not know how the women themselves labeled the incidents, because the researchers did not ask them directly whether they had been raped. The research director explained that

16. In fact, the rate of rape found in the National Victim Center study was 13 percent. Data on the age of the victims at the time of the rape are grouped; data on those younger than eleven are lumped together, as are data on those eleven to seventeen, eighteen to twenty-four, and twenty-five and older. To calculate the percentage of victims in the fourteen to twenty-four cohort, I took a proportional rate of the eleven- to seventeen-year-olds (18 percent) and added that to the 22 percent in the eighteen- to twenty-four-year-old group. Because these data on the age of rape victims include cases in which some women were raped more than once, the estimate is based on the assumption that the cases of multiple rapes were distributed proportionately among the age-groups.

17. When Nara Schoenberg and Sam Roe (1993) inquired about this item, the director of the study, Dean Kilpatrick, allowed that his definition "might be a tad broader" than the common legal standard.

there was not enough time in the thirty-five-minute telephone survey to include this question (Schoenberg and Roe, 1993). In an earlier survey conducted by the director of the National Victim Center study of 1992, respondents were classified as victims of rape if they had had an experience in which someone used force or the threat of force to make them have sexual relations (including intercourse and oral and anal sex) against their will. That 1985 survey of 2,004 women found a rape prevalence rate of 5 percent, less than half the rate found in 1992 (Kilpatrick et al., 1985). The findings from the 1985 survey are not mentioned in the 1992 report.

Koss and Cook also refer to a 1984 study in which Russell found a lifetime rate of rape that is twice as high as that found by the National Victim Center study. Despite the much higher prevalence rate, fewer than 1 percent of the rapes in Russell's sample were reported to have occurred when the victim was under eleven years of age, whereas 29 percent of the rapes reported in the National Victim Center study occurred during these childhood years. Claiming that the estimates of the prevalence of rape given in the *Ms.* survey "are well-replicated in other studies," Koss (1991b) refers us to Mary Craig's (1990) discerning review of the literature to confirm the consistency of prevalence data on college students. This citation is a curious one to make, for Craig holds a different opinion. She notes that the problems of definition "vary from use of force, to threat of force, to use of manipulative tactics such as falsely professing love, threatening to leave the woman stranded, or attempting to intoxicate the woman." Even when studies are conducted using the same general definitions, their authors often develop idiosyncratic measures to operationalize the terms—all of which leads Craig to conclude that "this lack of consistency limits the comparability of studies and makes replication of results difficult" (1990:403).

What can we make of these vast discrepancies? Only by ignoring key details can the results of studies like these be construed as independent confirmation of the *Ms.* findings. Moreover, if the works of Koss, Russell, and others suggest that anywhere from 15 percent to 50 percent of women have been the victims of rape and attempted rape, other studies—a nonsupporting literature—point to rates well below

10 percent. These studies with modest rates rarely make headlines. Linda George, Idee Winfield, and Dan Blazer (1992), for example, found in North Carolina a lifetime prevalence rate of 5.9 percent for sexual assault; the statistic was based on responses to the broad question "Has someone ever pressured you against your will into forced contact with the sexual parts of your body or their body?" Although regional differences may account for some of the disparity between the *Ms.* prevalence rate and the findings of the Duke University team, we should note that in 1990 the rate of rapes reported to the police in North Carolina was 83 percent of the national average.

An even lower rate was detected by Stephanie Riger and Margaret Gordon (1981), who report that among 1,620 respondents randomly selected in Chicago, San Francisco, and Philadelphia, only 2 percent had been raped or sexually assaulted in their lifetime. Riger and Gordon note, however, that among a small subsample of 367 respondents interviewed in person who were younger, wealthier, and better educated than those in the larger random sample, 11 percent mentioned having been raped or sexually assaulted. As we know, Kilpatrick and his colleagues (1985) found a rape prevalence rate of 5 percent in a representative sample of 2,004 women. And in a survey conducted by Louis Harris Associates (1993), only 2 percent of a random sample of 2,500 women responded affirmatively to the question "In the last five years have you been a victim of rape or sexual assault?" Because *sexual assault* might be interpreted as applying to a wide range of experiences, we would expect the victims of rape to account for considerably less than the entire 2 percent.

The most startling disparity emerges when we compare the *Ms.* study's finding on the annual incidence of rape and attempted rape with the number of such offenses actually reported to the authorities on college campuses. Koss found that 166 women in 1,000 were victims of rape and attempted rape in just one year on campuses across the country (each was victimized an average of 1.5 times). In sharp contrast, the FBI (1993) figures show that at 500 or so colleges and universities with an overall population of five million students, only 408 cases of rape and attempted rape were reported to the police — less than one incident of rape or attempted rape per campus. The number yields an annual rate of 0.16 in 1,000 for female students, which is *1,000 times smaller* than Koss's finding. Although it is generally agreed that many rape victims do not report their ordeal because of the embarrassment and because of the callous treatment frequently experienced at the hands of the police, no one to my knowledge publicly claims that the number of rapes is 1,000 times greater than the number of cases reported to the police—a rate at which almost every woman in the country would be raped at least once every year.

Finally, data collected annually by the Bureau of Justice Statistics (BJS) provide the most dependable figures on the changing rates of rape and attempted rape over the past two decades.[18] As Christopher Jencks (1991) points out, since the BJS surveys are conducted almost the same way every year, their biases are likely to be constant, making the data generated by these studies quite a reliable guide to trends in sexual assault over time (even if the magnitude is underestimated). As shown in Figure 4.1, the rates of rape and attempted rape for women over twelve years of age rose somewhat from 1973 to 1979, then declined, and eventually leveled off after the mid-1980s. From the peak in 1979 until 1992 the incidence of rape and attempted rape declined by more than one-third; between 1985 and 1990 the rate fluctuated slightly, but the differences were not statistically significant (Bureau of Justice Statistics, 1992, 1994). Whether we focus on the significant decline over the past decade or on the steady rate in recent years, the picture that emerges refutes advocates' accounts of an epidemic (Russell, 1984, 1991).

As for the magnitude of the problem in recent times, the BJS

18. In the BJS surveys, which are conducted by the Census Bureau, people in a random sample of about 62,000 households are interviewed every six months. The confidentiality of responses is protected by federal law, and response rates amount to 96 percent of eligible units. The interviewers ask a series of screening questions, such as "Did anyone threaten to beat you up or threaten you with a knife, gun or some other weapon? Did anyone try to attack you in some other way? Did you call the police to report something that happened to you that you thought was a crime? Did anything happen to you which you thought was a crime, but [which] you did not report to the police?" A positive response to any of these screening questions is followed up with other questions: "What actually happened? How were you threatened? How did the offender attack you? What injuries did you suffer? When, where did it happen, what did you do, and so forth?" (Bureau of Justice Statistics, 1992).

Fig. 4.1 Rates of Rape and Attempted Rape, 1973–1992

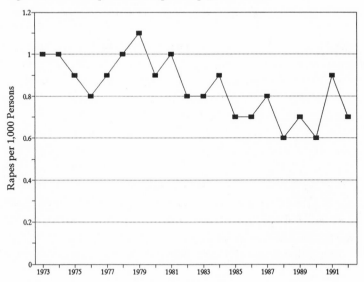

Source: Data from U.S. Bureau of Justice Statistics, 1994.

found that 0.7 people in 1,000 over twelve years of age were victims of rape or attempted rape. This amounts to 140,100 victims in 1992. No trivial number, that annual figure translates into roughly a 4 percent to 7 percent prevalence rate. Like other victimization surveys, the BJS studies have problems of subject recall, definition, and measurement, which—as Koss (1991) and others (Russell, 1984; Jencks, 1991) have pointed out—cause the amount of sexual assault to be underesti-mated. Less frequently pointed out is the fact that attempts to esti-mate the incidence of sexual assault are also contaminated by false reports of rape. According to the FBI (1993), for example, 8 percent of the rapes reported to the police in 1992 were later deemed unfounded because the alleged victim recanted or because investigators uncov-ered no evidence of a crime.

In light of these enormous discrepancies the average citizen, as well as the trained social scientist, must wonder what is really being measured. To advocacy researchers the discrepancies represent inconvenient details to be swept under the carpet of supporting literature. With neither the inclination nor the skill to systematically review and critically evaluate research literature, reporters are easily deceived by claims that other studies have independently verified certain findings. Repeating Koss's claim, for example, in an article for *Newsweek*, Susan Faludi (1993:61) confidently asserts, "Numerous other studies bear these figures out." Journalists evince much fuzzy thinking and writing on this matter. Katha Pollitt (1993:223), for one, writing in the *New Yorker*, disregards serious matters of detail and accuracy: "One in five, one in eight—what if it is only one in ten or one in twelve? Social science isn't physics. Exact numbers are important, and elusive, but surely what is significant here is that lots of different studies, with different agendas, sample populations, and methods tend in the same direction." Pollitt fails to explain, however, what direction she is referring to—toward one in five or one in twelve.

Journalists also have a difficult time sorting out the numbers because activist constituencies lend vocal support to claims made by advocacy researchers. Reporters seeking to verify reports about the prevalence of rape, for instance, find many social workers and therapists in rape prevention centers and counseling programs ready to confirm the figures. These workers have a vested interest in increasing public funds to address the problem. But their support of the data in the advocacy research reflects more than an occupational stake in the problem. Working daily with women who have suffered dreadful sexual abuses, many therapists and social workers truly believe that the number of victims is as huge as advocacy researchers profess. There is some evidence that their perceptions may be influenced not just by the stream of daily encounters with victims but also by personal experiences as victims themselves.[19] Thus, the initial absence of contradictory evidence and the presence of a constituency (often well organized) that will attest to their findings lend a degree of credibility to advocacy research.

19. In a survey of graduate students in social work, guidance and counseling, education, and business it was found that social-work students reported having been sexually molested three times as often, and counseling students twice as often, as students in education or business (Russel et al., 1993).

Although the media tend at first to promote advocacy findings, most journalists—liberal tendencies and readers' curiosity aside—ultimately are interested in the truth. When new data become available or advocacy claims stretch the suspension of disbelief so far that someone begins to wonder where the figures really came from, journalists will challenge the numbers that they originally promulgated.[20]

In 1993 the media began to challenge advocacy research on rape; a *New York Times Magazine* cover story proclaimed, "RAPE HYPE BETRAYS FEMINISM." In a critical analysis of "rape-crisis feminists," Katie Roiphe (1993a:26) recalls a poster at college announcing that one in four women had been a victim of rape or attempted rape. "If I were really standing in the middle of an 'epidemic,' a 'crisis'—if 25 percent of my women friends were really being raped—wouldn't I know it?" she wondered. Roiphe concludes, "These posters were not presenting facts. They were advertising a mood." It was a mood, I might add, that was stirred up by earlier stories in the *New York Times* (Lewin, 1991), *Time* (Gibbs, 1991), and many other periodicals, as well as television reports citing such findings as Koss's and Russell's as authoritative. Roiphe's article was followed by a new round of reports on television and radio and in the press that presented a more critical assessment of the problem of rape on college campuses. Nara Schoenberg and Sam Roe's (1993) three-part series in the *Toledo Blade* offers an unusually thorough and insightful coverage of the issue. Not only do they dissect the exaggerated figures of advocacy researchers, but they also show that although poor and minority women are much more likely to be victims of rape than middle-class college students, their stories are seldom told.

Debunking advocacy research is almost as approved as promoting it. There are even eminent rewards, to wit, the Pulitzer Prize won for the *Denver Post* series debunking the estimates of missing children. Advocacy research, then, is an excellent source of information for the media, often providing two lively stories—one with hype and the

20. Katherine Dunn (1993) offers several telling examples of advocacy claims initially accepted and later refuted by the press. Richard Cohen (1991) and Stephanie Gutmann (1990) were among the first columnists to criticize advocacy findings on date rape.

other with disputation. Whether this type of research serves as well to help fashion fair and responsive social policies is another question.

Consciousness-Raising or Consciousness-Changing?

Advocacy research is not unique to studies of rape. It is practiced in a wide variety of substantive problem areas and supported by groups who—to use Peter Rossi's (1987) phrase—share an "ideological imperative." That is, findings politically acceptable to the advocacy community are more important than the quality of research from which they derive; playing fast and loose with the facts is justifiable in the service of a noble cause; and data and sentiments that challenge conventional wisdom should be condemned or ignored. The folk singer Holly Dunn's hit "Maybe I Mean Yes" (when I say no) was denounced for expressing politically incorrect sentiments; the song was clearly out of tune with the feminist chant "No means no." The controversy over the lyrics ignored Muehlenhard and Hollabaugh's (1988) findings that 39 percent of 610 college women surveyed admitted to having said no to sexual advances when they really meant yes and fully intended to proceed.

Although advocacy studies do little to elevate the standards of social science research, they sometimes serve a useful purpose in bringing grave problems to public attention. Among social activists, this is known as consciousness-raising, and it is deemed a respectable function of advocacy research. Radical feminists may thus claim a measure of success, considering the proliferation over the past decade of publicly subsidized rape crisis centers and rape-prevention training programs, along with the growing support industry of consultants, books, videos, and other educational paraphernalia. One might say that even if rape research magnifies the problem to raise public consciousness, this is being done for a good cause, and, in any case, the difference is only a matter of degree. No matter how measured, rape—like child sexual abuse—is a serious problem that causes a great deal of human suffering. So why make an issue of the numbers?

But the issue is not that advocacy studies simply overstate the incidence of legally defined rape and child sexual abuse; it is the magnitude of the exaggeration and what it means. After all, the difference between boiling and freezing is only a matter of degree. In the case of sexual assault against women, advocacy researchers seek to alter public consciousness more than raise it, by molding social perceptions of the problem and what constitutes the common experience in heterosexual relations.

If one-third of female children are indeed sexually abused and almost half of all women will suffer an average of two incidents of rape or attempted rape at some time in their life, one is ineluctably driven to conclude that most men are pedophiles or rapists. This view of men is repeatedly expressed by advocates in the child sexual abuse prevention movement and the rape crisis movement.[21] As Russell (1984:65) puts it, "Efforts to explain rape as a psychopathological phenomenon are inappropriate. How could it be that all these rapes are being perpetrated by a tiny segment of the male population?" Her explanation (1984:290) of "the truth that must be faced" is that "this culture's notion of masculinity—particularly as it is applied to male sexuality—predisposes men to violence, to rape, to sexually harass and to sexually abuse children." In a similar vein, Koss (1988:23) notes that her findings support the view that sexual violence against women "rests squarely in the middle of what our culture defines as 'normal' interaction between men and women." And Naomi Wolf (1991:167) writes that "glamorized degradation has created a situation among the young in which boys rape girls and girls get raped *as a normal course of events*" (emphasis in original). Catharine MacKinnon (1991:15) offers a vivid rendition of the theme that rape is a social disease. Writing in the *New York Times*, she advises that when men charged with the crime of rape come to trial, the court should ask, "Did this member of a group sexually trained to woman-hating aggression commit this particular act of woman-hating sexual aggression?"

Under the influence of such views, the sexual politics of advocacy research on violence against women demonizes men and defines the

21. One explanation for such a hostile view of male behavior is that it suits the radical feminist ambition to achieve absolute control in sexual relations. To further this objective, Norman Podhoretz (1991:34) explains, "it became necessary to delegitimize any instance of heterosexual coupling that starts with male initiative and involves even the slightest degree of female resistance at any stage along the way. Hence almost the entire range of normal heterosexual intercourse must be stigmatized as criminal, and both women and men must be educated to recognize it."

common experience in heterosexual relationships as inherently menacing. When asked if college women should view every man they see as a potential rapist, a spokeswoman for the student health services at the University of California, Berkeley, responded, "I'm not sure that would be a negative thing" (Brydoff, 1991). This statement echoes the warning in one of the most popular college guidebooks on how to prevent acquaintance rape: "Since you can't tell who has the potential for rape by simply looking, be on your guard with every man" (Parrot, 1988). Thus, "the assumption that sexual relations among students at a progressive liberal-arts college should be thought of as per se fraught with the potential for violence is now taken for granted by about just everyone" (Menand, 1994:76).[22] The same message is being delivered to students at a very early age in sexual abuse prevention programs in the schools. Many of these programs (as noted in Chapter 2) make a point of teaching kids from the age of three years and up that male family members, particularly fathers, uncles, and grandfathers, may sexually abuse children.[23]

At the same time that all men are portrayed as dangerous predators, the most widely cited research on sexual violence conveys a view of women as helpless victims. In studies that, according to the researchers, uncover the highest rates of rape, female subjects typically do not realize that they have been raped; return to have sex again with the perpetrator because of guilt and self-doubt; are seen as substantially impaired by any amount of drinking; and are often psychologically coerced by men into having unwanted sex.[24] On the last

22. Experts on date rape advise college women to take their own cars on dates or to have a back-up network of friends ready to pick them up; to stay sober; to inform the man in advance what the sexual limits will be that evening; and to prepare for the worst by taking a course in self-defense beforehand (Warshaw, 1988). Separately, some of these instructions, such as staying sober, are certainly well advised. Collectively, however, this bundle of cautions transmits the unspoken message that dating men is very dangerous.

23. This is an example of the "new psychology," which Charles Krauthammer (1993:22) notes "is rooted in and reinforces current notions about the pathology of ordinary family life."

24. According to the "feminist analysis of rape," women "are socialized to be passive, good-willed, and compliant, and to assume the status of property" (Koss and Harvey, 1991:125).

point, Roiphe (1993b:67) declares: "The idea that women can't with-stand verbal or emotional pressure infantilizes them."

To protect women against nonphysical coercion and to empower those who might be hesitant to say no to sexual advances unless their oral permission is expressly requested, Antioch College has gone so far as to adopt a policy on sexual offense which maintains that anyone who initiates sexual activity must reaffirm the partner's verbal consent as the couple moves to each new level of physical intimacy: "May I kiss you, now may I unbutton your blouse, now may I touch you here, etc.?" But, as Cathy Young (1992) points out, if failure to object to unwanted sex can be attributed to verbal intimidation or deficient willpower, so can explicit consent. "Inevitably," she notes, "this patronizing line of thinking reaches the conclusion that in our oppres-sive society, *there can be no consensual sex*" (emphasis in original). Indeed, according to Susan Estrich (1987:102), "many feminists would argue that so long as women are powerless relative to men, viewing 'yes' as a sign of true consent is misguided." Estrich herself agrees that in sexual relationships a woman's yes often may mean no.

Besides depicting normal sexual relations between men and women as inherently brutish, advocacy researchers on rape and child sexual abuse redefine violations in ways that trivialize serious violence against women.[25] Their definitions equate vicious and appalling acts of rape and child molestation with such offenses as attempted petting, giving unwanted kisses, touching a ten-year-old's breast, forcing dig-ital penetration in the midst of heavy petting, having intercourse after the partner's inhibitions are lowered by a few drinks, and coercing a partner into sexual intercourse through verbal persuasion. This research strategy feeds off the suffering of real victims of sexual vio-lence, whose stories are often used to illustrate the larger problem, even though their painful experiences represent only a small fraction

---

25. Gillian Greensite (1991:15), founder of the Rape Prevention Education program at the University of California, Santa Cruz, writes that the seriousness of rape "is being undermined by the growing tendency of some feminists to label all heterosexual mis-communication and insensitivity as acquaintance rape." We might recall here that 49 per-cent of the students whom Koss defined as victims of acquaintance rape labeled their experience miscommunication.

of the cases included in the problem definition. Vivid anecdotes of real victims are used to support fragile numbers. But when policy implications are drawn from these advocacy studies, the real victims of profound violence are betrayed by what Charles Sykes (1992:19) calls "a victimist version of Gresham's Law: Bogus victims drive out genuine victims." The Violence Against Women Act is a case in point.

Distorted Measures and Inequitable Policy

In the deliberations on federal policy regarding violence against women, advocacy research on rape was accepted almost on face value. In the opening statement during the Senate Judiciary Committee hearings on the Violence Against Women Act in 1990, Chairman Joseph Biden explained: "One out of every four college women will have been attacked by a rapist before they graduate, and one in seven will have been raped. Less than 5 percent of these women will report these rapes to the police. Rape remains the least reported of all major crimes. . . . Dr. Koss will tell us today the actual number of college women raped is more than 14 times the number reported by official governmental statistics. Indeed, while studies suggest that about 1,275 women were raped at America's three largest universities last year, only three rapes—only three—were reported to the police" (U.S. Senate, 1991:3). Without a blink, the panel was informed that unreported rapes of college women are more than 20 times, more than 14 times, and—simultaneously—more than 400 times the number of incidents reported to the police. In fact, as we noted earlier, the unreported rate, according to Koss's figures, would be 1,000 times higher than the rate of rape and attempted rape reported on college campuses.

Expert opinions solicited for the hearings reinforced the figures presented by Chairman Biden as authoritative measures of rape; his data came directly from the *Ms.* study, whose severe shortcomings we have already examined. The first professionals testifying before the committee were introduced as "two nationally prominent experts in this field. . . . Ms. Warshaw is the author of the foremost book published on acquaintance rape and the attitudes that lead to it, entitled *I Never Called It Rape.*" And Dr. Koss "has studied the incidence and prevalence of rape more extensively than any other social scientist in

this country" (U.S. Senate, 1991:27). Robin Warshaw (1988) is a jour-
nalist, and the full title of her book is *I Never Called It Rape: The* Ms.
*Report on Recognizing, Fighting, and Surviving Date and Acquaintance
Rape*. Its afterward is by none other than Mary Koss, who directed the
Ms. study.

Owing in large part to the credibility attributed to advocacy
research, the Violence Against Women Act of 1993, under Title IV
(Safe Campuses for Women), proposes the appropriation of $20 mil-
lion for rape education and prevention programs to make college
campuses safe for women. Extrapolating from the 408 reported cases
of rape and attempted rape on 500 campuses with five million college
students in 1992 yields approximately 1,000 reported incidents at all
colleges in the United States. The appropriation proposed under Title
IV thus amounts to $20,000 per reported case (U.S. Senate, 1993).

Whatever the value of these programs, the cost is remarkably
high compared with the amount allocated per reported case of rape
victim off college campuses; among those cases, poor and minority
women are vastly overrepresented (Bureau of Justice Statistics, 1992).
According to FBI (1993) data, there were altogether 109,062 reported
cases of rape and attempted rape nationwide in 1992. Given these
rates, to make the rest of society as safe as college campuses would
require an expenditure of over $2 billion on education and prevention
programs (or more than twice the appropriations proposed under all
five titles of the act combined). Compared with the $20 million des-
ignated for college campuses ($20,000 per reported case), the Vio-
lence Against Women Act proposes an appropriation of $65 million
(approximately $650 per reported case) for prevention and education
programs to serve the broader community (U.S. Senate, 1993).[26]
Under this arrangement, the sum distributed for education and prevention programs on college campuses is disproportionate; worse,
most college victims, according to the *Ms.* study, do not know they

26. Although prevention and education funds are disproportionately targeted to college campuses, an appropriation of $100 million is earmarked for "high-density crime
areas" for the purposes of expanding police protection, prosecuting offenders, and
improving data collection.

have been raped. And relatively meager resources will be invested in similar programs for low-income and minority communities, where authentic victims need all the help that society can offer.

Some might argue that the need is really greater on college campuses because the rate of underreporting is much higher there than in other places. But we have little reason to assume that middle-class college students are less likely to report being raped than women from other backgrounds. Indeed, organized efforts have been made to facilitate reporting by college students. During the past decade, rape crisis counseling and supportive services have been established on most major campuses. Staffed by professionals highly sensitive to the social and psychological violations of rape, these services provide a sympathetic environment in which victims may come forward for assistance without having to make official reports to the police. Reliable data on how many rape victims are served by these programs are difficult to obtain, but individual accounts suggest that the demand is not excessive.[27] The director of counseling services at Lafayette College, for example, reports that over the course of five years services were provided to about a dozen students who confided that they were sexually assaulted (Forbes and Kirts, 1993). Offering an account of a typical Saturday night at the Rape Crisis Center at Columbia University, Peter Hellman (1993) reports: "Nobody called; nobody came."

Taking Back the Night

Yet a puzzling question remains: If the popular estimates of rape on campus are so greatly exaggerated compared with the relatively few cases reported to police and counseling centers, why are tens of thousands of female students across the country marching by candlelight to "take back the night"? Something is going on here. Radical feminists and advocacy researchers no doubt take this anguished behavior

27. In 1990, for example, the staff of the rape counseling program on the University of California, Berkeley, campus were unable to cite the exact number of women seen that year. They estimated having served forty to eighty cases, including some clients who were not students and some who were seen for problems other than rape. It was unclear whether the cases were counted according to number of contacts or number of individuals served.

as confirmation of widespread violence against college women. But several alternative explanations suggest a climate heavily influenced by the social dynamics of fear, power, conflict, and sex.

Inflated Fear   The view of take-back-the-night protests as confirmation of an epidemic of rape can be turned on its head. Claims that 33 percent of all children in the United States are sexually abused, that 25 percent of women students will be victims of rape or attempted rape, and that 50 percent of all American women will be raped during their lifetime have gained legitimacy and authority through repetition by public officials, journalists, television reporters, and well-known radical feminists with access to the media. Rather than responding to real violence against women on campus, these demonstrations may reflect a level of fear inflated by the exaggerated reports of violence. The reports create a premonition of danger that is grossly out of proportion to the actual risks of campus life. According to Katie Roiphe (1993b:58), a significant number of students are walking around with the alarming belief that 50 percent of women are raped. The "hyperbole" creates "a state of perpetual fear."

Power of Victimization   Some might argue, however, that demonstrations to take back the night are incited less by irrational fear than by the sense of righteousness and power that often accompanies the invocation of victim status. "Even the privileged," as Charles Sykes (1992:12) tells us, "have found that being oppressed has its advantage. On campuses of elite universities, students quickly learn the grammar and protocols of power—that the route to moral superiority and premier griping rights can be gained most efficiently through being a victim—which perhaps explains academia's search for what one critic calls the 'unified field theory of oppression.'"

Increased Gender Conflict   Over the past few decades, more women have entered college and joined the paid labor force than ever before. In 1960 most women married before their twenty-first birthday (Smith, 1994). Today at that age they are competing with men for graduate-school slots in almost every field and for jobs throughout the economy. An unprecedented number of women have also become heads of single-parent families to which absent fathers contribute often minimal support. These developments enlarge the occasions for friction and resentment in economic and social relationships between the sexes, particularly among the college-age group. The anxieties and animosities expressed in rallies to take back the night may in part reflect an increase in tensions between men and women. This explanation suggests that *sexual assault* has come to represent a broad and vaguely formulated category of offenses ranging from rape to the incivilities of heightened gender conflict in social and economic relationships.

Sexual Turmoil Explanations that refer to fear, power, and conflict downplay the extent to which sexual activities influence the highly emotional responses to the threat of rape on campus. Sexual relationships between young men and women, never exactly serene, have become more troublesome and confused in recent times. This is because there is more to manage, sex has become more dangerous, and it is harder to say no. Since 1960, as the median age for premarital intercourse has declined and the median age at first marriage has risen, the period of premarital sexual activity for women has grown from an average of 1.0 to 7.5 years (Smith, 1994). The sexual revolution in the late 1960s discounted the moral strictures against premarital sex. Without the shield of morality, it became more socially awkward to avoid having sex in situations where one's feelings were ambiguous or even strongly negative (Decter, 1972). (It is easier to take a moral stand and say no because premarital sex is wrong than to say no for all the other reasons: I don't love [or even like] you enough; you don't seem to love me enough; I am not ready yet.) Shortly after the time span for premarital sexual activity increased and the shield of morality fell, sexual encounters became more dangerous as the risks of contracting AIDS and other sexually transmitted diseases rose to alarming levels.

These explanations are not mutually exclusive. They describe a cultural climate of strained gender relationships under which advocacy research has successfully furthered the sexual politics of radical feminism. This politics is based on several convictions: that violence is the norm in heterosexual relationships, that all women are oppressed and deserve special treatment by the government, and that from an early age women need to be empowered by publicly supported training and prevention programs. The radical feminist agenda coincides with the interests of sexual-abuse-prevention professionals—therapists, counselors, sensitivity trainers, and consultants—who have developed a small industry of workshops, courses, videos, self-defense courses, and publications for schools and colleges. This agenda does not serve the interests of poor women, ethnic minorities, teenage boys, elderly people, and other groups in need of social protection from violence.

The radical feminist agenda has framed public discourse on violence against women since the 1980s. During the past few years, however, there has been a mounting challenge from other quarters of the feminist movement. Katie Roiphe (1993) and Stephanie Gutmann (1990) were among the first to question the sexual politics of those waving the rape crisis banner. In 1993 the Women's Freedom Network was organized by a prominent group of feminist thinkers, including Mary Ann Glendon, Elizabeth Fox-Genovese, Jeane Kirkpatrick, Edith Kurzweil, Sally Pipes, Virginia Postrel, Rita Simon, Christina Sommers, and Cathy Young. Among the principles to which they subscribe is the belief that "the rhetoric of victimization trivializes real abuse, demeans women, and promotes antagonism instead of real partnership between men and women" (Women's Freedom Network, 1994). This school of thought proposes an alternative approach to violence against women, one that promises to render a more rigorous account of the problem and more equitable policy solutions than have been shaped heretofore by advocacy research.

It is difficult to criticize advocacy research without giving the impression that one cares less about the problems of victims than do those engaged in magnifying the size of the problems. But a citizen or social scientist may be deeply concerned about problems like rape, child abuse, and homelessness yet still wish to see a rigorous and objective analysis of their dimensions. Advocacy researchers who uncover a problem, measure it with reasonable accuracy, and bring it to light perform a valuable service by raising public consciousness. Social equity is advanced when emerging problems are scrupulously assessed and brought to the attention of policymakers. The current trend in advocacy research, however, is to inflate problems and redefine them in line with the advocates' ideological preferences. The few impose their definitions of social ills on the many. Though creating sensational headlines, this type of advocacy research invites the formulation of social policies that are likely to be neither effective nor fair.

Chapter 5

Asking Who Benefits: Hidden Subsidies and Private Delivery

Most Americans earn an income and meet their needs for essential goods and services through market exchanges. Food, housing, clothing, and sundry personal services are purchased over the counter, so to speak, in discrete transactions between buyer and seller. Unlike the quid pro quo of exchange in the market economy, the welfare state distributes cash, goods, and services to individuals in unilateral transfers from public and private sources. The cash, goods, and services are allocated through what is sometimes described as the social market of the welfare state. From this perspective, the welfare state is a system for allocating resources that flow outside the regular channels of the market economy, mainly from the government to citizens.[1] Unchecked by the market forces of supply and demand, the allocation of welfare resources gives rise to concerns for social equity, voiced in such questions as Who gets what? Who pays? Is it fair to glean profit from delivering public aid to those in need?

Social and economic markets have different methods for allocating resources because they serve different purposes. In the simplest terms, transactions between providers and consumers in the economic market are influenced by prospects for growth, profit, and consumer satisfaction. Shaped by the forces of competition and consumer choice, the benefits of the market economy are typically described by its proponents as the product of enlightened self-interest. Opponents

1. The full range of welfare transfers would also include benefits in the form of power, opportunities, and vouchers (Gilbert, Specht, and Terrell, 1993).

would agree about the self-interest but would call it inordinate rather than enlightened.

With neither profit nor growth advanced as a legitimate motivating force in the welfare state, the allocation of resources through the social market is animated more by concerns for solidarity and communal benevolence than by individual self-interest. Here the unilateral transfer of welfare provisions performs several functions that are not filled very well by the economic market. In allocating a wide array of benefits to which people are entitled by virtue of their status as citizens, the social market promotes a sense of belonging to the community. It also creates a safety net protecting those unable to meet their basic needs through market exchanges because of disability, financial hardship, incompetence, or the failure of the economic market to produce the required commodities. By modifying the distribution of resources, the social market tends to reduce extremes of inequality, which arise when the market economy alone determines resource allocation. The extent to which the social market builds communal solidarity, provides a basic level of security, and reduces inequality varies within societies over time and among societies at any given time.

In the United States, as in other industrialized nations, the social market is closely identified with state agencies, but it also encompasses the family, voluntary organizations, and some elements of private enterprise—an arrangement often described as a mixed economy of welfare. The levels of activity and methods of contribution from these various sources have changed since 1900, producing new patterns of the public-private mix and reshaping the essential character of the welfare state.

The Shifting Balance Between Public and Private Activity

An examination of the mixed economy of welfare in the United States reveals three broad patterns during the twentieth century. From the turn of the century to 1935, welfare transfers were largely community based, with local governments, voluntary charitable institutions, family, and neighbors constituting the major sources of aid for those unable to meet their personal needs through the market economy.

Indeed, cases of local governments funding private welfare services can be traced back to colonial times, when public authorities contracted out with private parties to house and feed the poor. Although the federal government supported private welfare efforts as far back as 1819—when it provided assistance to the Hartford Asylum for the Deaf and Dumb—such support was intermittent and did not take on the character of a large-scale systematic effort until the mid-1930s. To the limited extent that the social market functioned, it was a distinctly local affair that depended heavily on voluntary charitable organizations and informal sources to finance and deliver welfare transfers (Leiby, 1978).

With the advent of the New Deal in the mid-1930s, the federal government assumed major responsibility for creating a national system that guaranteed a modicum of welfare for all citizens, financed and delivered chiefly through public agencies. Direct federal and state expenditures for social welfare climbed from 4 percent of the GNP in 1929, to 9 percent in 1940, to over 19 percent in 1976, after which it declined slightly, leveling off around 19 percent through 1991. The framework for the modern welfare state rose between 1935 and 1970s on the twin pillars of taxing and spending. The social market consisted of a public sector that financed and delivered welfare transfers through federal, state, and local units of government and a private sector in which transfers flowed through voluntary nonprofit agencies and informal networks of families and friends. These arrangements— government, voluntary nonprofit, and informal—operated in separate spheres that only occasionally joined together. For-profit enterprises were mostly excluded from the main line of activity in the social market.

Corresponding broadly to the conventional welfare-state model, the mixed economy that characterized the United States from 1935 to the mid-1970s differed from other systems in several aspects. It was more circumscribed than many of its European counterparts. Judging the United States a "laggard" in public spending on social security, Harold Wilensky (1975) saw it as a reluctant welfare state. Compared with most European welfare states, the United States had a government whose role was somewhat less vigorous, and voluntary nonprofit agencies performed more actively in the United States. But these differences were arguably matters of degree rather than kind. Through the early 1970s the United States followed the general welfare-state pattern for the most part: the government directly financed and publicly delivered welfare transfers, which were supplemented by the private activities of voluntary nonprofit agencies and informal networks.

Since the early 1970s the mixed economy has shifted toward market-oriented approaches to welfare transfers. Often described as the privatization of the welfare state, the shift puts public purchase-of-service policies that promote the delivery of social services by the private sector together with the increased use of fiscal instruments that dispense indirect transfers of cash (which subsidize the purchase of services on the private market by individual consumers).

A large measure of private activity was spurred by the advent of purchase-of-service arrangements under which government agencies contract for welfare services to be produced and delivered by private organizations (Gilbert, 1983). This development is evidenced, for example, in the experience of welfare agencies with Jewish sponsors; between 1962 and the early 1970s government payments for these agencies' services multiplied twentyfold, boosting the proportion of public funds from 11 percent to 51 percent of their total income (Chenkin, 1976). This case was not exceptional. By 1980 federal agencies provided 58 percent of the financial support received by private nonprofit social-service and community-development organizations (Salamon and Abramson, 1982).

At the same time that purchase-of-service arrangements enlarged the range of benefits provided under government contract with traditional nonprofit welfare agencies, they also created an opportunity for the delivery of welfare services by profit-making organizations. Between 1982 and 1987, for example, the number of paid employees in for-profit social-service agencies increased by 38 percent, compared with a 19 percent increase in the number of employees in voluntary agencies (Bureau of the Census, 1992). By 1990 proprietary agencies were prominently represented among the service providers in the areas of nursing-home care, homemaker aides, daycare, child welfare, health care, and housing (Gilbert and Tang, forthcoming). About 80 percent of nursing homes and related residential-care facilities are now operated for profit; the cost of nursing-home services amounted to more than $53 billion in 1990, half of which was paid for by public funds, mainly through the Medicaid program initiated in 1965 under Title XIX of the Social Security Act. In 1990 revenues and receipts from voluntary nonprofit and for-profit childcare agencies totaled $7.2 billion. A substantial portion of these private costs was subsidized by an indirect transfer of $3.9 billion through the childcare tax credit; in addition, daycare services were purchased with public funds under Title XX of the Social Security Act.

The move toward privatization is also reflected by the occupational choices of social workers, one of the primary groups who traditionally staff the public social services. In 1970 the proportion of social workers engaged in the private practice of psychotherapy on a full-time or part-time basis was 13 percent. By 1990 that proportion had increased to 40 percent (Specht and Courtney, 1994). The influx of profit-making activities into what was once the almost exclusive preserve of public and nonprofit service providers has blurred the boundaries between the social and economic markets (although fundamental differences remain between the core characteristics of these markets).

The case for greater involvement by profit-making organizations in the delivery of welfare services is supported by arguments about the shortcomings of government provisions and the advantages of private activity. On the shortcomings of government provisions, public-choice theorists like James Buchanan (1975) argue that democratic governments are susceptible to interest-group pressures that produce large inefficiencies in the allocation of societal resources. Each interest group has a strong incentive to demand as much as it can get from the government and little incentive to oppose demands of other groups which would have only a marginal impact on the overall tax situation. At the same time that all these demands add up, no interest group has much incentive to support an increase in general taxes, and individuals with similar needs who are unable to organize a strong interest group receive short shrift from the government. Given the politics of interest-group barter, both the absolute magnitude and the distribution of goods and services provided by the government are unlikely to be economically rational or efficient (Linowes, 1988). Besides these deficiencies is the apparent immunity of public bureaucracies to the constraints of cost, efficiency, and competition. Once government programs are established, they can rarely be dismantled (Friedman, 1962); bureaucrats form an interest group that advances their own demands for the growth of social programs and expenditures.

The argument for privatization rests squarely on the assumption that competition in the marketplace creates powerful incentives for firms to adopt cost-effective practices that reduce waste and to offer products that attract and satisfy consumers. The profit motive is seen as a further inducement to efficiency and responsiveness to consumer preferences.

Those opposed to privatization argue that market failure is likely to occur in the realm of social services. They proffer several reasons: competition to satisfy consumers is dampened by third-party purchase-of-service arrangements under which clients who consume certain services do not pay for them; the incentive for profit promotes avarice and low-quality services; and the vulnerable populations served by social welfare agencies are often ill-informed consumers who tend to be satisfied with any goods or services that are free or highly subsidized.[2] Richard Titmuss (1968) argues that in-kind social services, particularly medical care, have thirteen characteristics that differentiate them from typical private goods, characteristics related to the uncertainty and unpredictability of medical care systems and to the vulnerability of consumers. Many of these attributes of medical care reflect the more general problem of what Henry Hansmann (1980) terms contract failure, which occurs when consumers lack sufficient information to evaluate the quality or value of services. The case is also made that cash benefits to individuals, which subsidize demand, may not always elicit an increased supply of social services

2. Several researchers have found that, when surveyed, social-service consumers generally respond with favorable assessments of staff and service and that their assessments tend to be higher than those made by professionals. The tendency to express satisfaction has been attributed to gratitude for free or low-cost services, natural politeness, an inclination to rationalize personal involvement in a service, and a low level of expectations (Gilbert, 1983; Gilbert and Eaton, 1970).

sufficient to serve all those in need. Examining the increasing supply of childcare services, for example, Sheila Kamerman and Alfred Kahn (1989) conclude that it is unclear to what extent the overall increase in these services can be attributed to the Reagan administration policy of encouraging private-sector initiatives through consumer subsidies. Finally, some critics see privatization as simply a euphemism for cutting total public expenditures on social services (Walker, 1984; Bendick, 1989).

Weighing the Results
To what extent are the benefits and liabilities claimed for profit-making firms demonstrated by their performance in the production and delivery of social welfare provisions? Is profit making compatible with the delivery of social services? We ask such questions as the balance shifts between public and private responsibility for the delivery of social services.

The question of comparative quality and efficiency divides along two axes: public versus private (including both voluntary and for-profit providers) and profit versus nonprofit. In each case, the question involves which type of sponsorship is more efficient for the production and delivery of high-quality social services. On this issue the research findings are inconclusive, muddled by such intervening factors as agency size, geographic location, and the large differences in the categories of profit-oriented and nonprofit providers. A further complication is the difficulty of calibrating the quality of social welfare services (Kanter and Summers, 1987); it is easier to obtain a precise measure of service costs than of service quality. Over a dozen studies comparing the average price of care in nonprofit and for-profit nursing homes show that for-profits have lower costs (Marmor, Schlesinger, and Smithey, 1987). Generally, comparative analyses appear to favor for-profit over nonprofit providers of nursing homes and daycare *if cost is the only criterion.* But lower costs do not necessarily equate with higher efficiency when the products compared are of substantially different quality.

Frequently, the cost advantage of for-profit providers fades when measures of quality are introduced (Gilbert and Tang, forthcoming).

In daycare, for example, for-profit centers charge a lower hourly fee than do nonprofit centers under religious and independent sponsorship. But the for-profit centers have a higher child-to-staff ratio, a lower percentage of teachers with college degrees, a higher rate of staff turnover, and fewer physical and cognitive examinations of the clients (Kisker et al., 1991). Burton Weisbrod and Mark Schlesinger (1986) drew up a similar balance sheet for nursing homes. They found that proprietary facilities employed fewer professional and nonprofessional staff per patient than did nonprofit homes, and their staff administered considerably higher dosages of sleeping medication. When family members are asked about their level of satisfaction with nursing-home facilities, however, their overall ratings are fairly high for both profit and nonprofit facilities. Although church-owned nonprofit nursing homes are associated with the highest level of consumer satisfaction, Weisbrod (1993) reports that other nonprofits are virtually indistinguishable from proprietary facilities in degree of consumer satisfaction. In Austria proprietary retirement homes impose the highest charges, but both proprietary and voluntary nonprofit facilities charge higher prices and provide qualitatively better services than retirement homes run by government (Badelt and Weiss, 1991).

The largest body of research is in the area of hospital care, where some of the knottiest problems of measuring cost and quality are encountered. In the most comprehensive review of the evidence so far, the researchers at the Institute of Medicine at the National Academy of Science conclude: "Evidence on differences between for-profit and not-for-profit health care organizations is not sufficient to justify a recommendation that investor ownership of health care organizations be either opposed or supported by public policy" ("Review and Outlook," 1986:26). In a similar vein, Theodore Marmor and his associates (1987) found only minor, inconsistent differences in the costs of for-profit and nonprofit hospitals and few, if any, measurable differences in the quality of medical practice. For-profit facilities usually charged higher costs per day, but their costs per admission were often lower because of their patients' shorter lengths of stay.

In the interest of restoring social equity, we may ask whether it is fair to use public funds to support welfare transfers through profit-making enterprises. The taxpayer foots the bill to subsidize not only the services for welfare beneficiaries but also the profits for organizations delivering these services. The fairness of this arrangement ultimately depends on whether profit-making organizations are more efficient than other providers and can deliver services of equal or better quality at less cost. Overall, the various findings on the cost and quality of social services dispensed by public and private agencies do not yield a definitive answer. As Kamerman and Kahn (1989:262) observe, the evidence runs both ways, "varying with field, time, context, and scale." Since no decisive pattern emerges, the merits of profit-oriented and nonprofit service providers remain to be judged on a case-by-case basis.

At this stage, perhaps the best that can be said about the movement toward privatization is that opening new avenues for the delivery of social provisions has invited probing comparisons of service characteristics and outcomes under public, voluntary nonprofit, and for-profit auspices. Even if these comparisons fail to yield firm conclusions about the relative value of public and private service providers, they bring the issues of cost and quality into focus and help to clarify the changing pattern of service delivery.

Accounting for Welfare Expenditures

An increase in the government's purchase of services from private firms draws attention to the highly visible course of privatization. In contrast, another avenue toward market-oriented social welfare has opened, although it is largely concealed from public view. It is the conduit for a rising number of indirect transfers, which finance the private consumption of welfare. Recognition of these hidden social expenditures extends both the prevailing conception of who gains from welfare transfers and the nature of their social responsibilities.

Contemporary discussions about balancing social rights and obligations, as I suggested in Chapter 2, typically proceed from the assumption that we understand who gains from welfare transfers and need only to figure out what they owe society in return. But who gains and what social responsibilities they may be expected to fulfill in exchange are not entirely self-evident. Over the past two decades profound changes have occurred in the methods of financing welfare transfers, which have yet to be acknowledged in the standard accounting of welfare expenditures.

How much has government spending on social welfare changed over the years? To answer this question, policy analysts, researchers, and journalists ordinarily turn to the annual report of the Social Security Administration (SSA). It encompasses a broad range of transfers for health, housing, income maintenance, education, and social services and is generally considered the authoritative inventory for welfare spending in the United States.[3] According to the SSA ledger, government expenditure for social welfare surged from 10 percent of the GNP in 1960 to 19.5 percent by 1976 as new social benefits were awarded through an array of social legislation. The service amendments to the Social Security Act in 1962, the Economic Opportunity Act of 1964, the Model Cities legislation of 1966, the Food Stamp Act of 1965, the Older Americans Act of 1965, the Community Mental Health Centers Act of 1963, Medicare and Medicaid, and the Title XX amendments to the Social Security Act (in 1974) are only a sample of the major initiatives that formed a growing package of social provisions financed directly by government.

Through the early 1970s European countries and the United States both relied largely, though not exclusively, on the "direct expenditures" approach to welfare transfers. Taxes collected by the state financed cash benefits and social services produced by government. Measured by direct expenditures relative to GDP, the United States is usually judged inferior to European welfare states. But comparisons of this sort have become increasingly misleading.[4] Between 1970 and 1990 the U.S. social-welfare system has quietly evolved away from the traditional state-centered design of European models toward a market-oriented arrangement. The emphasis is on private activity and an expanding package of social welfare transfers through indirect mea-

3. The SSA data are regularly cited in the press (Rich, 1989), as well as in academic studies of welfare spending (Gough, 1979; Bell, 1983; Moroney, 1991).

4. The kinds of adjustments required for an unbiased measure of welfare expenditures are analyzed in Neil Gilbert and Ailee Moon's (1988) comparative study of welfare efforts.

sures, such as tax expenditures and credit subsidies. These benefits do not show up in the SSA's standard inventory of direct expenditures.

Judging by the SSA ledger of direct expenditures, public spending for social welfare over the past fifty years appears to have advanced from one plateau to another. As a percentage of the GNP, direct public expenditures for social welfare remained at nearly 10 percent between 1940 and 1960, climbed to over 19 percent by the mid-1970s, then dipped slightly, by 0.5 percent, and have since leveled off at the rate of 18.5 percent. After such a precipitous rise through the 1970s, liberals tend to interpret the steady level of expenditure as a reversal in progress, whereas conservatives are inclined to see it as progress toward a reversal in welfare spending. Both views are myopic. By narrowly focusing on direct grants to states and individuals, liberals and conservatives alike overlook the use of other fiscal instruments, which are reshaping the modern structure of welfare transfers. As the type of public spending that was most direct and most easily measured slowed down, less visible and more indirect forms of expenditure accelerated.

How much does the government really spend on social welfare? According to recent figures from the Social Security Administration, public spending on social welfare totaled $1,162 billion in 1991 (Bixby, 1994). But the bookkeeping here is incomplete. The SSA misjudges the full costs of social welfare transfers by an estimated 25 percent to 40 percent, depending on the range of indirect expenditures classified as serving social welfare purposes (Gilbert and Gilbert, 1989). The discrepancy between the SSA account and the actual level of government expenditure is attributable to a number of hidden transfers that are excluded from the conventional audit of welfare spending. Over the past two decades these ignored expenditures have multiplied and now form an almost invisible arm of the welfare state, which delivers substantial aid to recipients mainly in the middle and upper classes. Thus the SSA's focus on direct public expenditures conveys a distorted view not only of welfare expenditures but also of beneficiaries. It is a view that concentrates on the most visible form of social transfer, which is intended largely for poor, elderly, and dependent members of society. A more accurate account requires expanding the conventional ledger of direct financing to include the costs of indirect methods of government support for social welfare, especially the provision of social transfers through tax expenditures and credit subsidies.

That special deductions and exemptions in the tax code amount to a form of government transfer is hardly a new idea. It was recognized as early as the 1930s in Arthur Pigou's classic text *Economics of Welfare* (1938) and elaborated on by Richard Titmuss (1958) in the mid-1950s. The movement of this idea from academic discourse to public policy gained momentum in 1967, when Stanley Surrey, assistant secretary of the treasury, proposed that deductions, exemptions, and other tax expenditures be officially counted as federal revenue losses.[5] Only since 1974, however, have tax expenditure data been introduced as a regular component of the president's annual budget (Goode, 1977).

The case for an account of welfare spending that more precisely includes certain tax expenditures is underscored by the ongoing debate about preferred forms of public support for childcare (see Chapter 1). Policymakers are divided over whether this support should be delivered through tax credits to individuals or through direct grants for services. In 1990 they compromised by incorporating a package of childcare-related provisions into the Omnibus Budget Reconciliation Act. This package includes additional funding for childcare programs, such as Headstart and the Child Care Development Block Grant, and a substantial expansion of $18.3 billion in tax credits (through earned income tax credits and supplementary credits, both for young children, and through health insurance) over the next five years for low-income families with dependent children. Even though the tax-credit subsidy is among the most expensive social-welfare measures in recent decades, Committee on Ways and Means (1992) estimates show that approximately 12 percent of this benefit will not register in the conventional SSA account of welfare spending in 1993 nor be weighed in the typical comparisons of welfare expenditures on which the United States is continually ranked below the

5. Surrey wrote extensively on this subject. His best known works include *Pathways to Tax Reform* (1973) and *Tax Expenditures* (1985, with McDaniel).

European nations. None of the costs for most tax expenditures appear on the SSA ledger of social welfare spending. In this regard, the earned income tax credit is something of an exception. Because it is a refundable credit, beneficiaries receive a cash payment from the government for any portion of the credit that exceeds their tax liability.

The earned income tax credit is one of the many new items that has contributed to the growth in the number and size of tax expenditures since 1970. The federal income tax was initiated in 1909. By 1970 tax expenditures were specified in 53 provisions in the tax law. Between 1970 and 1988 the figure almost doubled, to 94 provisions, despite the tax reforms of 1986 that eliminated certain categories of tax expenditure.[6] Between 1970 and 1986, in addition to new items of expenditure there were 216 amendments to existing provisions, two-thirds of which resulted in expanded benefits. Thus, it comes as no surprise that between 1971 and 1988, tax expenditures rose from $52 billion to $289 billion, increasing their relative share of public costs from 22 percent to 28 percent of direct federal outlays (Moon, 1989).

There is one significant exception to the general trend of increasing tax expenditures worth mentioning. This involves the dependent exemption, which was $600 per person in 1948, an amount that equaled 40 percent of per capita personal income at that time. For the exemption to remain at the same proportion of per capita income that it represented in 1948, it would have had to rise to $7,800 by 1990. But in 1990 the dependent exemption amounted to only $2,050, or 10.5 percent of per capita income. The erosion in value was due largely to the failure to adjust for inflation and rising incomes (Ooms and Weinreb, 1992).

Although 82 percent of all federal tax expenditures in 1988 benefited individual taxpayers, items related exclusively to social welfare are not classified in a standard way.[7] Examining a few items most

6. The number of provisions for tax expenditures peaked at 104 in 1982 and then declined to 94 after the 1986 tax reforms, which were an attempt to reduce marginal tax rates and eliminate some controversial tax expenditures.

7. The Committee on Ways and Means (U.S. House of Representatives, 1992) gathers and reports data on many social-welfare-related tax expenditures dealing with retirement, health, poverty, employment, and disability. These data do not include tax expenditures related to veterans' benefits and education.

clearly related to social welfare, we see that the largest category of federal tax expenditures for individuals encompasses provisions for income maintenance, such as earned income tax credits and tax exclusions on retirement plans. Here, tax expenditures totaled $78.5 billion in 1988, which amounted to 24 percent of direct federal outlays for income maintenance. The second largest category of federal tax expenditure involves deductions and exclusions for housing; the total came to $50.4 billion in 1986—more than twice the amount spent in direct federal grants for housing and community development. And tax expenditures for education, training, employment, and social services totaled $19.0 billion in 1988, about two-thirds of direct federal outlays for these programs (Moon, 1989).

Credit subsidies, another indirect method of providing social transfers, are poorly understood and even harder to trace than tax expenditures. These hidden transfers derive from the difference between interest rates charged by the government, on the one hand, and market rates for similar loans, costs of loan defaults, reduction of loan fees, and other financial benefits of public guarantees, on the other. The federal credit budget, established in 1980, measures direct loan commitments but not the costs of public subsidies inherent in all these transactions. Efforts to take a systematic account of these subsidies are under way, however. In the area of housing, for example, the Office of Management and Budget (1988) estimates that the subsidies provided by federal loan guarantee programs netted borrowers benefits of $6.1 billion, or about 50 percent of direct federal expenditures on housing subsidies (Gilbert and Gilbert, 1989).

This brief comparison of direct expenditures with tax expenditures and credit subsidies suggests that the stream of social welfare transfers from the government to individual beneficiaries is considerably larger and more complex than the transfers represented in the standard SSA accounting of social welfare spending. Some benefits are more visible than others. Some costs are easier to calculate than others. Some recipients have greater public approval than others. The standard report on social welfare expenditures unwittingly conceals the full scope of these costs and benefits. At the same time, it narrows the policymaking window on how to finance social welfare and what the potential spending tradeoffs are.

To make informed judgments about welfare spending and potential tradeoffs, we must first get the numbers right. There are several difficulties besides technical matters of calculation. The middle and upper classes have gained substantially from the expansion of indirect government expenditures.[8] They are, however, unaccustomed to thinking of these financial advantages as welfare transfers. Farmers enjoying low-interest housing loans from federal programs, for example, typically fail to realize that they are being subsidized by the government for the costs of shelter just as residents of public housing are who pay below-market rent for their units. Liberals are hesitant to count the costs of indirect measures because doing so would dramatically increase the size of the welfare system, impugning their customary criticism that too little is being spent. Conservatives are not charmed by the idea that special tax preferences involve anything more than allowing citizens to keep what they have rightly earned.[9] Yet there is something to be said for a full disclosure of who benefits from the diverse forms of government assistance to individuals and what the assistance really costs. Aside from the need for accuracy in order to make informed judgments about spending, an accounting that captures the full range of welfare transfers helps to sharpen the discussion of social rights and responsibilities.

Inducing Social Responsibility

The growth of indirect welfare expenditures, which provide benefits that go almost unnoticed by the public, has been accompanied by an

8. Proportionately twice as many taxpayers filing joint returns in the $75,000 to $100,000 income class than in the $20,000 to $30,000 income class claimed a dependent-care tax credit in 1992, and the average amount awarded to individuals in the higher bracket was twice that awarded to those in the lower bracket. Because high-paying jobs are more likely to include pension benefits than low-paying jobs, taxpayers in the upper-income groups also gain disproportionately from pension-related tax expenditures (U.S. House of Representatives, 1992).

9. As Irving Kristol (1978:194) puts it, to think of tax concessions as subsidies is to tacitly assume that "all income covered by the general provisions of the tax law belongs of right to the government, and what government decides, by exemption or qualification, not to collect in taxes constitutes a subsidy."

increasing scrutiny of direct expenditures, which offer highly visible benefits. Programs that deliver the most visible welfare transfers are being reassessed by policymakers and citizens asking, What are the appropriate criteria of welfare entitlement? The question revives earlier distinctions between the deserving and the undeserving poor, the subject of a long-standing debate that was muted during the 1960s.

The central question of entitlement during the mid-1960s focused not so much on the worthiness of potential welfare recipients as on the range of benefits that they deserved (see Chapters 2 and 3). According to the conventional wisdom of that era, the poor were the innocent casualties of capitalism and were therefore entitled to be compensated for its failures. The pressing concern was how far to extend the "social rights of citizenship" (Marshall, 1950). Admonitions against blaming the victim struck a responsive chord in the 1960s and early 1970s. With a resurgence of popular support for capitalism in the 1980s, concerns about the nature of welfare entitlement shifted away from elaborations of social rights to delineations of the social responsibilities of citizenship.

Social rights are marked by a variety of tangible benefits to which citizens are legally entitled. Social obligations are acknowledged less frequently as a set of legal duties than as a normative consensus about how people should behave and what they owe each other. Although this normative attribute makes it difficult to gauge the full scope of social obligations, several duties constitute the core of expected behavior, as Lawrence Mead (1986) suggests. At the very least, according to Mead, able-bodied adults are expected to work in available jobs, to contribute to the support of their families, to acquire fluency in English, to learn enough in school to be employable, and to respect the law as well as the rights of others. The analysis of social obligations draws attention to the responsibilities that accompany the rights to various forms of public aid. Specifying these responsibilities might, it is thought, "induce private virtue through public policy" (Wilson, 1985:15). From this perspective, society is authorized to insist that entitlement to public aid be conditioned on the fulfillment of routine social obligations.

Efforts to balance social obligations and social rights, however, require a precise assessment of what to include on both sides of the ledger. To date, these efforts have concentrated primarily on rights embodied in the highly visible welfare transfers (such as cash grants and services to AFDC mothers) and on obligations essentially related to employment and financial support of one's family. The Family Support Act of 1988 (discussed in Chapters 2 and 3) is a case in point. In addition to requiring AFDC recipients with children over three years old to enroll in training programs and then seek employment, the act directs teenage mothers with children under three to complete their high school education or acquire an equivalency diploma, and it obliges single mothers applying for welfare to help establish paternity for purposes of eventually obtaining child-support payments. Stipulating workfare, a high school education, and establishment of paternity underscores the parental duty to provide economically for one's family. Although financial support is crucial, the social obligation to care for one's family has other dimensions that deserve serious consideration. Parents are expected to nurture and socialize their children and tend to their emotional needs. When children are young and most in need of socialization and emotional comfort, the single parent's obligation to take a paying job may be incompatible with these other dimensions of caring.

By focusing on obligations related to employment and financial support of one's family and on rights related to direct forms of welfare transfer, the moral calculus of social rights and responsibilities applies almost exclusively to the poor. But just as the full spectrum of benefits derived from social rights extends beyond benefits related to direct welfare expenditures, so, too, do the social obligations of community membership go well beyond the traditional duty to pay one's own way. In addition to caring for dependent members of one's family, the more general charge to assist the weakest and protect the most vulnerable members of the community is widely considered a basic responsibility of all who are able.

Revising the Ledger
The conventional estimate of welfare expenditure forms a narrow compass for mapping social rights, one that centers on the poor and

accentuates their social responsibility to be financially self-supporting. A broader, more balanced view of rights and responsibilities requires creating a new ledger for social accounting. Although some gaps remain, a growing body of information on tax expenditures and credit subsidies is available to take the full measure of government spending for social welfare.

The inclusion of benefits from tax expenditures and credit subsidies expands the moral equation of social rights and responsibilities in several ways. With regard to social rights, we begin to recognize a wider circle of beneficiaries, which encompasses such middle-class groups as homeowners and college students. As Michael Sherraden (1991) points out, most transfers to the poor, such as rent supplements to low-income households and AFDC grants, are for purposes of immediate consumption. In contrast, benefits for the nonpoor, such as tax deductions for interest payments on housing mortgages and credit subsidies for college loans, contribute to the accumulation of assets.

If efforts to correct the moral balance of rights and responsibilities weigh public relief for the poor against the recipients' performance of social duties, what about the reciprocal obligations of, for example, nonpoor homeowners and college students who are assisted by tax and credit-related subsidies? These groups profit immensely from indirect social transfers that allow them to accumulate assets over a lifetime. I can think of many ways that such middle-income beneficiaries might compensate the community for the financial advantages obtained through indirect transfers. Students subsidized by low-interest college loans, for instance, could be expected to perform some type of national service upon graduation, such as working in daycare centers, nursing homes, or inner-city schools. Those who benefit from tax deductions for homeowners might be charged a 1 percent or 2 percent federal transfer tax on profits from the sale of their property, which could go to finance housing vouchers for low-income tenants.

When indirect social transfers are included in assessments of social rights, issues also arise concerning the justification for subsidizing certain groups when need is not a compelling factor. In this regard, Peter Peterson, former secretary of commerce, proposes that the government set $250,000 as the limit on the amount of home mortgages on which interest is tax deductible—a measure that would save $10 billion over the next ten years. He would also limit tax expenditures on employer-paid health care. "This perverse subsidy," Peterson explains, "which in 1994 will cost the Treasury $76 billion in lost tax revenues, benefits relatively well-paid Americans the most while offering nothing to those who are poor, unemployed, or uninsured" (1994:44). Proposals like Peterson's prompt other questions: Should the government continue to subsidize mortgage-interest payments for people who own second homes? And why should a family with two children in which both parents work, earning more than, let us say, $70,000 a year, receive up to $960 in a childcare tax credit when families earning much less get no benefit because one parent remains at home to care for the children?

The growing value of indirect transfers raises compelling questions about how best to achieve a moral symmetry between welfare entitlements and social obligations. For a fair account of what is at stake, we need a ledger that incorporates the direct and indirect methods through which the government distributes cash and services to improve the welfare of individuals. Going beyond the conventional measure of welfare spending, this approach to accounting for expenditures would contribute to a more accurate reckoning of who benefits from social welfare transfers—a prerequisite for any effort to restore social equity.

Chapter 6

Enabling Citizens: Beyond the Welfare State

Many analytic schemes have been devised to classify modern welfare states. In one of the earliest efforts, Harold Wilensky and Charles Lebeaux (1958) distinguished between "institutional" and "residual" models. In the institutional model, welfare transfers are considered a normal ongoing function of the state, designed to meet a wide range of people's needs; in the residual model, welfare transfers are designed more as emergency measures to employ when family and market fail to perform adequately. Expanding the institutional-residual division, Richard Titmuss (1974) formulated a threefold scheme that included the industrial achievement-performance model, under which welfare transfers are an adjunct, or "handmaiden," to the market economy. These initial classifications were keyed to the extent to which human needs were met through the family, the state, and the market economy. The role of private voluntary organizations represents a fourth arena of welfare activity. Moving beyond the institutional-residual schema, Adelbert Evers and Ivan Svetlik (1991) characterize modern welfare states as pluralistic arrangements involving the state, the market, the family, and voluntary sectors, with state-coordinated and state-dominated models among the possibilities.

As welfare-state typologies became more intricate, greater efforts were made to specify their dimensions empirically. In an elaborate empirical analysis Gosta Esping-Andersen (1990) developed a scheme that differentiates among liberal, corporatist, and social democratic welfare states on the basis of variations in systems of stratification, the way social rights are promoted, and the public-private mix of social provisions. According to his scheme, the United States, Canada, and Australia exemplify the liberal welfare state, which restricts universal social rights, creates a sharp division between the class of welfare recipients and other citizens, and emphasizes private welfare schemes. In the corporatist welfare state, exemplified by France, Germany, and Italy, social rights are attached to class and status. Under this model, which supports existing class divisions, publicly subsidized welfare transfers are tempered by the principle of "subsidiarity," limiting state intervention to cases where the family and other traditional institutions are unable to care for members. Finally, there is the social democratic welfare state, represented by Sweden, Denmark, and Norway, which seeks to promote universal social rights and eliminate class distinctions by relying heavily on the public provision of welfare transfers. To these three models Norman Ginsburg (1992) adds a fourth, the British liberal-collectivist welfare state, a hybrid of the socialist and liberal types.

These models are a mere handful of the diverse typologies created to characterize modern welfare states.[1] Although the typologies embrace a wide range of variables, they yield classifications that tend to group the same countries together, as Demetrius Iatridis (1994) points out. This is because the analytic discourse is framed by at least three major assumptions about the core elements of the conventional welfare-state paradigm: first, that Marshall's (1950) proposition about the social rights of citizenship constitutes, as Esping-Andersen (1990) puts it, "the core idea of a welfare state"; second, that in welfare states the government bears the primary responsibility for delivering social provisions; and finally, that welfare transfers are financed mainly through direct public expenditures.[2]

1. Other approaches include Iatridis' (1994) fourfold classification of laissez-faire, institutional, interventionist, and authoritative models, based on degrees of market control by the government, and Therborn's (1987) models of interventionist, compensatory, and market-oriented welfare states, distinguished according to levels of social entitlement and full employment policies. For additional models see Alber, 1988; Barnes and Srivenkataramana, 1982; Leibfried, 1990; and Hurl and Tucker, 1986.

2. Esping-Andersen (1990) has developed as a measure of welfare entitlements a decommodification index to analyze the degree to which old-age pensions in eighteen industrial democracies permit the average person to opt out of the labor market. The index includes such variables as income-replacement rate, the years of contribution

The core elements of the welfare state—broad-based social rights, government delivery of services, and direct public expenditure— represent central tendencies. Variations come under the headings of welfare pluralism and the mixed economy of welfare. Thus, the welfare state as a theoretical construct has been applied to many systems of social protection with varying degrees of entitlements, levels of government activity, and direct public expenditure on social transfers. Yet, asked to identify the most progressive welfare states, respondents of all political stripes would agree that the Scandinavian countries fit this description. Here *progressive* connotes social welfare arrangements in which the core elements are well developed and come closest to the popular image conveyed by the concept of the welfare state. Typologies rarely employ the value-laden term *progressive*, because it suggests that some systems are better and more advanced than others.[3] Instead, what might otherwise be considered the less progressive systems—those with conspicuously lower degrees of social spending, government activity, and entitlement to welfare transfers— are affirmed merely as variants of the conventional paradigm.

Indeed, the conventional welfare-state paradigm offers a fairly accurate representation of the standard (not so much an average as an ideal-type in the Weberian sense) around which the systems of social protection clustered and against which they were judged in industrial democracies until the 1980s.[4] As Peter Baldwin (1992:69) points out:

required to qualify for pension benefits, and the percentage of pension financing paid by the individuals covered. In addition to old-age pensions based on direct public expenditures, however, in some countries, like the United States, a growing amount of replacement income in retirement is being furnished by private pension schemes, which are subsidized indirectly through tax expenditures (U.S. House of Representatives, 1992). These benefits (and the extent to which they add to the decommodification of labor) tend to be overlooked in the conventional welfare-state paradigm of rights manifest in social transfers delivered by the government and subsidized through direct expenditures.

3. Comparative analyses of welfare efforts, such as Harold Wilensky's classic study *The Welfare State and Equality* (1975), do rank welfare states according to their relative levels of social expenditure.

4. Max Weber's (Miller, 1963:31) ideal-type was not ideal in the sense of achieving perfection or representing exemplary values. The ideal-type was an analytic construct that captured the essential tendencies of a phenomenon. There were, as Weber explained, "ideal types of brothels as well as of religions."

"Until recently, much literature on the welfare state took the social citizenship model as the endpoint of social policy development. Sweden under the Social Democratic reign was the welfare Mecca that all other nations were striving towards or reacting against. The road to the welfare state was seen as a simple two-way street with movement possible only towards or away from the social citizenship model." Since the 1980s, however, the development of social protection in the United States has taken another road.

At some point, a change in degree becomes a change in kind. Molded in recent times by the demographic and ideological forces that have prompted the changing philosophy of social protection (discussed in Chapter 3), what is emerging in the United States is not just a variant of the conventional welfare state but an alternative form. It is a change in kind; the system of social protection is being transformed from that of a welfare state to that of an "enabling state." Although the transformation is not complete, we find the movement toward an enabling state unequivocally endorsed in mainstream political quarters.

The Progressive Policy Institute (PPI) is the policy arm of the Democratic Leadership Council, an organization that President Clinton helped organize in 1985 and chaired in 1991.[5] In a report to the Clinton administration the institute offers a "blueprint for a new America," recommending an approach that goes beyond incremental changes in the existing welfare system.

> To truly seize the initiative in the war on poverty, the new
> administration also must replace the welfare system with a new
> strategy for enabling America's poor. While the welfare state is
> organized around the goal of income maintenance, the enabling
> state should be organized around the goals of work and indi-
> vidual empowerment. Above all, it should help poor Americans

5. The Democratic Leadership Council was founded by moderate Democrats to move the party toward the center of the political spectrum. It is composed of over 750 elected Democratic officials from across the country and has been chaired by such party leaders as Senator Sam Nunn, House Majority Leader Richard Gephardt, and Senator Charles Robb, as well as President (then Governor) Clinton.

develop the capacities they need to liberate themselves from poverty and dependence. And it should do so directly, bypassing whenever possible public bureaucracies and service providers, and placing responsibility and resources directly into the hands of the people we are trying to help. An enabling strategy should see the poor as the prime agents of their own development, rather than as passive clients of the welfare system. (Marshall and Schram, 1993:228)

The last statement describing the institute report resonates with the efforts of the Organization for Economic Cooperation and Development (1989) to encourage a shift from a passive to an active society (discussed in Chapter 3). Ben Wattenberg (1993:12) describes the core ideas in the PPI's report as "representing nothing less than a new public value system for Democrats, a move from the 'welfare state' to the 'enabling state.'" Not only are Democrats embracing the virtues of an enabling state, but Charles Murray (1988:58) argues that good "government can do as much as it can to *enable*, but can do no more than enable." But Murray's threshold for enabling policies would surely be lower than that of the Democratic Leadership Council.

A similar trend toward an enabling role for the state can be seen in England, though it is perhaps not as advanced as in the United States. Both the Griffiths report in 1988 and the British government's 1989 white paper on community care emphasized the "enabling role" of local social-service authorities, encouraging their use of private and voluntary providers (Evandrou, Falkingham, and Glennerster, 1990). More generally, David Piachaud (1993:13) sees a need to rethink social policy in order to strengthen its link to economic growth. "If people can be enabled to or assisted to provide for themselves," he observes, "then this seems preferable from every point of view to relying on state support. Social policy thinking needs to move beyond redistribution, which has dominated thinking since the Second World War, and in a sense move back a step to think about people's capabilities and how those with limited capabilities—whether due to lack of skills, lack of child care, or lack of jobs—may be empowered to help themselves."

References to the enabling state are often couched in the language of "empowerment," "privatization," and "responsibility." The governing principle of this approach to social protection may be summed up in the phrase "public support for private responsibility" (Gilbert and Gilbert, 1989). But concerns for private effort and responsibility by citizens and nongovernmental organizations are embedded in a larger foundation of ideas and preferences that differentiate the enabling state from the conventional welfare state. As an alternative paradigm for social protection, the enabling state has essential tendencies that differ from those of the welfare state along several dimensions, as illustrated in Table 6.1. The characteristics of these alternative models of social protection are represented as tendencies because there are areas of overlap. Both the welfare state and the enabling state dispense social rights through transfers in the form of cash and services financed by direct and indirect expenditures and delivered through public and private vehicles; both forge social policies that support individuals and family units with welfare benefits for consumption and investment intended to achieve equality and equity. But for each variable, different preferences are advanced by the welfare state and the enabling state.

The enabling state does not exist in a pure form. Even in the United States, where much evidence supports the supposition that the system of social protection is evolving in this direction (Gilbert and Gilbert, 1989), there is still a distance to go. Many social policies do not coincide with those that would be derived from the central preferences listed in Table 6.1. The enabling state, for example, favors the two-parent family as a focal point for policy design because this unit is highly effective as a private source of economic and social support. Most families are able to nurture and care for their dependent members better than government agencies can. Unlike children raised entirely in two-parent families, the vast majority of those raised in single-parent homes will experience poverty during their childhood (Ellwood, 1988). From this perspective, policies that promote public support for private responsibility should not discourage the legal ties of marriage, which formalize a couple's commitment to care for each other, their children, and kin. Yet the income tax code imposes a

Table 6.1 The Welfare State and the Enabling State Compared

Welfare State	Enabling State
Expanding social rights	Linking rights to obligations
Relying on direct expenditures	Increasing indirect expenditures
Transfers in the form of service	Transfers in cash or vouchers
Delivery by public agencies	Delivery by private agencies
Policy focused on individuals	Policy focused on the family
Welfare benefits for consumption	Welfare benefits for investment
Reducing economic inequality	Restoring social equity

penalty on some two-earner married couples in the upper-income categories who must pay a higher tax than if they were able to file two single-person returns. This marriage penalty was reduced, though not eliminated, by the Tax Reform Act of 1986 but was increased under new rules in 1993 (Bernstein, 1993). Although the effects of the marriage penalty on decisions to wed are unknown, the inequity of the tax heightens with the increasing rates of cohabitation outside marriage.

Issues of Social Equity

Concerns for social equity are central to the philosophy of social protection in the enabling state. These concerns are exemplified by the recent emphasis on the design of policies that seek to balance rights and responsibilities in the allocation of welfare transfers (see Chapter 3). They are also reflected in the frequent pronouncement that citizens who work hard and play by the rules should be able to support their families above the poverty level (Ellwood, 1988). The enabling state is directed less toward equalizing the distribution of wealth than the welfare state is, and more toward giving people a fair shake. In this sense, social equity is the moral compass from which the enabling state takes its bearings.

Everyone does not always agree on what is fair. Formal discussions of equity distinguish between horizontal equity, or treating people in equal circumstances equally, and vertical equity, or differentiating as appropriate among people in unequal circumstances. With regard to social transfers, appropriate differentiation or fair treatment implies subsidizing the poor and the disadvantaged rather than the rich and the privileged. These general standards are widely accepted —until it is necessary to specify criteria by which equal and unequal circumstances are to be judged. Take the case, for example, of an African American from a high-income family who is admitted to a university over an equally qualified white person from a low-income family on the basis of affirmative action policy. Here, minority-group status is the criterion that defines the disadvantaged circumstances being redressed by the policy. Some might believe, however, that family income is a more appropriate criterion in this instance. Such questions gain saliency as the cases to which they are applicable increase with the rising number of minority-group families in upper-income categories.

Many social policies lead to instances where the treatment of a particular case may be deemed unmerited. These individual cases of unfair treatment represent the normal shortcomings of policy guidelines, which can rarely account for all possible contingencies. They become issues of social equity, however, when the policies produce a pattern of benefit distribution that denies fair treatment to a substantial segment of beneficiaries. As the enabling state evolves, those who advance social equity must come to grips with at least three challenges, which involve shifting circumstances, getting the numbers right, and managing dependency.

Shifting Circumstances

The issue of social equity is emerging in regard to public pensions in part because of the substantial increase in the number of working wives (see Chapter 1). Social security benefits account for more than half the direct federal expenditures for social welfare, making this a matter that touches vast numbers of citizens—and involves a sizable portion of all social transfers. When the Social Security Act of 1935 was first amended in 1939, the insurance principle of "individual equity"—that retired workers receive benefits roughly equal to their contributions—was compromised by concerns that benefits should provide an adequate standard of living (Pechman, Aaron, and Taussig,

1968). The extension of workers' benefits to dependents was among the revisions enacted in 1939 to achieve adequacy.

Dependents' benefits, however, as we saw in Chapter 1, create many inequities among married couples with different patterns of work and income. With the increasing proportion of wives joining the labor force, these individual cases form a pattern of social inequity, which is magnified by the differential benefit structure. Although weighted in favor of the low-income worker, social-security pension benefits rise with the wage level. By 1995 the nonworking wife whose husband earns an income of $60,600 will thus be entitled to a dependent's benefit of $7,470. This is about $1,000 more than an employed wife with an annual income of $11,400 will be entitled to on her own as a primary beneficiary (in a two-earner family with a husband earning $25,000 a year). And it is more than twice the dependent's benefit of $3,245 granted to a nonworking wife whose husband earns $11,400 (U.S. House of Representatives, 1992). Even though the husband with the higher income has paid higher social security taxes over the years, the pension benefits for his family (as in all other families) are partially subsidized by transfers from the next generation of contributors.[6]

Here, the circumstances that define the wives' entitlement are dependency status and economic class, with the dependent wife in the higher-income category receiving higher benefits than either the dependent or the employed wife in a lower-income family. Is this arrangement fair? Why should social policy provide subsidies that help upper-income groups maintain differential consumption patterns in old age?[7] Suggesting a much narrower range of benefits, which might offer a

6. Martha Ozawa (1982) estimates that a high wage earner retiring at age sixty-five with a dependent spouse receives $828 per month in unpaid-for benefits, compared with a monthly subsidy of only $482 for a low wage earner in similar circumstances.

7. Eveline Burns (1956) points out that in a large geographic area (like the United States) wage and income levels vary substantially from one part of the country to another. Thus, the case might be made that wage-related benefits help to ensure that pensions will be large enough to meet basic needs even in those sections of the country where average earnings are high. The variance of incomes within states is also quite large, however. Wage-related benefits probably do less to compensate for regional variations in average income than to maintain the relative position among local income groups during retirement.

modest standard of living for all, Mancur Olson (1983:358) argues for greater individual responsibility: "We do not need and should not have a Social Security System that guarantees the improvident high-income person enough retirement income to maintain his relative position in the consumption hierarchy. If some high-income people who had lived affluently during their working years became less well off in old age, that would be no catastrophe. Indeed, experiences of that kind would teach [other] people the value of being prudent and encourage them to plan for the future."

The social security system in the United States, as in most other industrialized democracies (see Chapter 3), is being reshaped by immense fiscal pressure caused by the maturation of pension schemes and the aging of the population. In addition to raising the standard age of retirement to sixty-seven by the year 2026, the value of pension benefits is declining relative to the wages they replace. In 1980 the pension benefits of low-wage earners amounted to 68 percent of their salaries in the year prior to entitlement; the wage-replacement rate for workers who earned an average income was 51 percent. By 1995 these wage-replacement rates will fall by about one-sixth, to 57 percent for low-income workers and 42 percent for average-income workers (Committee on Ways and Means, 1992).[8]

While the social-security replacement rate declines, the aggregate income of the elderly from other sources is increasing, as Table 6.2 shows. The change is not large. But if the absolute differences among various sources of income would grow at the same rate over the next four decades as they grew between 1980 and 1990, workers entering the labor force today would retire on a mix of income from social security, assets, and other pensions—a mix substantially different than that of the current generation of retirees. Instead of being the major source of income for elderly people, social security would fall to third place, behind income from assets and private pensions. This would shift the source of financial security in old age from public

8. The figures are based on a low-income earner's wage of $5,166 in 1980 and $11,425 in 1995; the average earner's wage was $11,479 in 1980 and $25,390 in 1995 (U.S. House of Representatives, 1992).

Table 6.2 Sources of the Aggregate Income of Elderly People, 1980 and 1990

Source of Income	1980 (%)	1990 (%)
Social security	39	36
Pension	16	18
Earnings	19	18
Asset income	22	24
Other	4	3

Source: Adapted from Reno, 1993.

Note: Elderly people are defined as those sixty-five years of age and older. The percentages do not total 100 because of rounding.

to private sources of funding.[9] Of course, sources of income for the elderly are unlikely to change at the same rate over the course of forty years. Trends of this sort seldom maintain such consistency for that long a time. (Even over one decade, 1980 to 1990, the rates fluctuated; asset income rose to 28 percent of aggregate income in 1984 and then declined to 24 percent in 1990.) What we can expect in the near term, however, is that more retirement income will come from private sources; the shift will continue to be in the direction of privatization.

Because low-paid workers have limited access to private pensions and asset income, the trend toward privatization increases their dependence on social security benefits relative to high-income groups. This development is illustrated in Table 6.3, where the change in the aggregate income of the elderly that comes from social security is analyzed according to level of income. Between 1980 and 1988 social security benefits actually formed an increasing share of the aggregate income for those elderly people in the lowest three-tenths of the

9. In 1990 social security and public pension funds accounted for over 50 percent of the aggregate income received by the elderly outside of earnings. At the current rate of change, in forty years over 50 percent of elderly people's aggregate income outside of earnings would be derived from private pensions and assets. As Virginia Reno (1993) explains, private pensions may also account for much of the asset income, which may reflect private pension payouts in lump sums that are held as income-producing assets.

Table 6.3 Social Security Benefits as a Percentage of the Aggregate Income of Elderly People by Decile, 1980 and 1988

Level of Income	1980	1988
1	72	74
2	78	83
3	79	82
4	76	74
5	66	66
6	61	59
7	53	48
8	43	41
9	32	29
10	14	14

Source: Calculated from Current Population Survey, 1980–1988.

Note: Elderly is defined to mean those sixty-five years of age and older. Level of income is grouped by decile from lowest to highest.

income levels. At the higher-income levels, social security benefits declined as a percentage of aggregate income (from 66.05 percent to 65.95 percent at the fifth level); the exception comes for the elderly people in the top tenth, for whom social security benefits initially represented a small fraction (less than 15 percent) of aggregate income.

The rising costs of social security and the increasing reliance of the low-income elderly on these public benefits are likely to intensify pressures to reduce the inequities that stem from dependents' benefits and the differential benefit structure. Whatever shape the reforms take, the future of social security will no doubt continue to involve the transfer of resources from the working to the dependent population. But as the secretary general of the International Social Security Association, Dalmer Hoskins, observes, it is time to reexamine these arrangements. "Social security provisions must be constantly adapted and modified to reflect the changing circumstances in society" (Hoskins, 1992:40).

The shifting public-private mix in retirement income and the increasing labor-force participation of women suggest two directions for social security reforms: (1) toward family accounts under which entitlements are split equally between husband and wife in the place of dependents' benefits; and (2) toward a flat-rate benefit structure that serves more fully as a safety net, ensuring a decent level of protection, and less as a replacement of former income in old age. In addition to these reforms, the expanding coverage by private pension plans raises the issue of whether greater public regulation is needed. According to the Pension Benefit Guarantee Corporation (1993), underfunding among private pension plans has more than doubled, from $18 billion in 1982 to about $40 billion in 1991, for single-employer plans. Another $11 billion in underfunding among multi-employer plans brought the total underfunding in federally insured pensions to $51 billion in 1991. Although most of the underfunding is concentrated in a relatively small number of companies, public liability is substantial and warrants reforms to strengthen the funding rules for private plans.

Getting the Numbers Right
An implicit assumption of social equity is that welfare transfers ought to result in a fair distribution of public resources among those with competing needs and problems. On one side of the equation we must calculate the full range of transfers and how they are distributed. On the other side we must enter the needs and problems to which transfers are addressed and how well they contribute to a solution. Measuring all the needs, resources, and outcomes of welfare transfers is not feasible, so efforts to achieve social equity aim not to balance the equation exactly but to produce a reasonable allocation of resources within the limits of knowledge. Fairness here reflects a certain proportionality between needs and the resources necessary to meet them. To make informed decisions in allocating social transfers, policymakers should have data on how big the problem is, what is already being spent on it, and to what extent it is being resolved by existing efforts.

Getting the numbers right on the expenditure side of social transfers requires going beyond the conventional accounting of welfare spending. As suggested earlier (see Chapter 5), a new ledger is required to take the full measure of welfare transfers, one that includes direct and indirect expenditures that benefit, for example, homeowners, students, employees, veterans, and farmers, as well as poor and dependent groups. Much information is available and needs only to be pulled together in an inclusive annual report on social welfare expenditures. Because there is no consensus on the full range of expenditures to include in a complete accounting, such a report might develop two or three models of welfare spending based on different assumptions about how to classify transfers related to social welfare.

Estimating expenditures is often easier than measuring the problems addressed, whose dimensions are often inflated by advocacy research. As was previously discussed, interest groups and their supporters frequently overstate social ills to gain public attention and to expand the resources allocated to their cause. Social scientists identified with the partisan agendas of various interest groups lend advocacy research the aura of scientific activity. As Irving Louis Horowitz (1993:183) observes for one academic discipline: "The identification of social science with social advocacy has reached such pandemic proportions in American sociology that it is time, indeed the time is long overdue, to step back from the precipice of partisanship if the worth of serious analysis is itself to be preserved." Nor is social research that is inspired more by politics than by science limited to the United States. "In the post-war history of British social policy studies," Robert Pinker (1991:287) notes, "the political disagreements became so embedded in the academic debate that they often impeded the process of scientific enquiry itself."

Buttressed by the academic authority of people with Ph.D.s, the claims of advocacy research are often accepted by the media with little probing or critical scrutiny. This is reflected in advocacy studies that magnify the size of social problems, as was illustrated in Chapter 4. Reporters are also susceptible to advocacy research that appraises the impact of service programs operated by interest groups and viewed as the preferred solutions to specific problems. Programs to prevent child sexual abuse are a perfect example. Despite their widespread use, the evidence reviewed in Chapter 2 shows that there is a serious debate among professionals about whether prevention programs work and should be expanded or whether the vast amount of resources that they consume might not be used in other ways to protect children more effectively. Findings from a major study claim to settle the issue with the discovery that comprehensive prevention programs really do protect children. These findings have gained the kind of authority that is attributed to facts endorsed by the *New York Times*. Under the headline ABUSE-PREVENTION EFFORTS AID CHILDREN, the *Times* devotes almost a quarter of a page to an article extolling the benefits of sexual-abuse-prevention training programs (Goleman, 1993). A close look at the study, however, reveals a different story than the one told to the public. It is a story of how journalists are bamboozled by advocacy research advanced under the mantle of social science and, in the process, how public funding is promoted for programs of dubious value.

The opening sentence of the *Times* article declares, "The first national survey to assess the effectiveness of school-based programs to prevent sexual abuse confirms that they help children in real-life encounters with potential child molesters." Based on the results from a representative national sample of 2,000 children contacted in a telephone survey, the study's senior author says "that the kids who have gotten the better sexual abuse prevention programs do act better in the crunch" (Goleman, 1993). By "better programs" he means those that were longest and most comprehensive in coverage of prevention concepts.

What are the effects of these programs? According to the *Times* article, the study found that "the more comprehensive the training the more likely it was that the children would use strategies like yelling, saying no or running away when threatened with sexual abuse. They also knew more than other children about the topic, felt more confident about their abilities to protect themselves, and were more likely to report any actual or attempted abused to adults. On the other hand, children who had received the training were slightly more likely to suffer injury once a sexual assault began because they were more prone to fight back" (Goleman, 1993).

This version of the research findings magnifies small differences that are insignificant and underplays large differences that may be seriously dangerous. Let's look at the facts. Did children who participated in the comprehensive program have more knowledge about sexual abuse prevention? Yes. On a sixteen-point scale they scored an average of half a point higher than children who had never had any training. At the same time, the children who had never been trained actually scored a whit higher than those who had participated in the prevention programs that were judged less comprehensive (Finkelhor, Asdigian, and Dziuba-Leatherman, 1993). If these findings are correct, about one-half of the schools that mandate this training are spending millions of dollars on brief, less-comprehensive prevention programs from which students emerge with no more knowledge than those who never participated. And even more funds are being spent on longer programs that increase knowledge by just a fraction of a point.

But what about the other outcomes? Does this slight increase in knowledge matter? Do the children who receive comprehensive sexual abuse prevention training really act better in the crunch? The researchers' rigorous analysis of the data simply does not coincide with their optimistic interpretation of the results. Regarding the positive outcomes cited in the *Times*, for all of the children abused or threatened by sexual abuse the data show no statistically significant differences between the behavior of those who received no or minimal prevention training and those who participated in the most comprehensive programs, when such relevant factors as age and gender are controlled for. That is, among the sexually victimized respondents, children receiving comprehensive training did not differ significantly from the others with regard to (1) the number of preferred strategies recommended by prevention programs which they employed during the incident (such as saying no or running away), (2) their sense of confidence in coping with their abusers, (3) their disclosures of actual or attempted abuse, and (4) their success in thwarting attempted abuse.

There were small differences among the respondent groups on these outcome variables. In some cases—for example, those marked by success in thwarting attempted abuse—children who received no training were a little more effective than those who had participated in minimal or comprehensive prevention programs. This finding was not mentioned in the *Times* article. But in every case, judging by conventional scientific standards, we must conclude that the small differences found were likely to occur by chance.[10]

On several other outcome variables, however, the differences were more pronounced and statistically significant. Whereas the *Times* article reports that the children who received comprehensive training were only "*slightly more likely* to suffer injury once a sexual assault began," the data show that in fact 15 percent of these children were injured, a rate more than three times that for those who received no training. And when threatened with sexual victimization, children who had participated in comprehensive prevention training programs were more likely to employ the less preferred strategies of crying and fighting back (which may account for their being injured). Although fighting back was considered one of the less preferred responses (see Chapter 2), it is a protective strategy taught to children as young as preschool age by one of the most widely used programs in the country. Rather than acting better in the crunch, the firmest conclusion that can be drawn from these findings is that when faced with the danger of sexual abuse, children who receive comprehensive training use less preferred strategies and get injured more than three times as often as children who received no training. The *Washington Post* offers a somewhat more accurate rendition of this study, but even here the findings are jumbled (Evans, 1993).[11]

Are sexual abuse prevention programs really that dangerous? These findings should not be taken too seriously. Professionals know that telephone surveys are rather unreliable as a method to evaluate

10. Controlling for age and gender, the level of significance for differences in the use of preferred strategies by children in the more comprehensive programs was .35; the level of significance for differences in their sense of confidence in coping with abuse was .41; and the level of significance for differences in disclosure rates was .16 (Finkelhor, Asdigian, and Dziuba-Leatherman, 1993).

11. Sandra Evans (1993) reports, for example, that well-trained children are no more successful in thwarting abuse and are more likely to be injured during a sexual assault. Nonetheless, she notes, "the well-trained children were more knowledgeable about abuse, more likely to disclose incidents, and had more of a sense of control when facing assault." Later, in contradiction, she observes about disclosures that "fourteen percent said they told an adult about an incident as a result of what they learned in the program. But *those figures did not vary significantly* from the group of children who had received no training" (emphasis added).

anything as complex as the effectiveness of prevention programs or the way children respond to actual threats.

To protect against misleading data and wasteful policies, journalists should learn more about the limits of social research. Advocacy researchers will continue to ply their trade as long as funding sources drive research, as long as ideologies inspire research more than science does, and as long as interest groups are firmly entrenched in many problem areas. The modern brand of advocacy often operates beyond the pale of objective social science research, only to be rewarded by easy access to an indulgent media. The media can restrain the excessive claims of advocacy researchers about the size of social problems and the efficacy of public aid in solving these problems. Some restraint is no doubt already taking place, but not enough to discourage the exaggerations of social ills that appear regularly in the news and undermine rational discourse on social policy. Efforts to advance social equity in the enabling state would benefit from a more temperate brand of advocacy research and a higher threshold of media skepticism, bolstered by more rigorous standards of accuracy.

Managing Dependency
Social equity is about more than auditing categories of expenditure and deciphering the numbers of victims reported in the media. It embodies a give-and-take between welfare entitlements and the duties of citizenship, particularly the duty to be self-sufficient. Formulating equitable welfare policies to cope with dependency presents a tremendous challenge to the enabling state.

There is a tacit optimism about the enabling state which presupposes that the correct blend of well-designed social policies will enable people to be independent. The elements of well-designed policies include consumer choice, private delivery of social services, indirect transfers of welfare provisions, subsidies oriented to strengthening families, the creation of human capital, asset accumulation, and incentives to work. Where the welfare state was seen as a corrective for the dysfunctions (some would say evils) of capitalism, the enabling state builds on the virtues of the market economy and the aptitude of its citizens to be self-sufficient. In this context, able-bodied citizens who do not have paid employment, particularly those receiving public assistance under the AFDC program, pose the foremost problem of welfare reform in the 1990s. For the reasons discussed in Chapters 2 and 3, policymakers on both sides of the political spectrum concur that work must replace welfare and that dependency on public aid must be abolished. This sentiment is explicit in the call for reform made by the Progressive Policy Institute: "An enabling strategy for welfare reform should buttress America's basic values, especially reciprocal responsibility. . . . Social responsibility is a two-way street: Government can help those determined to help themselves. An enabling state should condition social supports on recipients' willingness to work and strive toward self-sufficiency" (Marshall and Schram, 1993:233).

During the 1992 presidential campaign, Bill Clinton promised a New Covenant, emphasizing the bond between work and public aid. The government would serve the needs of those who hold down jobs and play by the rules, but there would be, he proposed, a two-year limit on welfare dependency, after which recipients would be expected to find employment. Both Democrats and Republicans have embraced the idea of a two-year limit on welfare, during which time AFDC recipients would be given education, training, childcare, and job-placement counseling. Afterward, upon entering the labor force, they would continue to qualify for transitional services, such as childcare and Medicaid insurance, for a specified period, as is currently the case under the Family Support Act.

The questions on everyone's mind are, What happens to those who fail to participate in the training programs? And what happens to those who are unable to secure employment after the two years are up? The usual response to the second question is that those who have not found a job after two years would be required to participate in some form of public works program established by the state. This is a tough-sounding quick fix that will create more problems than it solves. Those unemployed after two years are likely to include many of the least skilled and least motivated in the welfare population. The reading skills of the typical AFDC mother between the ages of seventeen and twenty-one, for example, are below the sixth-grade level (Pryor, 1994). At least 37 percent of AFDC mothers between the ages of eighteen and twenty-four abuse or are addicted to alcohol and drugs (Center on Addiction and Substance Abuse, 1994). The social and economic costs of employing these AFDC mothers in public works are staggering. Estimates by the Congressional Budget Office indicate that expenditures for supervision and daycare would amount to $6,300 per participant. With the average AFDC grant amounting to about $5,000, participation in mandatory work programs would more than double the costs for each welfare recipient, without any increase in their basic grant (Besharov, 1993a). Fiscal concerns aside, the cynicism and demoralization bred by make-work would surely undermine the already shaky standards of public bureaucracies.

With the imposition of mandatory requirements, another issue arises: what to do about AFDC recipients who may refuse to participate in either the training or the public works. Answers are rather harsh and unsatisfactory. The proposal put forth by the Republican Task Force on Welfare Reform (H.R. 3500, 1993), for example, would penalize those who fail to participate by initially reducing the family's AFDC grant and food stamp benefit by 25 percent, then, after six months, by dropping nonparticipants from AFDC rolls altogether. Proposals of this sort tend to be extremely quiet about what will happen to the children in these families, for whom the program was originally devised. They also neglect the knotty question of how to deal with passive resistance to social engineering among AFDC recipients who may participate in public works but malinger on the job.

As the focus of concern shifts from protecting children to requiring that AFDC parents go to work, efforts to enforce a two-year limit on welfare highlight the impediments to social engineering. This is not a new story. Analyzing the costs and results of the early workfare reforms more than twenty years ago, Gilbert Steiner (1971:74) observed: "Unfortunately, the sorry history and limitations of day care and work training as 'solutions' to the welfare problem could not be faced by the administration's welfare specialists in 1970. . . . But after a few years it will inevitably be discovered that work training and day care have had little effect on the number of welfare dependents and no depressing effect on public relief costs. Some new solution will then be proposed, but the more realistic approach would be to accept the need for more welfare and to reject continued fantasizing about day care and 'workfare' as miracle cures." The new solutions that have since arrived involve variations on workfare that are more stringent in their demands and more generous in their incentives but no more likely to succeed than earlier schemes. Current welfare reforms organized around incentives to work and a two-year limit on public support are plagued by three problems: they ignore successes, they create perverse effects, and they require a level of callousness that social workers are unlikely to countenance.

For many families, AFDC serves not as a poverty trap but as a temporary support in hard times. About 48 percent of all spells on the AFDC rolls last less than two years. True, this figure of success for short-term cases can be somewhat misleading, for one-third of these people will enroll in the program again at some time in the future; and, in any event, most AFDC costs are attributable to the long-term recipients.[12] Nevertheless, reform measures that ignore the substantial number of successful cases are likely to increase program expenses still further. Providing various transitional incentives to work after two years on AFDC raises the costs of public support for all those families who would previously have left the rolls in the absence of those benefits. At the same time, incentives that are high enough may have the perverse effect of encouraging those in low-paying occupations to leave work for AFDC and then recycle back into the labor force in order to qualify for the transitional benefits, as noted in Chapter 3.

Finally, whatever hard lines policymakers may draw for those who refuse to participate in workfare, those who work on the front lines in welfare agencies are unlikely to impose sanctions that would drive families with children into the streets. If the sanctions are enacted, the two-year limit will be to welfare in the 1990s what deinstitutionalization was to mental illness in the 1960s, the deferred costs of which now plague U.S. cities. The essential problem with the tran-

12. Although over a ten-year period, 48 percent of all persons on welfare are enrolled for less than two years altogether and 17 percent for eight years or more, the proportions are reversed in the short term. At any given point in time, the long-term (eight years or more) cases account for 50 percent of the AFDC recipients and consume a disproportionate share of the program's resources (U.S. House of Representatives, 1992).

sitional incentives and time limits is that they do not distinguish among recipients in terms of competence and motivation. This approach to welfare reform deals too generously with those who are the most competent and motivated and too harshly with those who are the least competent and motivated.

Can anything be done to make welfare more equitable without transitional incentives and public works programs that will increase the cost of benefits and without time limits backed by financial sanctions that would impose hardships on children? An alternative approach to welfare reform begins with the need to distinguish among AFDC families and aims to ensure the well-being of children.

This is no easy matter. Inspired by norms of equal treatment and welfare entitlement, a democratic government often finds it awkward to accept the need for tailored policies and target-specific programs (Finn, 1991). But families enter the AFDC program for different reasons and remain on the rolls for varying lengths of time. About 60 percent of the stays on AFDC rolls begin because of a decline in family earnings or because of the divorce (or separation) of a married couple with children. An argument can be made that initially these cases should be treated differently from the 30 percent of AFDC cases that begin when an unmarried woman has a child. Welfare applicants who were married or employed for some period of time—say, at least eighteen months—prior to enrollment in the AFDC program are generally independent citizens who had been abiding by social conventions. They should be considered separately. As Mickey Kaus (1986a:23) explains: "Well, they tried to play by the rules—they got married, they or their husbands worked, and now they need only temporary help." It is reasonable to assume that they are competent and motivated to become self-sufficient. Thus, applicants who are pushed into the program because of a marital breakup or a decline in family income should be awarded AFDC benefits and left alone for two years to reorganize their lives. A high proportion of them will be among the 48 percent of recipients who leave the welfare rolls of their own volition in less than two years. Those remaining in the AFDC program after two years would then be enrolled in the first phase of intervention, which leads to what might be termed managed dependency.

Women who enter the AFDC program because of out-of-wedlock births are another matter. They are younger and more likely to be long-term recipients than those in the other group; and, as we saw in Chapter 2, their children are at greater risk of harm.[13] This is the segment of the welfare population that policymakers are most interested in getting tough with, in part because their long-term spells on welfare are very costly. The appeal of a firm two-year limit and mandated public work for those who would otherwise be unemployed after two years on the welfare rolls is that it will seemingly put an end to the pattern of long-term welfare dependency by never-married single mothers. Although AFDC no doubt contributes to the pattern of dependency, it did not create the single-mother culture of poverty and will not eliminate it with time limits. Still, this group should be targeted for special intervention, if for no other reason than to protect the children at risk.

Instead of forced labor and make-work schemes, there would be two phases of social supervision for the group of potentially long-term welfare recipients. The first phase would involve a service strategy aimed at providing practical assistance to mothers and protection to their children. These efforts would include regular home-health visiting (described in Chapter 2), encouraging school dropouts to complete their high-school-degree requirements, assistance in home management, and developing systematic plans for the mothers' integration into the labor force. After three years, those still on AFDC would enter the second phase. Greater social controls would be invoked, reflecting the recipients' emerging status as "wards of the state," rather than temporary dependents. Home visiting to monitor the well-being of children would continue, and the level of public-assistance grants would remain the same. During this phase, however, a case manager would be assigned to regulate each family's financial affairs; the manager would pay rent and utilities and make weekly allocations of food stamps. There would also be increased monitoring of

13. Estimates of the risk for long-term welfare receipt indicate that over 40 percent of never-married women with a young child who enroll in AFDC under the age of twenty-six will spend ten years or more on the welfare rolls (U.S. House of Representatives, 1992).

any outside resources available to recipients, which would reduce their AFDC grants.

Tightening social control through case managers and home-health visitors would certainly raise the cost of AFDC, though with brief training, welfare recipients might fill many of the casework jobs. But it would still be a relatively inexpensive way for society to protect vulnerable children while giving notice that long-term public dependency would be accompanied by greater public surveillance. Increasing the role of public authority in recipients' lives would make welfare less attractive to some who might otherwise be employed. Closer monitoring would also limit the amount of unreported income, which is quite frequently available to supplement AFDC grants (Jencks and Edin, 1990; Harris, 1993).

The goal here is modest. Those who demand more would do well to heed Gilbert Steiner's (1971) counsel against "tireless tinkering with dependent families." Welfare programs contribute to the never-married single-parent culture of poverty. Just as AFDC alone did not create the culture of poverty, forces larger than those generated by AFDC reform will be required to curtail this deleterious pattern of behavior. Ultimately, any strategy to reduce welfare must go well beyond adjustments in AFDC. Make-work, time limits, and transitional benefits are no substitutes for employment in the private sector that leaves working people substantially better off than those receiving a combination of welfare grants, food stamps, and Medicaid. The best and fairest incentive is to increase the work-related benefits of the low-paying jobs that many welfare recipients might perform. Progress along these lines is already under way with the expansion of tax-based social transfers, such as the earned income tax credit.

Policy analysts like David Ellwood (1988) and Christopher Jencks (1992b) urge an increase in indirect social transfers and the addition of other tax-based supports so that working families are lifted above the poverty level. Working families also need the security of medical protection, which welfare recipients receive through Medicaid. Finally, there is widespread agreement that absent fathers should be held responsible for providing financial support for their children, although the resources for such support may be rather limited among fathers of children in the AFDC population.

Even with all these aids and supports, dependency will not disappear. The quest for social equity in the enabling state will run a gentler course if it is tempered by the realization that whether because of personal deficiencies or because of forces beyond their control, people in need of care will always be with us.

References

Aaron, Henry. 1978. *Politics and the Professors: The Great Society in Perspective*. Washington, D.C.: Brookings Institution.

Abramovitz, Mimi. 1986. "The Privatization of the Welfare State: A Review." *Social Work* 34(4), pp. 257–64.

Ageton, S. 1983. *Sexual Assault Among Adolescents: A National Study*. Final Report to the National Institute of Mental Health.

Ahn, Helen. 1994. "Cultural Diversity and the Definition of Child Abuse." In R. Barth, J. D. Berrick, and N. Gilbert, eds., *Child Welfare Research and Policy Review Bi-Annual*. New York: Columbia University Press.

Ahn, Helen, and Neil Gilbert. 1992. "Cultural Diversity and Sexual Abuse Prevention." *Social Service Review* 66(3), pp. 410–27.

Alber, Jens. 1988. "Continuities and Change in the Idea of the Welfare State." *Politics and Society* 16(4), pp. 451–60.

Amir, D., and M. Amir. 1979. "Rape Crisis Centers: An Arena for Ideological Conflicts." *Victimology* 4(2), pp. 247–57.

Applebaum, Paul. 1987. "Crazy in the Streets." *Commentary* 83(5), p. 37.

"Baby Death Study Indicating Risks." 1985. *New York Times*, November 17.

Badelt, Christoph. 1992. "Austria: Family Work, Paid Employment, and Family Policy." In Sheila Kamerman and Alfred Kahn, eds., *Child Care, Parental Leave, and the Under Threes: Policy Innovation in Europe*. New York: Auburn House.

Badelt, Christoph, and Peter Weiss. 1991. "Nonprofit, For-Profit, and Government Organizations in Social Service Provision: Comparison of Behavioral Patterns in Austria." *Voluntas* 1(1), pp. 77–96.

Baldwin, Peter. 1992. "Beveridge in the *Longue Durée*." *International Social Security Review*, 45(1–2), pp. 53–72.

Baldwin, Wendy, and Virginia Cain. 1980. "The Children of Teenage Parents." *Family Planning Perspectives* 12 (January–February), pp. 34–43.

Barnes, John, and Talapady Srivenkataramana. 1982.

174

"Ideology and the Welfare State: An Examination of Wilensky's Conclusions." *Social Service Review* 56(2), pp. 230–45.

Barr, Nicholas, and Fiona Coulter. 1990. "Social Security: Solution or Problem?" In John Hills, ed., *The State of Welfare: The Welfare State in Britain Since 1974.* Oxford: Oxford University Press, Clarendon Press.

Baum, Alice, and Donald Burnes. 1993. "Facing the Facts About Homelessness." *Public Welfare* 51(2), pp. 20–27.

Bell, Winifred. 1983. *Contemporary Social Welfare.* New York: Macmillan.

Belsky, Jay. 1986. "Infant Day Care: A Cause for Concern?" *Zero to Three: Bulletin of the National Center for Clinical Infant Studies* 6(5), pp. 1–7.

———. 1988. "The Effects of Infant Care Reconsidered." *Early Childhood Research Quarterly* 3(3), pp. 235–72.

———. 1990. "Parental and Nonparental Child Care and Children's Socioemotional Development: A Decade in Review." *Journal of Marriage and the Family* 52 (November), pp. 885–903.

Belsky, Jay, and J. D. Steinberg. 1978. "The Effects of Day Care: A Critical Review." *Child Development* 49(4), pp. 929–49.

Belsky, Jay, J. D. Steinberg, and A. Walker. 1982. "The Ecology of Day Care." In M. Lamb, ed., *Childrearing in Nontraditional Families.* Hillsdale, N.J.: Erlbaum.

Bendick, M., Jr. 1989. "Privatizing the Delivery of Social Welfare Services: An Idea to Be Taken Seriously." In S. Kamerman and A. Kahn, eds., *Privatization and the Welfare State.* Princeton: Princeton University Press.

Berger, Brigitte. 1987. "Limits of Doing Good." *Society* 24(3), pp. 25–27.

Berkowitz, Monroe. 1981. "Social Policy and the Disabled: The Main Issues." In International Social Security Association, ed., *Social Security and Disability: Issues in Policy Research.* Geneva: International Social Security Association.

Bernstein, Allen. 1993. *Tax Guide for College Teachers.* Washington, D.C.: Academic Information Services.

Berrick, Jill Duerr, and Neil Gilbert. 1991. *With the Best of Intentions: The Child Sexual Abuse Prevention Movement.* New York: Guilford.

Besharov, Douglas. 1990. "Gaining Control Over Child Abuse Reports." *Public Welfare* 48(2), pp. 34–40.

———. 1992. "Cautions for the New Paternalism." *Washington Post,* January 5.

———. 1993a. "Escaping the Dole." *Washington Post,* December 12.

———. 1993b. "Risks and Realism: Teen Sex." *American Enterprise* (March–April), pp. 52–59.

Besharov, Douglas, and Michelle Dally. 1986. "How Much Are Working Mothers Working?" *Public Opinion* 9(4), pp. 48–51.

Besharov, Douglas, and Karen Gardiner. 1993. "Teen Sex." *American Enterprise* (January–February), pp. 52–59.

Best, Joel. 1988. "Missing Children, Misleading Statistics." *Public Interest* 92 (Summer), pp. 84–92.

———. 1990. *Threatened Children: Rhetoric and Concern About Child-Victims.*
Chicago: University of Chicago Press.

Bixby, Ann. 1994. "Public Social Welfare Expenditures, Fiscal Year 1991." *Social Security Bulletin* 57(1), pp. 96–104.

Board of Trustees, Federal Old-Age and Survivors Insurance and Disability Trust Fund. 1991. *The 1991 Annual Report of the Board of Trustees.* Washington, D.C.: Government Printing Office.

Booth, Charles. 1892. *Life and Labour of the People in London.* London: Macmillan.

Borkin, Joyce, and Lesley Frank. 1986. "Sexual Abuse Prevention for Preschoolers: A Pilot Program." *Child Welfare* (January–February), pp. 75–81.

Bradshaw, Jonathan, and Jane Millar. 1990. "Lone-Parent Families in the U.K.: Challenges for Social Policy." *International Social Security Review* 43(4).

Breakey, Gail, and Betsy Pratt. 1991. "Healthy Growth for Hawaii's Healthy Start: Toward a Systematic Statewide Approach to the Prevention of Child Abuse and Neglect." *Zero to Three: Bulletin of the National Center for Clinical Infant Programs* 11(4), pp. 15–22.

Briere, John, and Marsha Runtz. 1989. "University Males' Sexual Interest in Children: Predicting Potential Indices of 'Pedophilia' in a Nonforensic Sample." *Child Abuse and Neglect* 13(1), pp. 65–75.

Brocas, Anne-Marie. 1988. "Equal Treatment of Men and Women in Social Security: An Overview." *Equal Treatment in Social Security.* Studies and Research no. 27. Geneva: International Social Security Association.

Brydoff, Carol. 1991. "Professor: Rape Figures Are Inflated." *Oakland Tribune,* March 30.

Buchanan, James. 1975. *The Limits of Liberty.* Chicago: University of Chicago Press.

Buckley, Stephen. 1992. "Unfounded Reports of Rape Confound Area Police Investigations." *Washington Post,* June 27.

Burns, Eveline. 1956. *Social Security and Public Policy.* New York: McGraw-Hill.

Burt, Martha, and Barbara Cohen. 1989. *America's Homeless: Numbers, Characteristics, and Programs That Serve Them.* Washington, D.C.: Urban Institute.

Cantillon, Bea. 1990. "Socio-Demographic Changes and Social Security." *International Social Security Review* 43(4), pp. 399–425.

Center on Addiction and Substance Abuse. 1994. *Substance Abuse and Women on Welfare.* New York: Center on Addiction and Substance Abuse at Columbia University.

Chenkin, Alvin. 1976. "Government Support to Jewish-Sponsored Agencies in Six Major Fields of Service, 1962–1973." Background paper prepared for the Sidney Hollander Colloquium, April 24–25. Mimeo.

Cherlin, Andrew, ed. 1988. *The Changing American Family and Public Policy.* Washington, D.C.: Urban Institute Press.

Child Abuse Prevention Training Center of Northern California. 1983. *Preschool Project Training Manual.* Berkeley, Calif.: Child Abuse Prevention Training Center.

Cohen, Richard. 1991. "The Wrong Rape Statistics." *Sacramento Bee*, June 3.

Cohen, Roger (1993). "Europe's Recession Prompts New Look at Welfare Cuts." *New York Times*, August 9.

Collins, Barbara, and Mary Whalen. 1989. "The Rape Crisis Movement: Radical or Reformist?" *Social Work* 34(1), pp. 61–65.

Collins, Mary. 1990. "A Guaranteed Minimum Income in France." *Social Policy and Administration* 24(2).

Craig, Mary. 1990. "Coercive Sexuality in Dating Relationships: A Situational Model." *Clinical Psychology Review* 10(4), pp. 395–423.

Crystal, Stephen. 1987. "Elder Abuse: The Latest 'Crisis.'" *Public Interest* 88 (Summer), pp. 56–66.

Daro, D., K. Casey, and N. Abraham. 1990. *Reducing Child Abuse 20% by 1990: Preliminary Assessment*. Chicago: National Committee for the Prevention of Child Abuse.

Davidoff, Paul. 1965. "Advocacy and Pluralism in Planning." *Journal of the American Institute of Planners* 31(4), pp. 331–37.

Decter, Midge. 1972. *The New Chastity and Other Arguments Against Women's Liberation*. New York: Coward, McCann, and Geoghegan.

Demause, Lloyd. 1991. "The Universality of Incest." *Journal of Psychohistory* 19(2), pp. 123–64.

Denmark. Ministry of Social Affairs. 1992. *Danish Strategies: Families with Children at Work and at Home*. Copenhagen: Danish Ministry of Social Affairs.

Derthick, Martha. 1975. *Uncontrollable Spending for Social Services Grants*. Washington, D.C.: Brookings Institution.

Dingwall, Robert. 1992. "Family Policy and the Liberal State." In Hans-Uwe Otto and Gaby Flosser, eds., *How to Organize Prevention*. Berlin: Walter de Gruyter.

Dunn, Katherine. 1993. "Fibbers." *New Republic*, June 21, pp. 18–19.

Dworkin, Andrea. 1988. *Letters From a War Zone*. London: Secker and Warburg.

Dworkin, Ronald. 1993. "Feminism and Abortion." *New York Review of Books* 11(11).

Eberstadt, Nicholas. 1990. "The American Infant Mortality Rate in International Perspective." *Raising Children for the Twenty-first Century*. Washington, D.C.: American Enterprise Institute.

Ellwood, David. 1988. *Poor Support: Poverty in the American Family*. New York: Basic Books.

Epstein, Cynthia Fuchs. 1988. "Toward a Family Policy: Changes in Mothers' Lives." In Andrew Cherlin, ed., *The Changing American Family and Public Policy*. Washington, D.C.: Urban Institute Press.

Esping-Andersen, Gosta. 1990. *The Three Worlds of Welfare Capitalism*. Princeton: Princeton University Press.

———. 1991. "The Welfare State in the Reorganization of Working Life." In Peter Sanders and Diana Encel, eds., *Social Policy in Australia: Options for the*

1990s. New South Wales: Social Policy Research Centre, University of New South Wales.

Estrich, Susan. 1987. *Real Rape*. Cambridge: Harvard University Press.

Etzioni, Amitai. 1991. "What Community? Whose Responsiveness?" *Responsive Community* 1(2), pp. 5–8.

Etzler, Cecilia. 1987. "Education, Cohabitation, and the First Child: Some Empirical Findings From Sweden." *Stockholm Research Reports in Demography* 34. Stockholm: Section of Demography, University of Stockholm.

Euzeby, Alain. 1988. "Unemployment Compensation and Unemployment in Industrialized Market-Economy Countries." *International Social Security Review* 41(1).

Evandrou, Maria, Jane Falkingham, and Howard Glennerster. 1990. "The Personal Social Services: Everyone's Poor Relation but Nobody's Baby." In John Mills, ed., *The State of Welfare: The Welfare State in Britain Since 1974*. Oxford: Oxford University Press, Clarendon Press.

Evans, Sandra. 1993. "Do Abuse Prevention Programs Work?" *Washington Post*, November 30, p. 93.

Evers, Adelbert, and Ivan Svetlik, eds. 1991. *New Welfare Mixes in Care for the Elderly*. Vienna: European Center for Social Welfare Policy and Research.

Fallows, Deborah. 1985. *A Mother's Work*. Boston: Houghton Mifflin.

Faludi, Susan. 1991. *Backlash: The Undeclared War Against Women*. New York: Crown.

———. 1993. "Victimization Is No Fantasy." *Newsweek*, October 25, p. 61.

Family Welfare Research Group. 1992. *GAIN Family Life and Child Care Study*. Berkeley: School of Social Welfare, University of California.

Federal Bureau of Investigation. 1993. *Crime in the United States: Uniform Crime Reports, 1992*. Washington, D.C.: Government Printing Office.

Felson, Richard. 1991. "Blame Analysis: Accounting for the Behavior of Protected Groups." *American Sociologist* 22(1), pp. 5–23.

Finkelhor, David, and Associates. 1986. *A Sourcebook on Child Sexual Abuse*. Beverly Hills, Calif.: Sage.

Finkelhor, David, Nancy Asdigian, and Jennifer Dziuba-Leatherman. 1993. *The Effectiveness of Victimization Prevention Instruction: An Evaluation of Children's Responses to Actual Threats and Assaults*. Durham: Family Research Laboratory, University of New Hampshire.

Finkelhor, David, Gerald Hotling, I. A. Lewis, and Christine Smith. 1990. "Child Abuse in a National Survey of Adult Men and Women: Prevalence, Characteristics, and Risk Factors." *Child Abuse and Neglect* 14(1), pp. 19–28.

Finkelhor, David, and Nancy Strapko. 1991. "Sexual Abuse Prevention Education: A Review of Evaluation Studies." In D. Willis, E. Holden, and M. Rosenberg, eds., *Child Abuse Prevention*. New York: Wiley.

Finn, Chester, Jr. 1991. "When Families Fail." *First Things* 9 (January), pp. 20–25.

Fischer, Pamela, and William Breakey. 1991. "The Epidemiology of Alcohol, Drug, and Mental Disorders Among Homeless Persons." *American Psychologist* 46 (November).

Florio, James. 1992. "New Jersey's Different Approach." *Public Welfare* 50(2), p. 7.

Forbes, Karen, and Donald Kirts. 1993. "Letter to the Editor." *The Lafayette*, October 29, p. 5.

Fox-Genovese, Elizabeth. 1992. "Feminist Rights, Individualist Wrongs." *Tikkun* 7(3), pp. 29–34.

Fraiberg, Selma. 1977. *Every Child's Birthright: In Defense of Mothering*. New York: Basic Books.

Freedburg, L. 1991. "Rape Expert Accuses UC of Barring Her Lecture." *San Francisco Chronicle*, November 9.

Friedman, Milton. 1962. *Capitalism, Freedom, and Democracy*. Chicago: University of Chicago Press.

Fryer, George, Sherryll Kraizer, and Thomas Miyoshi. 1987. "Measuring Actual Reduction of Risk to Child Abuse: A New Approach." *Child Abuse and Neglect* 11(2), pp. 173–80.

Gallup Organization. 1980. *American Families—1980*. Report submitted to the White House Conference on Families, June 5. Princeton: Gallup Organization.

Galston, William. 1992. "Clinton and the Promise of Communitarianism." *Chronicle of Higher Education*, 39(15), p. 52.

Garfinkel, Irwin. 1992. "Bringing Fathers Back In." *American Prospect* 9 (Spring), pp. 74–83.

Garfinkel, Irwin, and Elizabeth Uhr. 1984. "A New Approach to Child Support." *Public Interest* 75 (Spring), pp. 111–22.

George, Linda, Idee Winfield, and Dan Blazer. 1992. "Sociocultural Factors in Sexual Assault: Comparison of Two Representative Samples of Women." *Journal of Social Issues* 48(1), pp. 105–25.

Gibbs, Nancy. 1991. "When Is It Rape?" *Time*, June 3, pp. 48–54.

Gilbert, Neil. 1977. "The Transformation of Social Services." *Social Service Review* 51(4), pp. 624–41.

———. 1983. *Capitalism and the Welfare State: Dilemmas of Social Benevolence*. New Haven: Yale University Press.

———. 1991a. "The Campus Rape Scare." *Wall Street Journal*, June 27, p. 10.

———. 1991b. "The Phantom Epidemic of Sexual Assault." *Public Interest* 103 (Spring), pp. 54–65.

———. 1992. "The Governor's Got It Half Right." *Los Angeles Times*, January 10.

Gilbert, Neil, Jill Duerr Berrick, Nicole LeProhn, and Nina Nyman. 1989. *Protecting Young Children From Sexual Abuse: Does Preschool Training Work?* Lexington, Mass.: Lexington Books.

Gilbert, Neil, and Joseph Eaton. 1970. "Who Speaks for the Poor?" *Journal of the American Institute of Planners* 36 (November), pp. 411–16.

Gilbert, Neil, and Barbara Gilbert. 1989. *The Enabling State: Modern Welfare Capitalism in America*. New York: Oxford University Press.

Gilbert, Neil, and Ailee Moon. 1988. "Analyzing Welfare Effort: An Appraisal of Comparative Methods." *Journal of Policy Analysis and Management* 7(2), pp. 326–40.

Gilbert, Neil, and Kwong Leung Tang. Forthcoming. "Privatization of Social Welfare in the United States: Scope, Rationale, and Performance." In N. Johnson, ed., *Private Markets in Health and Welfare: An International Perspective*. London: Berg.

Gilbert, Neil, Harry Specht, and Paul Terrell. 1993. *Dimensions of Social Welfare Policy*. Englewood Cliffs, N.J.: Prentice Hall.

Gilder, George. 1987. "Welfare's New Consensus." *Public Interest* 89 (Fall), pp. 20–25.

Gill, Richard, and T. Grandon Gill. 1994. "A Parental Bill of Rights." *Family Affairs* 6(1–2), pp. 1–6.

Ginsburg, Norman. 1992. *Divisions of Welfare*. London: Sage.

Giovannoni, Jeanne, and Rosiana Becerra. 1979. *Defining Child Abuse*. New York: Free Press.

Glazer, Nathan. 1975. *Affirmative Discrimination: Ethnic Inequality and Public Policy*. New York: Basic Books.

———. 1988. *The Limits of Social Policy*. Cambridge: Harvard University Press.

Glenn, Norval. 1992. "What the Numbers Say." *Family Affairs* 5(1–2), pp. 5–7.

Glendon, Mary Ann. 1991. *Rights Talk*. New York: Free Press.

Goleman, Daniel. 1993. "Abuse-Prevention Efforts Aid Children." *New York Times*, October 6.

Goode, Richard. 1977. "The Economic Definition of Income." In Joseph Pechman, ed., *Comprehensive Income Taxation*. Washington, D.C.: Brookings Institution.

Goode, William. 1993. *World Changes in Divorce Patterns*. New Haven: Yale University Press.

Gordon, Suzanne. 1992. "Feminism and Caring." *American Prospect* 10 (Summer), pp. 119–27.

Gough, Ian. 1979. *The Political Economy of Welfare*. London: Macmillan.

Graycar, Adam, ed. 1983. *Retreat From the Welfare State*. Sydney: Allen and Unwin.

Greensite, Gillian. 1991. "Acquaintance Rape Clarified." In *Student Guide*. Santa Cruz: University of California.

Greenstein, Robert. 1992. "Cutting Benefits vs. Changing Behavior." *Public Welfare* 50(2), pp. 22–23.

Gutmann, Stephanie. 1990. "How Date Rape 'Education' Fosters Confusion, Undermines Personal Responsibility and Trivializes Sexual Violence." *Reason* 22 (July), pp. 22–27.

———. 1993. "The Breeding Ground." *National Review*, June 21, pp. 47–55.

180

Haanes-Olsen, Leif. 1993. "Sweden Decides Against a Retirement Age Increase—For Now." *Social Security Bulletin* 56(3), p. 106.

Hansmann, Henry. 1980. "The Role of Nonprofit Enterprise." *Yale Law Journal* 89, pp. 835–99.

Hardy, Dorcas. 1988. "Financing of Retirement Pensions in the United States of America." *International Social Security Review* 41(1), pp. 10–29.

Harrington, Michael. 1962. *The Other America: Poverty in the United States*. New York: Macmillan.

Harris, Kathleen. 1993. "Work and Welfare Among Single Mothers in Poverty." *American Journal of Sociology* 99(2), pp. 317–52.

Harris, Louis, and Associates. 1993. *The Commonwealth Fund Survey of Women's Health*. New York: Commonwealth Fund.

Hart, R. A. 1984. *Shorter Working Time: A Dilemma for Collective Bargaining*. Paris: Organization for Economic Cooperation and Development.

Hartman, Ann. 1992. "Murphy Brown, Dan Quayle, and the American Family." *Social Work* 37(5), pp. 387–88.

Heller, Walter. 1964. "Employment and Manpower." In Stanley Lebergott, ed. *Men Without Work*. Englewood Cliffs, N.J.: Prentice Hall.

Hellman, Peter. 1993. "Crying Rape: The Politics of Date Rape on Campus." *New York*, March 8, pp. 32–37.

Hennessey, John, and Janice Dykacz. 1989. "Projected Outcome and Length of Time in the Disability Insurance." *Social Security Bulletin* 52(9), pp. 2–41.

Heyns, Barbara. 1982. "The Influence of Parents' Work on Children's School Achievement." In Edward Zigler and Edmund Gordon, eds., *Day Care: Scientific and Social Policy Issues*. Boston: Auburn House.

Hoem, Jan, and Bo Rennermalm. 1985. "Modern Family Initiation in Sweden: Experience of Women Born Between 1936 and 1960." *European Journal of Population* 1, pp. 81–112.

Hojat, Mohammadreza. 1993. "The World Declaration of the Rights of the Child: Anticipated Challenges." *Psychological Reports* 72, pp. 1011–22.

Holmes, P., M. Lynch, and I. Molho. 1991. "An Econometric Analysis of the Growth in the Numbers Claiming Invalidity Benefits." *Journal of Social Policy* 20(1), pp. 87–105.

Holzmann, Robert. 1988. *Reforming Public Pensions*. Paris: Organization for Economic Cooperation and Development.

Horowitz, Irving. 1993. *The Decomposition of Sociology*. New York: Oxford University Press.

Hoskins, Dalmer. 1992. "Developments and Trends in Social Security, 1990–1992." *Social Security Bulletin* 55(4), pp. 36–42.

Hunter, Robert. 1965. *Poverty: Social Conscience in the Progressive Era*. Ed. Peter d'A. Jones. New York: Harper Torchbook Edition. Originally published in 1904 by Macmillan.

Hurl, L. F., and D. Tucker. 1986. "Limitations of an Act of Faith: An Analysis of the MacDonald Commission's Stance on Social Services." *Canadian Public Policy* 12(4), pp. 606–21.

Iams, Howard. 1993. "Earnings of Couples: A Cohort Analysis." *Social Security Bulletin* 56(3), pp. 22–32.

Iatridis, Demetrius. 1994. *Social Policy: Institutional Context of Social Development and Human Services*. Pacific Grove, Calif.: Brooks/Cole.

International Social Security Association. 1989. "Developments and Trends in Social Security, 1978–1989." *International Social Security Review* 42(3), pp. 247–349.

International Social Security Association. 1991. "United Kingdom: New Disability Allowances." *International Social Security Review* 44(1–2), pp. 137–38.

Jamrozik, Adam. 1983. *The Economy, Social Inequalities, and the Welfare State*. Social Welfare Research Centre Reports and Proceedings, no. 31. Australia: University of New South Wales.

Jencks, Christopher. 1985. "How Poor Are the Poor?" *New York Review of Books* 32(8) (May 9), p. 44.

———. 1991. "Is Violent Crime Increasing?" *American Prospect* 4 (Winter), pp. 98–109.

———. 1992a. "Can We Put a Time Limit on Welfare?" *American Prospect* 11 (Fall), pp. 32–40.

———. 1992b. *Rethinking Social Policy*. Cambridge: Harvard University Press.

Jencks, Christopher, and Kathryn Edin. 1990. "The Real Welfare Problem." *American Prospect* 1 (Spring), pp. 34–50.

Johnson, Allan. 1980. "On the Prevalence of Rape in the United States." *Signs* 6(1), pp. 137–45.

Kalisch, David. 1991. "The Active Society." *Social Security Journal* (August), pp. 3–9.

Kamerman, Sheila, and Alfred Kahn. 1987. "Mother-Only Families in Western Europe: Social Change, Social Problem, and Societal Response." A report prepared for the German Marshall Fund of the United States. November.

———, eds. 1989. *Privatization and the Welfare State*. Princeton: Princeton University Press.

Kaminer, Wendy. 1990. *A Fearful Freedom: Women's Flight From Equality*. New York: Addison-Wesley.

Kanter, Rosabeth, and D. Summers. 1987. "Doing Well While Doing Good: Dilemmas of Performance Measurement in Nonprofit Organizations and the Need for a Multiple-Constituency Approach." In Walter Powell, ed., *The Nonprofit Sector: A Research Handbook*. New Haven: Yale University Press.

Kates, Nancy. 1990. *Buying Time: The Dollar-a-Day Program*. Written at the direction of Marc Roberts. Cambridge: Case Program, Kennedy School, Harvard University.

Kaus, Mickey. 1986a. "Welfare and Work: A Symposium." *New Republic*, October 6, pp. 22–23.

———. 1986b. "The Work Ethic State." *New Republic*, July 7, pp. 27–28.

Kersten, Katherine. 1991. "A Conservative Feminist Manifesto." *Policy Review* 56 (Spring), pp. 4–15.

Kilpatrick, Dean, Connie Best, Lois Veronen, Angelynne Amick, Lorenz Ville-ponteaux, and Gary Ruff. 1985. "Mental Health Correlates of Criminal Victimization: A Random Community Survey." *Journal of Consulting and Clinical Psychology* 53(6), pp. 866–73.

Kirby, D. 1984. *Sexuality Education: An Evaluation of Programs and Their Effectiveness*. Santa Cruz, Calif.: Network Publications.

Kisker, E., et al. 1991. *A Profile of Child Care Settings: Early Education and Care in 1990—Executive Summary*. Washington, D.C.: U.S. Department of Education.

Kleiman, Lorraine. 1993. "The Relationship Between Adolescent Parenthood and Inadequate Parenting." *Children and Youth Services Review* 15(4), pp. 304–20.

Koss, Mary. 1988. "Hidden Rape: Sexual Aggression and Victimization in a National Sample of Students in Higher Education." In A. W. Burgess, ed., *Rape and Sexual Assault II*. New York: Garland.

———. 1990. "Testimony in Senate Hearings on Women and Violence." In *Women and Violence: Hearings Before the Committee on the Judiciary*, 101st Cong., 2nd sess. Part 2. Washington, D.C.: Government Printing Office.

———. 1991a. "Letters to the Editor." *Wall Street Journal*, July 25.

———. 1991b. "Rape on Campus: Facing the Facts." University of Arizona, Tucson. Mimeo.

———. 1991c. "Statistics Show Sexual Assaults Are More Prevalent Than Many Realize." *Los Angeles Daily Journal*, July 17.

———. 1993. "Letters to the Editor." *Wall Street Journal*, August 3.

Koss, Mary, and Sarah Cook. 1993a. "Facing the Facts: Date and Acquaintance Rape." Final draft of chapter prepared for *Current Controversies on Family Violence*.

———. 1993b. "Facing the Facts: Date and Acquaintance Rape Are Significant Problems for Women." In Richard Gelles and Donileen Loseke, eds., *Current Controversies on Family Violence*. Beverly Hills, Calif.: Sage.

Koss, Mary, Thomas Dinero, Cynthia Seibel, and Susan Cox. 1988. "Stranger and Acquaintance Rape: Are There Differences in the Victim's Experience?" *Psychology of Women Quarterly* 12, pp. 1–24.

Koss, Mary, and Christine Gidycz. 1985. "Sexual Experiences Survey: Reliability and Validity." *Journal of Consulting and Clinical Psychology* 53(3), pp. 422–23.

Koss, Mary, Christine Gidycz, and Nadine Wisniewski. 1987. "The Scope of Rape: Incidence and Prevalence of Sexual Aggression and Victimization in a National Sample of Higher Education Students." *Journal of Consulting and Clinical Psychology*, 55(2), pp. 162–70.

Koss, Mary, and Mary Harvey. 1991. *The Rape Victim*. Newbury Park, Calif.: Sage.

Koss, Mary, and Cheryl Oros. 1982. "The Sexual Experiences Survey: A Research

Instrument Investigating Sexual Aggression and Victimization." *Journal of Consulting and Clinical Psychology* 50(3), pp. 455–57.

Krauthammer, Charles. 1993. "Defining Deviancy Up." *New Republic*, November 22, pp. 21–25.

Kristol, Irving. 1978. *Two Cheers for Capitalism*. New York: Basic Books.

Krucoff, Carol. 1985. "The Effects of Day Care on Children." *Washington Post*, December 27.

Kutchinsky, Berl. 1994. "The Prevalence and Incidence of Child Sexual Abuse: The Child Sexual Abuse Panic." Paper presented at the Conference on Sexual Missbrauch—Evaluation of der Praxis und Forschung, Berlin, January 20–21.

Le Grand, Julian. 1982. *The Strategy of Equality*. London: Allen and Unwin.

Leibfried, Stephan. 1990. *Income Transfers and Poverty Policy in E.C. Perspective: On Europe's Slipping into Anglo-American Welfare Models*. Germany: Center for Social Policy, Bremen University.

Leibfried, Stephan, and Paul Pierson. 1992. *The Prospects for Social Europe*. Center for European Studies Working Paper Series no. 34. Cambridge: Harvard University.

Leibmann, George. 1993. "The AFDC Conundrum: A New Look at an Old Institution." *Social Work* 38(1), pp. 36–43.

Leiby, James. 1978. *A History of Social Welfare and Social Work in the United States*. New York: Columbia University Press.

Leira, Arnlaug. 1994. "The Women-Friendly Welfare State?" Paper presented at the Peder Sather Symposium on Gender Equality, Children and the Family entitled "Evolving Scandinavian and American Social Policy." University of California, Berkeley, April 6–7.

Lerner, Jacqueline, and Nancy Galambos. 1986. "Child Development and Family Change: The Influences of Maternal Employment on Infants and Toddlers." In Lewis Lipisitt and Carolyn Rovee-Collier, eds., *Advances in Infancy Research*. Vol. 4. Hillsdale, N.J.: Ablex.

Letwin, Shirley. 1992. *The Anatomy of Thatcherism*. London: Fontana.

Levin, Michael. 1986. "Feminism Stage Three." *Commentary* 82(2), pp. 27–31.

Levitan, Sar, and Robert Taggart. 1971. *Social Experimentation and Manpower Policy: The Rhetoric and the Reality*. Baltimore: Johns Hopkins University Press.

Lewin, Tamar. 1990. "Suit Over Death Benefits Asks, What Is a Family." *New York Times*, September 21.

———. 1991. "Tougher Laws Mean More Cases Are Called Rape." *New York Times National*, May 27.

Lichter, Robert, Stanley Rothman, and Linda Lichter. 1986. *The Media Elite*. Bethesda, Md.: Adler and Adler.

Liddell, T., B. Young, and M. Yamagishi. 1988. "Implementation and Evaluation of a Preschool Sexual Abuse Prevention Resource." Department of Human Resources, Seattle. Mimeo.

Lingg, Barbara. 1990. "Women Beneficiaries Aged 62 or Older, 1960–1988." *Social Security Bulletin* 53(7), pp. 2–12.

Linowes, David. 1988. *Privatization: Toward More Effective Government*. Chicago: University of Illinois Press.

Lonsdale, Susan. 1993. *Invalidity Benefit: An International Comparison*. London: Analytical Services Division, Department of Social Security.

Lowi, Theodore. 1969. *The End of Liberalism*. New York: Norton.

Lubran, Barbara. 1990. "Alcohol and Drug Abuse Among the Homeless Population: A National Response." In Milton Argeriou and Dennis McCarty, eds., *Treating Alcoholism and Drug Abuse Among Homeless Men and Women: Nine Community Demonstration Grants*. Binghampton, N.Y.: Haworth.

Luker, Kristin. 1991. "Dubious Conceptions: The Controversy Over Teen Pregnancy." *American Prospect* 5 (Spring), pp. 73–83.

McCurdy, Karen, and Deborah Daro. 1993. *Current Trends in Child Abuse Reporting and Fatalities: The Results of the 1992 Annual Fifty-State Survey*. Chicago: National Committee for Prevention of Child Abuse.

MacKinnon, Catharine. 1991. "The Palm Beach Hanging." *New York Times*, December 15, p. 15.

Marklund, S. 1992. "The Decomposition of Social Policy in Sweden." *Scandinavian Journal of Social Welfare* 1(1), pp. 2–11.

Marmor, Theodore, Mark Schlesinger, and Richard Smithey. 1987. "Nonprofit Organizations and Health Care." In Walter Powell, ed., *The Nonprofit Sector: A Research Handbook*. New Haven: Yale University Press.

Marshall, T. H. 1950. *Citizenship and Social Class*. Cambridge: Cambridge University Press.

Marshall, Will, and Martin Schram, eds. 1993. *Mandate for Change*. New York: Berkley.

Mason, Mary Ann. 1990. "Motherhood vs. Equal Treatment." *Journal of Family Law* 29(1), pp. 1–50.

Mead, Lawrence. 1986. *Beyond Entitlement: The Social Obligations of Citizenship*. New York: Free Press.

———. 1992. "How Should Congress Respond?" *Public Welfare* 50(2), pp. 14–17.

Melton, Gary. 1991. "The Improbability of Prevention of Sexual Abuse." In D. Willis, E. Holder, and M. Rosenberg, eds., *Child Abuse Prevention*. New York: Wiley.

Menand, Louis. 1994. "Behind the Culture of Violence." *New Yorker*, March 14, pp. 74–85.

Meyers, Marcia. 1990. "The ABCs of Child Care in a Mixed Economy: A Comparison of Public and Private Sector Alternatives." *Social Service Review* 64(4), pp. 559–79.

Miller, Henry. 1991. *On the Fringe: The Dispossessed in America*. Lexington, Mass.: Lexington Books.

Miller, S. M. 1963. *Max Weber: Selections From His Work*. New York: Crowell.

Mishra, Ramesh. 1981. *Society and Social Policy*. London: Macmillan.

Moon, Ailee. 1989. "Analysis of Tax Expenditures." Ph.D. diss., University of California, Berkeley.

Moore, Kristen, and Martha Burt. 1982. *Private Crisis, Public Cost*. Washington, D.C.: Urban Institute Press.

Moore, Kristen, and Sandra Hofferth. 1979. "Women and Their Children." In Ralph Smith, ed., *The Subtle Revolution*. Washington, D.C.: Urban Institute.

Moroney, Robert. 1991. *Social Policy and Social Work: Critical Essays on the Welfare State*. New York: Aldine de Gruyter.

Moskowitz, J. 1989. "The Primary Prevention of Alcohol Problems." *Journal of Studies on Alcohol* 50, pp. 54–88.

Moynihan, Daniel P. 1969. *Maximum Feasible Misunderstanding*. New York: Free Press.

Muehlenhard, C., and L. Hollabaugh. 1988. "Do Women Sometimes Say No When They Mean Yes? The Prevalence and Correlates of Women's Token Resistance to Sex." *Journal of Personality and Social Psychology* 54, pp. 872–79.

Munnell, Alicia. 1977. *The Future of Social Security*. Washington, D.C.: Brookings Institution.

Murray, Charles. 1984. *Losing Ground: American Social Policy 1950–1980*. New York: Basic Books.

———. 1985. "Helping the Poor: A Few Modest Proposals." *Commentary* 69(5), p. 30.

———. 1988. *In Pursuit of Happiness and Good Government*. New York: Simon and Schuster.

Musick, L. 1990. "Adolescents as Mothers: The Being and the Doing." *Zero to Three: Bulletin of the National Center for Clinical Infant Programs* (December).

Myrdal, Gunnar. 1960. *Beyond the Welfare State*. New Haven: Yale University Press.

National Victim Center. 1992. *Rape in America: A Report to the Nation*. Arlington, Va.: National Victims Center.

The Netherlands. Ministry of Social Affairs and Employment. 1991. "Cabinet Proposals About Absenteeism due to Sickness and Disablement." *The Hague* (November).

Novak, Michael. 1987. "Welfare's New Consensus: Sending the Right Signal." *Public Interest* 89 (Fall), pp. 26–30.

Oellerich, Donald, and Irwin Garfinkel. 1983. "Distributional Impact of Alternative Child Support Systems." *Policy Studies Journal* 12(1), pp. 119–29.

Okin, Susan. 1992. *Justice, Gender, and the Family*. New York: Basic Books.

Olmstead, Bob. 1986. "Teacher's Hugging Ban Hit." *Chicago Sun Times*, April 3, p. 22.

Olson, Mancur. 1983. "Social Security Survival: A Comment." *CATO Journal* 3(2), pp. 355–59.

Ooms, Theodora, and Jennifer Weinreb. 1992. *Reducing Family Poverty: Tax-Based and Child Support Strategies: Briefing Report, Family Impact Seminars*. Washington, D.C.: Research and Education Foundation, American Association for Marriage and Family Therapy.

Organization for Economic Cooperation and Development. 1985. *The Integration of Women into the Economy*. Paris: OECD.

———. 1988a. *The Future of Social Protection*. Paris: OECD.

———. 1988b. *Reforming Public Pensions*. Paris: OECD.

———. 1989. "Editorial: The Path to Full Employment: Structural Adjustment for an Active Society." *Employment Outlook* (July).

———. 1990. "Editorial: Labour Markets in the 1990s: Challenges and Opportunities." *Employment Outlook* (July).

———. 1991a. *Economic Surveys: Netherlands*. Paris: OECD.

———. 1991b. *Shaping Structural Change: The Role of Women*. Paris: OECD.

Ozawa, Martha. 1982. "Who Receives Subsidies Through Social Security and How Much?" *Social Work* 27(2), pp. 129–36.

Parrot, Andrea. 1988. *Acquaintance Rape and Sexual Assault Prevention Training Manual*. Ithaca, N.Y.: Cornell University.

Pechman, Joseph, Henry Aaron, and Michael Taussig. 1968. *Social Security: Perspectives for Reform*. Washington, D.C.: Brookings Institution.

Pension Benefit Guarantee Corporation. 1993. *Annual Report 1992*. Washington, D.C.: Pension Benefit Guarantee Corporation.

Peterka, Josef. 1988. "Equality of Treatment of Men and Women in the Pension Insurance Scheme in Austria." In *Equal Treatment in Social Security*. Geneva: International Social Security Association.

Peterson, L. 1984. "Teaching Home Safety and Survival Skills to Latch-Key Children." *Journal of Applied Behavior Analysis* 17, pp. 279–93.

Peterson, Peter. 1994. "Entitlement Reform: The Way to Eliminate the Deficit." *New York Review of Books* 41(7), pp. 39–47.

Piachaud, David. 1993. "Social Policy—Parasite or Powerhouse of the Economy?" In Peter Saunders and Sheila Shaver, eds. *Theory and Practice in Australian Social Policy: Rethinking the Fundamentals*. Proceedings of the National Social Policy Conference, Sydney, July 14–17.

Piaget, Jean. 1954. *The Construction of Reality in the Child*. Trans. M. Cook. New York: Basic Books.

Pigou, Arthur. 1938. *Economics of Welfare*. New York: Macmillan.

Piliavin, Irving, and Alan Gross. 1977. "The Effects of Separation of Services and Income Maintenance on AFDC Recipients." *Social Service Review* 51(3), pp. 389–406.

Pinker, Robert. 1991. "On Discovering the Middle Way in Social Welfare." In Thomas Wilson and Dorothy Wilson, eds., *The State and Social Welfare*. London: Longman.

Poche, C., P. Yoder, and R. Miltenberger. 1988. "Teaching Self-Protection to Children Using Television Techniques." *Journal of Applied Behavior Analysis* 12(3), pp. 253–61.

Podhoretz, Norman. 1991. "Rape in Feminist Eyes." *Commentary*, October, pp. 29–35.

Polansky, Norman. 1987. "Cynical Notes on Change." *Society* 24(3), pp. 40–44.

Pollitt, Katha. 1993. "Not Just Bad Sex." *New Yorker*, October 4, p. 222.

Popenoe, David. 1988. *Disturbing the Nest: Family Change and Decline in Modern Societies*. New York: Aldine De Gruyter.

———. 1992. "Family Decline: A Rejoinder." *Public Interest* 109 (Fall), pp. 117–22.

———. 1993. "Parental Androgyny." *Society* 30(6), pp. 5–11.

Prins, Rienk. 1990. *Sickness Absence in Belgium, Germany (FR) and the Netherlands: A Comparative Study*. Amsterdam: Netherlands Institute for the Working Environment.

Prins, Rienk, T. J. Veerman, and S. Andriessen. 1992. *Work Incapacity in a Cross-National Perspective: A Pilot Study on Arrangements and Data in Six Countries*. Amsterdam: Netherlands Institute for the Working Environment.

Proch, Kathleen, and Merlin Taber. 1987. "Helping the Homeless." *Public Welfare* 45(2), pp. 5–9.

Pryor, Lloyd. 1994. "The Single Welfare Mother and Deficiency in Reading." *Youth Policy* 15(10), pp. 38–56.

Rains, Prudence. 1975. "Imputations of Deviance: A Retrospective Essay on the Labelling Perspective." *Social Problems* 23(1), pp. 1–11.

Rapoport, Rhona, and Peter Moss. 1990. *Men and Women as Equals at Work*. London: Thomas Coram Research Unit.

Reinhard, Hans-Joachim. 1988. "The Splitting of Pension Credits in the Federal Republic of Germany and Canada—An Appropriate Way to Achieve Equality in Social Security Treatment for Men and Women?" In *Equal Treatment in Social Security*. Studies and Research no. 27. Geneva: International Social Security Association.

Reno, Virginia. 1993. "The Role of Pensions in Retirement Income: Trends and Questions." *Social Security Bulletin* 56(1), pp. 29–43.

Reppucci, N. Dickon, and Jeffrey Haugaard. 1993. "Problems With Sexual Abuse Prevention Programs." In Richard Gelles and Donileen Loseke, eds., *Current Controversies on Family Violence*. Newbury Park, Calif.: Sage.

"Responsive Communitarian Platform." 1992. *Responsive Community* 2(1), pp. 4–20.

"Review and Outlook: Medical Benefits." 1986. *Wall Street Journal*, June 12.

Rich, Spencer. 1989. "Social Welfare Spending." *Washington Post*, April 11.

Riger, Stephanie, and Margaret Gordon. 1981. "The Fear of Rape: A Study of Social Control." *Journal of Social Issues* 37(4), pp. 71–92.

Roiphe, Katie. 1993a. "Date Rape's Other Victim." *New York Times Magazine*, June 13, pp. 26–28, 40–41.

———. 1993b. *The Morning After: Sex, Fear, and Feminism on Campus*. Boston: Little, Brown.

Ross, Jane, and Melinda Upp. 1988. "The Treatment of Women in the United States Social Security System, 1970–1988." In *Equal Treatment in Social Secu-*

rity. Studies and Research no. 27. Geneva: International Social Security Association.

Rossi, Peter. 1987. "No Good Applied Social Research Goes Unpunished." *Society* 25(1), pp. 73–79.

Rossi, Peter, Gene Fisher, and Georgianna Willis. 1986. *The Condition of the Homeless in Chicago*. Amherst.: Social and Demographic Research Institute, University of Massachusetts.

Rubin, Alan, and Earl Babbie. 1989. *Research Methods for Social Work*. Belmont, Calif.: Wadsworth.

Russel, Robin, Phyllis Gill, Ann Coyne, and Jane Woody. 1993. "Dysfunction in the Family of Origin of MSW and Other Graduate Students." *Journal of Social Work Education* 29(1), pp. 121–29.

Russell, Diana. 1975. *The Politics of Rape*. New York: Stein and Day.

———. 1982. *Rape in Marriage*. New York: Macmillan.

———. 1984. *Sexual Exploitation: Rape, Child Sexual Abuse, and Workplace Harassment*. Beverly Hills, Calif.: Sage.

———. 1991. "The Epidemic of Sexual Violence Against Women: A National Crisis." Seabury Lecture, University of California, Berkeley, November 25.

Ryan, William. 1971. *Blaming the Victim*. New York: Random House.

Safilios-Rothschild, Constantina. 1974. *Women and Social Policy*. Englewood Cliffs, N.J.: Prentice Hall.

Salamon, L., and A. Abramson. 1982. *The Federal Budget and the Nonprofit Sector*. Washington, D.C.: Urban Institute Press.

Schlesinger, Arthur M., Jr. 1965. *A Thousand Days: John F. Kennedy in the White House*. Boston: Houghton Mifflin.

Schoenberg, Nara, and Sam Roe. 1993. "Rape: The Making of an Epidemic." *Toledo Blade*, October 10, 11, 12.

Schorr, Alvin. 1965. "Income Maintenance and the Birth Rate." *Social Security Bulletin* 28(12), pp. 2–10.

———. 1986. *Common Decency: Domestic Policies After Reagan*. New Haven: Yale University Press.

Schumpeter, Joseph. [1942] 1950. *Capitalism, Socialism, and Democracy*. 3rd ed. New York: Harper and Row.

Segal, Steven, and Harry Specht. 1983. "A Poorhouse in California, 1983: Oddity or Prelude?" *Social Work* 28(4), pp. 319–23.

Sherraden, Michael. 1991. *Assets and the Poor: A New American Welfare Policy*. Armonk, N.Y.: M. E. Sharpe.

Smedmark, Goran. 1992. "Survivors' Pensions in Sweden: A Recent Adaptation to Changed Conditions." In *Survivors' Benefits in a Changing World*. Studies and Research no. 31. Geneva: International Social Security Association.

Smith, Tom. 1994. "American Sexual Behavior." In Jayne Garrison, Mark Smith, and Douglas Besharov, eds., *Sexuality and American Social Policy: The Demography of Sexual Behavior*. Menlo Park, Calif.: Kaiser Family Foundation.

Social Security Administration. 1981. *Annual Statistical Supplement, 1980.* Washington, D.C.: Government Printing Office.

Sommers, Christina. 1994. *Who Stole Feminism?* New York: Simon and Schuster.

Specht, Harry, and Mark Courtney. 1994. *Unfaithful Angeles: How Social Work Has Abandoned Its Mission.* New York: Free Press.

Steiner, Gilbert. 1971. *The State of Welfare.* Washington, D.C.: Brookings Institution.

Stets, Jan. 1991. "Cohabiting and Marital Aggression: The Role of Social Isolation." *Journal of Marriage and the Family* 53, pp. 669–80.

Stevenson, Richard. 1993. "Swedes Facing Rigors of Welfare Cuts." *New York Times,* March 14.

"The Supply Side of OECD." 1987. *Wall Street Journal,* May 11.

Surrey, Stanley. 1973. *Pathways to Tax Reform.* Cambridge: Harvard University Press.

Surrey, Stanley, and Paul McDaniel. 1985. *Tax Expenditures.* Cambridge: Harvard University Press.

Svensson, Sven. 1987. "Vardnadsbidrag Fore Dagis." *Dagens Nyheter,* April 12.

Swan, Helen, Allan Press, and Steven Briggs. 1985. "Child Sexual Abuse Prevention: Does It Work?" *Child Welfare* (July–August), pp. 395–405.

Swedish Institute. 1978. *Taxes in Sweden.* Stockholm: Swedish Institute.

———. 1992. *Childcare in Sweden.* Stockholm: Swedish Institute.

Swedish National Insurance Board. 1992. "Memorandum: Developments in Swedish Social Insurance." Stockholm, April 30.

Sykes, Charles. 1992. *A Nation of Victims: The Decay of the American Character.* New York: St. Martin's.

Testa, Mark. 1992. "Introduction." In Margaret Rosenheim and Mark Testa, eds., *Early Parenthood and Coming of Age in the 1990s.* New Brunswick, N.J.: Rutgers University Press.

Tharinger, A. J., J. J. Krivacska, M. Faye-McDonough, J. Jamison, G. G. Vincent, and A. D. Hedlund. 1988. "Prevention of Sexual Abuse: An Analysis of Issues, Educational Programs, and Research Findings." *School Psychology Review* 17(4), pp. 614–34.

Therborn, G. 1987. "Welfare State and Capitalist Markets." *Acta Sociologica* 30, pp. 237–54.

Tilly, Louise, and Joan Scott. 1989. *Women, Work, and Family.* London: Routledge.

Titmuss, Richard. 1958. *Essays on the Welfare State.* London: Unwin University Books.

———. 1968. *Commitment to Welfare.* New York: Pantheon.

———. 1974. *Social Policy.* Ed. Brian Abel-Smith and Kay Titmuss. London: Allen and Unwin.

Townsend, Peter. 1968. "Does Selectivity Mean a Nation Divided?" In *Social Services for All?* London: Fabian Society.

Tracy, Martin. 1987. "Credit-Splitting and Private Pension Awards in Divorce: A Case Study of British Columbia." *Research on Aging* 9(1), pp. 148–59.

———. 1988. "Equal Treatment and Pension Systems: A Comparative Study." In *Equal Treatment in Social Security*. Studies and Research no. 27. Geneva: International Social Security Association.

Tracy, Martin, and Paul Adams. 1989. "Age at Which Pensions Are Awarded Under Social Security: Patterns in Ten Industrial Countries, 1960–1986." *International Social Security Review* 42(4), pp. 447–78.

Tracy, Martin, and Patsy Tracy. 1987. "The Treatment of Women as Dependents Under Social Security: After 50 Years How Does the United States Compare to Other Countries." *Journal of Applied Social Sciences* 11(1) , pp. 5–16.

Treas, Judith. 1993. "Money in the Bank: Transaction Costs and the Economic Organization of Marriage." *American Sociological Review* 58(5), pp. 723–34.

Trombley, William. 1990. "Budget Cloud Brings Gloom to Successful State Program." *Los Angeles Times*, July 2.

U.S. Bureau of the Census. 1981. *Statistical Abstract of the United States, 1981*. Washington, D.C.: Government Printing Office.

———. 1986. *Statistical Abstract of the United States, 1987*. Washington, D.C.: Government Printing Office.

———. 1990. *Statistical Abstract of the United States, 1990*. Washington, D.C.: Government Printing Office.

———. 1992. *Statistical Abstract of the United States, 1992*. Washington, D.C.: Government Printing Office.

U.S. Bureau of Justice Statistics. 1991. *Criminal Victimization in the United States, 1989*. Washington, D.C.: Government Printing Office.

———. 1994. *Criminal Victimization in the United States, 1992*. Washington, D.C.: Government Printing Office.

U.S. Department of Health and Human Services. 1988. *Study of National Incidence and Prevalence of Child Abuse and Neglect*. Washington, D.C.: Government Printing Office.

U.S. House of Representatives. Committee on Ways and Means. 1992. *The Green Book: Overview of Entitlement Programs*. Washington, D.C.: U.S. Government Printing Office.

U.S. Office of Management and the Budget. 1988. *Special Analysis: Budget of the U.S. Government FY 1988*. Washington, D.C.: Government Printing Office.

U.S. Senate. 1991. *Women and Violence: Hearings Before the Committee on the Judiciary*, 101st Cong., 2nd sess. Part 2. Washington, D.C.: Government Printing Office.

———. 1993. *S.11 Violence Against Women Act 1993*, 103rd Cong., 1st sess. Washington, D.C.: Government Printing Office.

Vlastos, Gregory. 1962. "Justice and Inequality." In Richard Brandt, ed., *Social Justice*. Englewood Cliffs, N.J.: Prentice Hall.

Wagner, Marsden, and Mary Wagner. 1976. *The Danish National Child-Care System*. Boulder, Colo.: Westview.

Walker, Alan. 1984. *Social Planning: A Strategy for Socialist Welfare*. Oxford: Blackwell.

Warshaw, Robin. 1988. *I Never Called It Rape: The* Ms. *Report on Recognizing, Fighting, and Surviving Date and Acquaintance Rape*. New York: Harper and Row.

Wattenberg, Ben. 1993. "Let Clinton Be Clinton." *Wall Street Journal*, January 20.

Weaver, Carolyn. 1992. "Reassessing Federal Disability Insurance." *Public Interest* 106 (Winter), pp. 108–21.

Weisbrod, Burton. 1993. "Does Institutional Form Affect Behavior? Comparing Private Firms, Religious Nonprofits and Other Nonprofits." Working paper, Department of Economics and Center for Urban Affairs and Policy Research, Northwestern University, Evanston, Ill.

Weisbrod, Burton, and Mark Schlesinger. 1986. "Nonprofit Ownership and the Response to Asymmetric Information: The Case of Nursing Homes." In S. Rose-Ackerman, ed., *The Economics of Nonprofit Institutions*. New York: Oxford University Press.

Whitehead, Barbara. 1992. "A New Familism?" *Family Affairs* 5(1–2), pp. 1–5.

Whitehead, Barbara, and David Blankenhorn. 1991. "Man, Woman, and Public Policy: Difference and Dependency in the American Conversation." Working paper, Institute for American Values, New York.

Wilensky, Harold. 1975. *The Welfare State and Equality*. Berkeley: University of California Press.

Wilensky, Harold, and Charles Lebeaux. 1958. *Industrial Society and Social Welfare*. New York: Russell Sage.

Wilson, James Q. 1985. "The Rediscovery of Character: Private Virtue and Public Policy." *Public Interest* 81 (Fall), pp. 3–16.

Wolf, Naomi. 1991. *The Beauty Myth*. New York: Morrow.

Wolfe, Alan. 1991. "The Right to Welfare and the Obligation to Society." *Responsive Community* 1(2), pp. 12–22.

——. 1993. "Whose Body Politic?" *American Prospect* 12 (Winter), pp. 99–108.

Women's Freedom Network. 1994. "Statement of Purpose." *Women's Freedom Network Newsletter* 1(1), p. 1.

Wright, James. 1988. "The Worthy and Unworthy Homeless." *Society* 25(5), p. 69.

Yegidis, Bonnie. 1986. "Date Rape and Other Forced Sexual Encounters Among College Students." *Journal of Sex Education and Therapy* 12, pp. 51–54.

Young, Cathy. 1992. "Women, Sex, and Rape." *Washington Post*, May 31.

Zelnick, Melvin, John Kanter, and Kathleen Ford. 1981. *Sex and Pregnancy in Adolescence*. Beverly Hills, Calif.: Sage.

Index

196